A Child's History of Spain

John Bonner

A
Child's
History
of
Spain

COLUMBUS AS A YOUTH.

A

CHILD'S HISTORY OF SPAIN

BY

JOHN BONNER

AUTHOR OF "A CHILD'S HISTORY OF ROME"
"A CHILD'S HISTORY OF FRANCE" ETC.

ILLUSTRATED

NEW YORK

HARPER & BROTHERS PUBLISHERS

1894

CONTENTS

SPAIN—FROM THE BEGINNING TO THE ROMAN CONQUEST

500 B.C. – 50 A.D.

AWAY down in the south-western corner of Europe, cut off from the rest of the continent by a range of mountains six to twelve thousand feet high, is the beautiful country of Spain. It is a country of lofty and rugged mountain chains and long level plains. Some of the latter lie low, and are watered by flowing rivers; here the climate is genial and the rainfall copious, so that the fields are fat and rich; others, in the centre of the country, stand higher above the level of the sea; these have a scanty rainfall, excessive beat in summer, and extreme cold in winter, and are sometimes baked and sometimes frozen, but always dry and poor. In the north the Basque peasant in his long ragged black cloak cowers from the bleak winds from the Atlantic and the biting gales from the snow-clad ridge of the Pyrenees and the Cantabrians; in the south, the gay Andalusian is warmed by balmy breezes from the Mediterranean, and sleeps his noonday sleep under groves of gently waving palms or orange-trees, or beneath broad vine-leaves, or in orchards laden with fragrant fruit, or in snug corners of fields yellow with golden wheat. Thus Spain is divided into a paradise and a wilderness.

Long, long ago, before history began to be written, Spain was probably part of Africa. On the Cape of Gibraltar live thirty or forty monkeys of the African breed; an old Spanish legend says that they still visit their old home, from time to time, by a submarine tunnel under the Mediterranean. In old prehistoric times the country was overrun with mammoths and other enormous preadamite monsters, whose bones are still found in great heaps in the mountains. After their day came volcanic convulsions which altered the shape of the country, uptwisted mountain ranges, burst yawning chasms, tilted great layers of rock on edge, cut channels for rivers, and perhaps opened a way for the waters of the Mediterranean to empty into the Atlantic through the Straits of Gibraltar.

We first bear of Spain four or five hundred years before Christ, when the Phoenicians of Tyre planted a colony near the present seaport of Cadiz. Two or three hundred years later we again bear of it, when

1

the mighty trading city of Carthage founded the town which is now called Carthagena, and sent a general with an army of fifty thousand men and two hundred elephants to conquer the coasts of Spain.

THE BAY OF BISCAY.

At that time the peninsula was inhabited by two races, who were know as Iberians and Celts, and who afterwards blended and were then called Celtiberians. The Iberians came from Africa, and were short, dark-skinned men, though not negroes; the Celts came from the North, were tall and white, wore their hair in long braids, and dressed in leathern coats, over which they threw long black cloaks. They spent their time in war or at the chase, while their women tilled the fields. Their weapons were swords and spears of iron, and they were skilled horsemen. They lived chiefly on vegetables, fruits, acorns, and chestnuts, and were not acquainted with strong liquor. In some respects they may remind you of some of our Indian tribes.

These races were intermarrying, or living peaceably side by side, and growing in numbers, when the Carthaginians invaded Spain. The latter were a very superior people to the Celtiberians; highly educated, far-seeing, good soldiers, good sailors, and, above all, good merchants. They taught the natives how to work their mines of silver and gold and lead and iron; they bought the produce of the mines and the fields and the orchards, and gave in exchange the goods of Carthage and of Tyre; they kept order with their armies, and when Greek marauders landed they drove them off with their well-drilled regiments and their elephants; they treated the Celtiberians so fairly that the two races became friends, and when the Carthaginian general proposed that Spain should become a province of Carthage the Celtiberians agreed. Thus, for the first though not for the last time in history, Spain came to be ruled by men of the Arab race from Africa.

It did not all become Carthaginian, however. There were a few Greek settlements here and there along the coast, and as Greece went down and Rome rose up, some of these became more Roman than Greek. Such a place was Saguntum. On the place where it stood there is now a small Spanish town called Murviedro, or Old Walls; something over twenty-one hundred years ago it was a rich and powerful city, with high stone-walls, an amphitheatre, an aqueduct, temples, and other fine buildings. It was full of brave people, who were stanch friends of Rome. Now it befell at this time that Rome and Carthage were foes. They had waged one war which had lasted twenty-three years, and had ended in the defeat of Carthage. A young Carthaginian general, named Hannibal, who was then in Spain, resolved to reopen the fight, and to begin by attacking Saguntum.

For the work he mustered one hundred and fifty thousand troops, most of whom were Spaniards. A Spanish poet, writing many centuries afterwards, sang:

"Lord Hannibal upon the town
His hirelings brings from far;
The men of Ocana come down
To serve him in the war.
With all that Andalusia yields
Her trooping soldiers come;
From rich Granada's fertile fields,
From Cadiz washed with foam,
With guards and spears and helms and shields
They march to fight with Rome."

Hannibal attacked the place with high towers which overtopped the walls, and from which huge stones, thrown by machinery upon the parapet, cleared it of defenders; while an immense battering-ram with a steel head, and driven by two-score men, working day and night, at length made a breach in the wall. Then the leading Saguntines kindled a great fire in the public square, and after throwing their gold and silver into it, leaped into the flames themselves. The victorious army swarmed into the city and showed no mercy. Saguntum was burned, and though the Romans long afterwards undertook to rebuild it, it never regained its former state.

This was the beginning of the second war between Rome and Carthage. It opened with splendid victories by young Hannibal, who overran Italy and defeated army after army. But the dogged tenacity of the Romans won at last; Carthage received her death-blow, and Hannibal himself committed suicide in exile. You will find a trace of his service in Spain in the town of Barcelona, which was named after his family—Barca.

While Hannibal was winning victories in Italy, the Romans resolved to carry the war into Spain. They sent an army there under Publius Scipio, and he was defeated and killed; then another army, under his brother Cneius Scipio, and he was defeated and killed; then a third, under Publius Cornelius Scipio, who was afterwards known as the African, and be conquered the country, though be was only twenty-four years old. When he landed, with eleven thousand men, somewhere near Barcelona, nine-tenths of Spain was Carthaginian; in seven or eight years all Spain, except a town or two here and there, was Roman. This he accomplished not so much by fighting as by policy and kindness. Then, as now, the Spaniards were a hot-headed, impulsive people; they had never warmed to the Carthaginians, who were harsh and cruel. Scipio was gentle and generous.

When the Carthaginians won a victory they held the finest youths among their vanquished foes as hostages for the good behavior of their tribe. Scipio asked for no hostages. Among the Carthaginians beautiful maidens were always spoil of war. After a battle, when a lovely Spanish girl was brought to Scipio as his prize, he restored her to her lover, and gave her a dowry. He was always just and kind;

and this was so surprising to the simple Spaniards, accustomed to the rough ways of a brutal age, that they regarded Scipio as more than a man, and offered to make him king. He refused the title, saying:

"No Roman can endure the name of king. If you think that the royal spirit is the noblest spirit of man, I shall be glad if you think that such a spirit is mine. But you must never call me king."

So completely did he win their hearts that for his sake they became firm friends of Rome. And you will find, as you read this history, that of all people the Spaniards are the most faithful. They have often given their lives rather than break their troth. They were, moreover, at this time a rich people. When Scipio took the city which is now known as Carthagena, he received as part of the government's share of the plunder two hundred and seventy-six golden bowls, each weighing about a pound, nine tons of wrought and coined silver, and one hundred and thirteen merchant vessels.

Before he died he saw Roman authority firmly planted over Eastern and Southern Spain. In the North and West some native tribes were still independent. They were generally a people of herdsmen and shepherds—poor, with no great city and no treasure that was worth stealing. They were, moreover, brave and skilful fighters, and by going to war with them the Romans stood to win more hard-knocks than plunder. Therefore the Roman legions kept away from the bulk of the regions which are now known as Portugal, Estremadura, the Asturias, Galicia, Leon, Castile, and the windy plateau on which Madrid stands, and clung to the sunny slopes which lean to the Mediterranean.

On those purple hills which look into the Southern Sea, and in the leafy valleys between them, where summer is long and life is sweet, and fragrant odors and the buzz of many insects lull the idler to sleep, the Roman soldier, weary of war, took to his broad breast a blushing Spanish maiden, who in his arms became a Roman matron, as he in hers became a Spanish citizen. Thus Spain became Roman, and for four or five hundred years, when Rome itself was ravaged spring and fall by barbarian invaders, it was a home of Roman civilization, a refuge of Roman letters, a centre of Roman spirit.

Some of the wisest statesmen, several of the most skillful generals, a few of the most brilliant writers of the later ages of Rome, were born in Spain. The Emperors Trajan and Hadrian were both born near Seville; Marcus Aurelius was born at Rome of Spanish parents; the Senecas and the poet Lucan at Cordova; the poet Martial in Aragon; Quintilian, the grammarian, in Navarre. These great men generally spent their lives at Rome; but some of them, as death approached, returned to lay their bones in the country of their birth, by the side of the flowing rivers they loved, and under the kindly skies they had gazed at in their boyhood. During the first centuries of the Christian era Spain was a more peaceful and happier country to live in than Italy.

THE GOTHS IN SPAIN

A.D. 200—700

FOR over five hundred years after the Roman conquest Spain was tranquil. The only interruption to peace was an uprising by a proconsul named Sertorius, who for a time established an independent government in the North. He defied the utmost power of Rome for ten years, and alight have founded an empire, for he was brave, wise, and honest, had he not, in a moment of forgetfulness, accepted a bidding to a banquet given by some refugees from Rome, who murdered him as he sat at table.

He was adored by his people. There is a legend that one of the secrets of his power was his ownership of a white fawn, which he had tamed, and which came at his call and ate out of his hand. He persuaded the ignorant Spaniards that this creature came to him from Heaven, held converse with the gods, and advised him in moments of trouble. The Spaniards, like most dwellers in mountainous, volcanic regions, have always been a superstitious people, prone to believe things incredible. It would have been well for them if they had never cherished wilder delusions than the one about the white fawn.

During the first centuries of the Christian era unending conflict raged between the Roman Empire and wild tribes of Northern Europe, who bore various names, among others Vandals, Sueves, Franks, Alemans, Saxons, Burgundians, and especially Goths. These last came from the shore of the Baltic, and were sometimes distinguished as Visigoths and Ostrogoths. They and rough races like them ravaged the Roman country, from the turbulent Bay of Biscay to the Danube, and plundered in turn the regions which we now call France, Germany, Italy, and Austria. For a long time the lofty wall of the Pyrenees kept them out of Spain; but an hour came when the barbarous tribes, thirsting for new towns to sack, scaled the mountain wall and poured into the valley of the Ebro. They were terrible visitors; often giants in size and strength, with blue eyes, long yellow hair, and coats of sheepskin or fur on their backs. They could neither read nor write, but they could fight from the dawn of day to the setting of the sun.

The first tribes which settled in Spain were Sueves and Vandals. They roamed through the North, robbing cities and carrying off flocks and herds. The Spaniards called upon Rome for help; but Rome could not even defend herself. She was glad when a Gothic chief, Ataulph, or Adolphus, a brother of Alaric the Goth, offered to drive the Vandals and Sueves out of Southern France and Spain, on the condition that Rome should give them to him, and with them the Emperor's sister, Honoria, a lady of remarkable beauty, to be his wife. The bargain was closed on these terms. At the head of an army of Goths Ataulph scattered the other barbarians; not, however, until the Vandals had given their name to the most lovely portion of the country, which to this day is known as Andalusia.

Then Ataulph founded a Gothic empire in Spain, and chose for his capital the beautiful city of Barcelona, on the Mediterranean. His Goths mingled and intermarried with the Spaniards, and in course of time it was difficult to distinguish one people from the other. The Goths had conquered the Spaniards on the battle-field, but the Spaniards had civilized their conquerors, and forced upon them the manners and customs and language of Rome.

During several hundred years many kings succeeded each other on the Gothic throne. Ataulph did not reign long. As he was reviewing his troops a dwarf crept up behind him and stabbed him in the back. His successor, Sigeric, thought to make himself secure on his throne by causing the six little children of Ataulph to be put to death; but the people said this was going too far, and they killed the murderer. A good riddance! Then there came a king named Wallia, who waged successful war upon the remnant of the Vandals and Sneves, and penned then up in corners of Spain; and after him came Theodoric, also a valiant fighter, who helped defeat Attila, King of the Huns, the Scourge of God, on the battle-field at Chalons. Both Attila and Theodoric died of wounds received in this battle. The next Gothic king, Evaric, was the most powerful and the wisest of the Gothic monarchs. All nations sent embassies to make treaties with him. He drew the Gothic code of laws, which was in force for many centuries, and is the basis of the system of laws which is in force in Spain to-day.

We are told there were thirty-two Gothic kings in all, and that of these eight were usurpers, four were dethroned, and eight were murdered. As they did little except to quarrel and make war on their neighbors, I do not think you would care to hear much about them. There was a king named Leovigild, who, like Evaric, became a monarch of repute. He held his court at Toledo, dressed in purple, and sat on a throne. He levied heavy taxes on his people, and seized the estates of traitors, by which means he was enabled to gather a vast sum of money into his treasury. It was in his reign that the dispute became hot between two sects into which the Christians were divided—Arians and Catholics. The king was an Arian, his people Catholics. While he reigned the Arians were in the ascendant. After he died, A.D. 586, the Catholics got the upper hand and did not delay to crush out Arianism, though it was the ancient faith of the Goths.

He had a wife whose name was Goswinda, and whose temper was hot. She was an Arian. Her son married a French princess named Ingunda, who was a Catholic. Goswinda ordered her daughter-in-law to become an Arian; Ingunda, who was only seventeen, respectfully declined to do anything of the kind. Thereupon the mother-in-law seized her by the hair of her head, threw her down, trampled on her, and held her in the water while she was baptized by an Arian priest. The young lady appealed to her husband and father-in-law for redress, but got none. In those days such pleasantnesses were not unusual at courts.

It was a son of Leovigild, Ricared by name, who declared Catholicism to be the religion of Spain. He had been an Arian, but renounced his faith. He was so fortunate as to be able to effect the religious union of his people without war. He died A.D. 601, having built a cathedral at Toledo, which was consecrated to the Virgin Mary. According to the legend, the Virgin herself came down from heaven to inspect it when it was finished, and if you go to see it, you will be shown the footprint of her step on the stair.

Seventy-one years after Ricared, in the year A.D. 672, the Gothic lords elected a farmer named Wamba to be king. The story goes that their messengers found Wamba ploughing his field; that when they told him their errand he laughed, saying that he would be king when leaves grew on his staff. With which words he smote the earth with the staff, and green leaves forthwith sprouted from it.

Whatever you may think of this story, you will have to admit that the old ploughman was a valiant and gallant soldier. He carried on many wars, and was always victorious. A rebellion breaking out at Nismes, which then formed part of the Spanish dominion, Wamba marched swiftly to the city and stormed it. Numbers of the defenders were killed in the attack; their leader was brought before Wamba in chains.

"Thy life," said the king, "will I spare, though the mercy is ill deserved."

He ordered the prisoners' heads to be shaved and their beards to be cut off—it was esteemed a disgrace to wear a bare chin—and when he returned to Toledo he required them to march in front of the army with bare feet and clothed in hair. The leader wore a leather crown, which I suppose corresponded to the leather medal of our day.

I wish Wamba had been as merciful to the Jews as he was to the rebels. But he hated them with a hatred which nothing could appease, and, as was the custom of that day, he persecuted them cruelly. Toledo was said to have been an ancient Jewish city, founded before Christ. How the Jews got there, in the very heart of Spain, we are not told. But in the time of Wamba they were numerous at Toledo, and, as is their custom, they had grown rich. The king robbed them of their wealth, and gave them the choice of turning Christians or going into exile. Thus Toledo lost many of its most useful and enterprising citizens.

One day King Wamba fell ill. His disease deprived him of consciousness; he could neither see what was going on round him, nor hear what was said. Now there was a curious custom in Spain that when a person became unconscious on his death-bed his friends could shave his head, and the priests could ordain him, unconscious as he was, as a monk of the church; the object being to secure him easy entrance into heaven, whose door always stood wide open for the priesthood. King Wamba's courtiers, being sure that he was going to die, shaved his head, and the Archbishop of Toledo received him into the Church as a monk, and ordained him with the usual ceremonies.

Fancy their surprise next day when the king got better! His majesty was a good deal nonplussed when he passed his hand over his head and found his hair gone; likewise when he observed that he was dressed in the costume of a monk. A council of bishops and lawyers was summoned to consider the case, and they decided that the rule—once a priest, always a priest—must apply. So King Wamba was told that his reign was over, and that there was nothing for him to do but to retire to a monastery at Burgos, which he did.

THE MOORISH CONQUEST

A.D. 710-711

WHEN the Goths first became masters of Spain they were a rude tribe of savages, without learning or culture. After they had mixed with the natives for a century or so they became a refined and polished people, speaking Latin, and trained in letters, law, and religion; and they still remained warlike and manly. But after they had been two or three centuries in possession of the rich valleys of Spain they acquired idle and luxurious habits, spent their lives in drinking and feasting and dancing, and thus became as weak and helpless as the people of Italy.

It was the old story. Powerful chiefs, with men-at-arms under their command, seized the richest lands, and made the common people till then for their food and clothes. The man who drove the plough was cowed, houseless, hungry, ragged, unkempt, filthy, and ignorant. The man who owned the land lived in a splendid castle, with soldiers guarding the gate. He wore clothes of silk and rich stuffs, ate choice food, drank fine wines, took his siesta in the shade of olive groves, where fragrant flowers perfumed the air, listened to the sweet music of lutes, or lazily watched lovely girls dancing on Persian carpets for his delight. You know that there was too much contrast here for such a society to last. When the pillars of the arch are so very far apart the corner-stone is apt to fall in.

At the close of the Gothic period in Spain a good deal of fable is mixed with the history. The Gothic king was named Roderick; of that there can be no doubt. He is said to have been brutal, reckless, headstrong, and incapable; of that there is no certainty at all.

The legend says that at Toledo there was a house which had been built by Hercules, the strong man of Greece, and which was called "The House of God." It was the law that no one should enter that house; and for the better assurance of this, every king set his seal upon the door. Roderick had set his seal with the others. But afterwards, consumed with curiosity to know what was in the house, he broke his own and the other kingly seals and forced his way in. First he saw the statue of a man of prodigious size lying in bed, and he knew that this was Hercules. Then be went on, and he came to a room of which one wall was dazzling white, another pitch-black, the third an emerald-green, and the fourth blood-red. In this room stood a tall pillar; in the pillar a niche; in the niche a casket of gold, studded with precious stones and closed with a lock of mother-of-pearl; and in the casket a white cloth, on which were drawn pictures of strange men with turbans on their heads, banners in their hands, swords hanging from their necks, bows tied to their saddles, and a scroll underneath, saying: "Whosoever shall see this cloth shall also see men like these conquer Spain and become the lords thereof."

You do not need to be told that there was no house of Hercules, no colored walls, no pillar, no casket, no pictures on cloth, and no scroll, but that all these were invented long afterwards by the rich Moorish fancy. I cannot be as sure that another story of the same time was also a fable, but I suspect it was.

Over against Spain, on the northern coast of Africa, dwelt tribes of Moors who constantly threatened to invade Europe. To hold them in check, Roderick built forts in Africa, and filled them with fighting men under a captain named Julian. Now this Julian had a lovely young daughter, named Clorinda, whom he sent to Toledo to be educated, and placed under the guardianship of the king.

Forgetting his duty, Roderick fell in love with her, and, though he had a wife already, carried her off from her boarding-school. Her relations flew to arms to rescue her, but when they broke into the place where she was shut up she refused to leave, and said she would cast her lot with the king. At this her kinsmen left her with curses, and from that time to this the Spaniards have never christened a girl-baby by the name of Clorinda, but have taken pleasure in giving the name to dogs.

I suspect myself that this story was made up long afterwards to excuse the treachery of Julian; for, according to the story, just at this time that officer sent word to the Moorish chief that he would surrender his forts if the Moors would despatch a force into Spain to overthrow Roderick. The chief's name was Mousa or Musa. He delayed till he could consult the Caliph; then, receiving a favorable reply, he sent into Spain an officer named Tarif with five hundred men, and on his report despatched another army of seven thousand under another officer named Tarik.

These invaders are called Moors, because they embarked for Spain from Mauritania, which we call Morocco. They were a mixed race, part Arab and part African, of whom I will tell you more in the next chapter. Swarthy but not black, fierce, warlike, unruly; tireless on the march, and fearless in battle; living for a day on a handful of fruit, with a mouthful of water; devoted heart and soul to the Moslem faith, which they believed it to be their duty to spread through the world by fire and sword, they may perhaps remind you of the Carthaginians, who sprang from the same stock and lived also in Northern Africa. They were indeed terrible foes for the weakened Spanish Goths to encounter.

When Roderick heard of their landing he mastered all the troops he could gather, and marched down to Xeres, near Cadiz, with ninety thousand men. It is said that he went into battle in an ivory chariot drawn by two milk-white mules, but this is not certain. What is certain is that, though his force far outnumbered that of the Moors, even after the latter had been reinforced with five thousand fresh troops, he was beaten, after a desperate fight which lasted eight days.

There is an old Spanish ballad which tells the story of the end of the battle, and describes the despair of Roderick:

> "He climbed into a hill-top,
> The highest he could see,
> Thence all about of that wide rout
> His last long look took lie;
> He saw his royal banners,
> Where they lay drenched and torn,
> He heard the cry of victory,
> The Arabs' shout of scorn.
> 'Last night I was the King of Spain:
> To-day no king am I.
> Last night fair castles held my train:
> To-night where shall I lie?
> Last night a hundred pages

Did serve me on the knee;
To-night not one I call my own,
Not one pertains to me.
Oh! Death, why now so slow art thou,
Why fearest thou to smite?"

The story goes that the king was drowned in the Guadalquivir in trying to escape. His body was never found, hut his crown and his royal robe fell into the hands of the Moors.

His army scattered; neither officers nor men were true to Roderick. He had taught them to hate him by his cruelties and his folly. The Jews, especially, whom he had oppressed, openly took sides with the Moors, in order to he revenged on their Christian oppressors.

Musa, the chief general of the Moors in Africa, had ordered his lieutenant Tarik, when he left Africa, to give one battle, if he thought it safe, but not to follow up his victory, if he won. Musa wanted the glory of conquest for himself. Tarik, looking out for his own glory, chose to disobey. Without an hour's delay, after the battle of Xeres, be marched north, and took city after city. The Spanish spirit had been broken.

But Musa had no idea of letting Tarik play the part of conqueror. He placed himself at the head of an army, crossed into Spain, marched on the trail of his lieutenant, took Seville and Merida, and came up with Tarik outside the walls of Toledo.

The Moorish chief, seated on a prancing charger, met his lieutenant with a black frown on his brow and bitter words on his tongue. He charged Tarik with having secreted plunder for himself. When this was disproved, Musa accused him of having aimed at making himself ruler of Spain. When this was also denied, Musa slashed him across the face with his whip and ordered him into prison.

While the Moorish conquerors were quarrelling among themselves the Spaniards submitted quietly to be conquered. They were tired of the Goths and of their government, which latterly had neither preserved the peace nor protected the peasant. All they asked of the Moors was to be allowed to keep their old laws and their lands on the old terms; these conditions the conquerors granted. As to their religion, the Moors promised that it should not be interfered with, but so long as a Spaniard remained a Christian he must pay head-money. This was not so bard to bear as some of the oppressions they had endured when the Gothic chiefs had been warring against each other.

THE EVENING PRAYER.

As you read Spanish history you will find no trait in the Spanish character more clearly marked than an unconquerable hatred of foreign control. That trait had not developed when the Moors overran Spain in the year of our Lord seven hundred and eleven.

WHO WERE THE MOORS?

A.D. 630-711

IN order that you shall understand something of the people who conquered Spain nearly twelve hundred years ago, and who held the best part of it for over seven hundred years, I must tell you something of their origin.

A MOORISH FORT.

In the deserts of Arabia, where a tropical sun scorches vast stretches of sand, divided from each other by bare mountain ranges, and grass and trees only grow round a well or spring, to which the traveller, choked with dust or sickened by breathing air which is full of sulphur and salt, staggers at the close of a sultry day's march, in order to camp for the night. In these deserts wandering tribes of dark-faced men, with their wives, their children, their servants, their horses, their camels, and their flocks and herds, lived as long ago as history remembers. They were Arabs of the Desert. They rarely ventured out of their country, and strangers seldom visited them. They were not barbarians. In their lonely life they had studied many things, among others astronomy, mathematics, and poetry. They lived so close to Nature that their minds inclined to thoughts of God.

They were brave and warlike, hardened to fatigue, and, like all natives of barren regions, they could live on a few dates, or a *frijole*, on which others would have starved.

Among these Arabs there appeared, in the first quarter of the seventh century, a teacher whose name was Mahomet, or Mohammed. He proclaimed to the Arabs a new religion, which was based on the Old Testament. It differed from Christianity in that it did not admit the divinity of Christ, but it resembled Christianity in that it declared there was but one God. It also declared that Mahomet was his prophet. The general rules of life which this new religion proclaimed were much like the rules of Christ, though it did not forbid the Eastern practice of marrying more than one wife, and did forbid the use of wine. It enjoined three chief duties: the duty of prayer, the duty of self-denial, and the duty of charity.

Such a religion was a vast improvement upon the religions which the Eastern nations had professed. After a few years' consideration the Arabs embraced it; and having embraced it, they resolved to spread it through the world by force of arms. In this enterprise they were surprisingly successful. In a few years they overran Syria, Persia, Egypt, and the whole of Northern Africa, and made the people adopt their faith. It looked at one time as though Mahometanism, or Moslemism, was going to supersede Christianity.

The chief holy city of the Moslem Church was Mecca, in Arabia; but when the Moslems began to conquer territory, their chief ruler resided at Damascus, in Syria. He was called a caliph, which means a successor, and he was so called to indicate that he was a successor of Mahomet. He was, in fact, a Moslem Pope, with temporal as well as spiritual power. He gave orders to the Moslem armies wherever they were; his authority extended from the Indus to the Atlantic Ocean. After a time the caliphs removed from Damascus to Bagdad. I dare say you have read in story-books accounts of one of the caliphs of Bagdad who used to go round in disguise to see how his officers performed their duties, and to hear what people said of him.

These Arabs had long led contented lives in their barren country, surrounded by their children, their fleet horses, and their tireless camels. There was no distinction of rank among them. All dressed alike, ate the same food, bore the same privations with the same fortitude. They were hospitable to the stranger, and merciful to the prisoner. In speech they were courteous. They loved poetry, and well knew the books of the Old Testament. When Mahomet roused them to undertake the spread of their religion by the invasion of other countries, and they enlarged their minds by mixing with foreigners, the Moslem Arabs became admirable soldiers, capable of long marches on short rations, unconscious of fear, and submissive to discipline. Their swift horsemen were the terror of an enemy. In peace they were patient, intelligent workers. They farmed their lands with skill, and toiled with unceasing industry. They made fine cloths of silk and wool and linen. They forged steel swords which have not been surpassed in temper by the best weapons of our day. They knew much, for the times in which they lived, of various sciences. It is from the language they used that we borrowed such words as alphabet, algebra, and alchemy; and with the names we borrowed the first rudiments of the things. They invented the numerals we use. You will see, as we go on with this Child's History, that they were at one time the most learned people in the world.

The Moors who invaded Spain in the year 711 were a branch of these Moslem Arabs. They were called Moors by the Christians, because they embarked for the enterprise from ports in Morocco, and also because a considerable number of them were natives of that country. Musa and Tarik were Arabs, born in Asia; but many of their regiments consisted of Berbers, who were men of the Arab race, born and bred in Northern Africa.

You have already learned what manner of people they found in Spain. At this time the Goths and the native races had completely blended into one race—Spaniards. Four or five hundred years before the Moors came Spain was a centre of elegant Roman civilization. Learning was general, manners were polished, letters were cultivated, fine cities had been built with splendid adornments, and rich people lived in luxurious villas, in which life was a dream of pleasure. At that time, too, the poor were not to be pitied, for everybody had or could have a farm; nor were the Spanish soldiers to be despised, for they could hold their own against any foe.

MOSQUE OF MEDINA, CONTAINING THE PROPHET'S TOMB.

But by the beginning of the eighth century vast changes had taken place. Luxury had ruined the rich, and brought the poor to the verge of starvation. The earnings of the farmer were taken by nobles, to be spent in riotous living. Feuds between family and family constantly turned whole sections of the country into a wilderness. No Spaniard could tell when he might be called out to fight in a quarrel which was not his own. No one could go to bed sure that his vineyard and his wheat-field would not be ravaged in the night-time by an enemy. No father of a family could feel certain he would not be stabbed in the back as he filled his water-pail, or that a band of marauders would not carry off his daughters.

Of course, when such confusion prevailed, farming was difficult, industry slow, and education impossible. The Spaniards forgot how to read. The science of war was lost when there were no armies, and everybody was skirmishing on his own account. Courage died out when people fell into the way of stabbing each other from behind. Even the national spirit, exhausted by never-ending misery, faded out of existence, and the old Spanish love of country, which had taught the men of Saguntum to die rather than to surrender to Hannibal, had become a dim tradition.

You must remember these contrasts if you wish to understand the remaining chapters of this book.

THE CONQUEST

A.D. 711-717

YOU read in the chapter before the last that, after the battle in which King Roderick lost his life, Tarik swiftly moved forward and captured city after city. Malaga made no resistance, Granada was stormed; against Cordova Tarik sent seven hundred cavalry, who found a breach in the walls, and broke into the place. The Jews, who were numerous, sided with the Moors, and the Christians made but a feeble resistance. So the city fell, the governor and bishop fled for refuge to a convent, where they stood a three months' siege, and the Jewish rabbi was set in their place.

At only one town was any semblance of resistance. This was Orihuela. The Christian commander was one Theodemir. He sallied forth, gave battle to the Moors, and lost his whole army. Returning to the town with a single page, he closed the gates and bade every woman in the place dress in the attire of a man. He placed sticks in their hands to resemble lances, and had each draw her long hair under her chin so that as the Moors approached in the dusk of the evening it resembled a beard. Then he paraded his female army in a long line on the parapet. Surprised at the appearance of troops they had not expected, the Moors halted and camped for the night.

Before they slept Theodemir entered the camp under a flag of truce. Stating that he came on behalf of the commander of the city, he offered to evacuate it next morning, provided the army and the inhabitants were allowed to go out with all their property. If this were denied, they would fight till the last man fell. The Moors accepted the offer.

Next morning they were surprised to observe Theodemir, followed by a single page and a crowd of women, emerge from the gate. They asked him where was his army that was going to fight to the death.

"There," replied Theodemir, patting his page on the head, "is my army."

The Moors admired his stratagem so much that they made him Moorish Governor of Murcia.

THE ENTRANCE TO TOLEDO.

On from Orihuela the Moors pushed to Toledo, the Gothic capital. There they expected resistance. But the Jews, who had been so cruelly persecuted there, took up arms and opened the gates; the Christian nobles and churchmen fled to the mountains, and Tarik found himself in possession of the most splendid and the strongest city of Spain without striking a blow. It was there that Musa, who bad stopped on his way to capture Seville, rejoined his disobedient lieutenant and disgraced him, as you read in the third chapter of this Child's History.

From that time all Southern Spain, from the Guadarrama Mountains to the Cape of Gibraltar, fell under Moorish control. Here and there a band of Christians, under a dar¬ing leader, would rise against the invaders, but after a few skirmishes the uprising would be quelled. The Moors held all of Andalusia, with the fertile valleys of the Guadalquivir and the Guadiana, and the fine cities of Cadiz, Malaga, Granada, Seville, and Cordova; all the country afterwards known as New Castile, with the valley of the Tagus and the cities of Toledo and Madrid; all of Murcia, Aragon, and Catalonia, with the valley of the Ebro, and the towns of Carthagena, Valencia, and Barcelona. The Christians were driven back into the northern provinces of Galicia, the Asturias, Leon, Old Castile, and Navarre—a region which was cold, bleak, and broken. All of Spain that was worth having belonged to the Moors.

I must say that in the beginning they governed it well. They laid a poll-tax on Christians and Jews, but afterwards both were placed on the same footing as Moslems. The Christians had their own churches. Their priests and their bishops, their magistrates and their judges were of their own choosing. The land-tax was the same for Moslem, Christian, and Jew. Every man, whatever his religion, could own his land and sell it. Under the Gothic rule the Christians had owned large numbers of slaves, some of whom were sold with the farms on which they worked, and could not be separated from them. The Moslem faith did not approve of slavery. Any Spanish slave could obtain his freedom by going before a magistrate and saying, with his right hand uplifted,

"There is no God but God, and Mahomet is his prophet."

I am not surprised to learn that conversions among the slaves were frequent.

But the splendid victory of the Moors did not benefit those who had planned it and carried it out. Tarik, with the sting of Musa's whip still tingling on his cheek, sent trusty messengers to the Caliph at Damascus to complain of tithe treatment he had endured. The Caliph ordered Musa to repair to Damascus forthwith, to justify himself, if he could. He went, laden with treasures. Scores of wagons, filled with gold and silver ornaments; four hundred Gothic nobles forming his body guard, and several thousand male and female slaves of matchless beauty followed him to the city of the Caliph. He fancied that he could buy his grace; but the Caliph saw in the conqueror of Spain a dangerous rival.

Musa was heard, and bidden to await his sentence. Meanwhile trusty officers were sent to Spain with a message for Musa's son, Abdelaziz. They found him at the palace at Cordova, struck him down, cut off his head, embalmed it, and bore it to Damascus. Next day Musa was sent for, and shown his son's head.

"Dost thou recognize him?"

"I do," said the father. "He was innocent, and I invoke God's curse on his assassin."

He was an old man. His head, which was snow-white, he dyed, after the fashion of his times, with a red powder. In battle he was as fierce and valiant as he had been in his youth. But at the sight of the head of his dearly loved son he broke down and buried his face in his robe. The Caliph was not moved by his grief. He sentenced him to pay a fine which took everything he had. Then he ordered him to go in exile to Mecca. There he died of a broken heart.

Nor did his enemy Tarik meet a much better fate. He, too, was ordered to Damascus to give an account of Iris doings in Spain. He was acquitted of wrong, and as a mark of favor was allowed to become one of the Caliph's slaves in the palace.

After Musa several Moorish governors, some appointed by the Caliph, others selected by their tribes, ruled over Spain. The news of the wealth of the new Moslem province drew to it Moslems from far and wide. Bodies of fighting men from Syria, from Egypt, from Damascus, from North Africa poured into Spain and fought with each other for the rich valleys. In their fights governor after governor was killed. None of them claimed to rule the whole country; the authority of many did not extend beyond a bowshot from the castle where they lived.

About the only one who deserves your attention was named Abderrahman. He led an army of Moors into France in 730, and captured cities and spoil. He had planned the conquest of the country to the shore of the Baltic, and resolved that he would not rest till there was not a Chris¬tian left in Western or Southern Europe. Unluckily for him, when he got as far as the valley of the Loire, in France, in 732, he ran against an army of Franks and Gauls, under the command of Charles Martel or Charles the Hammer. Where the two armies met is not now exactly known. It was somewhere near Tours. But wherever it was, Charles the Hammer hammered the Moors with such tremendous blows, and so many other stalwart Franks and Gauls hammered after him, that when the sun went down the followers of Mahomet were flying in all directions, and when the sun rose again nothing was to be seen of them anywhere. Abderrahman was killed in the battle, and his Moors made the best of their way back again to Spain, having concluded to postpone the destruction of Christianity till a more convenient season.

Forty-five years afterwards the grandson of Charles the Hammer, who is known in history as Charlemagne, undertook to avenge the Moorish invasion of France by a Frank invasion of Spain. He crossed the Pyrenees in 777, there expecting to find allies among the Moors who were fighting among themselves. But bitterly as the Moorish chiefs bated each other, they bated the Christian Franks more bitterly, and Charlemagne was disappointed in their aid. He did not stop to give battle but faced north and recrossed the mountains; there, in the pass of Roncesvalles, his rear guard fell into an ambuscade, and was cut off to a man. It is, said that thirty thousand were destroyed by rocks and darts and arrows, which the Spaniards poured upon them from the mountain heights as they wound through the defile beneath.

The Spaniards who planned this ambuscade and destroyed the Franks were largely from the province of Leon, and were probably not Moors. They fought simply for their country. They have an old legend which says:

> "With three thousand men of Leon,
> From the city Bernard goes,
> To protect the Spanish soil
> From the spear of Frankish foes;
> From the city which is planted
> In the midst between the seas,
> To preserve the name and glory
> Of old Pelayo's victories.
> At least King Charles, if God decrees
> He must be lord of Spain,
> Shall witness that the Leonese
> Were not aroused in vain;
> He shall bear witness that we died
> As lived our sires of old
> Not only of Numantian pride
> Shall minstrel tale be told."

You will not read of another invasion of Spain by the French till near the close of this history.

AT THE FOUNTAIN, CORDOVA.

ABDERRAHMAN THE FIRST

A.D. 750-788

IN the year 750 the Caliph of Damascus was overthrown and killed by a rival who was called the Butcher, and who proved his right to the title by murdering every member of the Caliph's family except two. Of these two one was a young man named Abderrahman, who saved himself by running away to the desert, where he took refuge with an Arab family. Hunted by the Butcher, he ran away again, and this time he did not stop till he reached Africa, where he found a home with some kindly Berbers.

The Governor of the Berber country, who was a friend of the Butcher, heard of him, and sent a party of soldiers to seize him. But the Berbers gave him warning; he escaped again, and this time he did not rest till he reached the sea-coast of Mauritania. While he was there certain of the Moors in Spain, who had been loyal to the murdered caliph and hostile to his assassin, heard of Abderraham and sent him word to come to Spain. The Moors had ruled Spain for forty-four years, and in those forty-four years they had no less than twenty governors or emirs, most of whom had died violent deaths. Warlike as the Moors were, they sighed for peace.

Abderrahman landed in Andalusia in September, 755. He was only twenty years old, was blind of one eye, and devoid of the sense of smell. But he was tall, stout, strong, and brave. His judgment was sound, and his energy prodigious. I am sorry to say that with these good qualities he coupled want of principle and cruelty. His word was not to be trusted, and no man's life was safe in his hands. He was not a good type of the Moorish chief.

He took with him seven hundred and fifty horsemen, and the blessing of the old Berber chief, whose last words to him were:

"'Tis the finger of Heaven which beckons you. Your cimeter shall restore the honor of your family."

Great numbers of Moors in Andalusia flocked to his standard, Seville opened her gates to him, and next spring, when he had got his army in shape, he marched on Cordova. Governor Yusuf, who had been appointed over Spain by the Butcher, came forth to meet him. The two armies were separated by the river Guadalquivir, swollen by the spring rains. As they gazed at each other across the rolling flood Abderrahman offered to treat for peace if Yusuf let him cross without resistance; the offer was accepted, and when Abderrahman's troops got across they fell upon Yusuf's army and cut it in pieces. This treachery gave him possession of Cordova.

Most of Spain submitted with little hesitation. Nearly fifty years of war had inclined the Moors to peace. They secretly respected the vigor with which Abderraham put down rebellions against his authority; they said to each other that such a man knew how to rule. One party of Moors, who were friends of the Butcher, beset him at Carmona. He attacked them and defeated them. Then cutting off the heads of the officers, he labelled them and sent them in sacks to the Butcher. The latter inspected them with a grim face, and said:

"Thank God, there is a sea between that man and me!"

Toledo was one of the last cities to yield. It opened its gates at last on promise of fair treatment by the conqueror. But he no sooner entered the city than he seized the chief citizens and crucified them.

He chose as his capital the city of Cordova, and when you visit that grand old city you will see many traces of his work, and of the work of his successors. He built dikes along the Guadalquivir, and planted on its banks gardens in which Eastern trees and plants grew. It is said that he was the first to plant the palm-tree in Spain. It reminded him of his Arabian home, though, as he said, the palm and the Euphrates had forgotten his early griefs.

He loved poetry, and wrote verse which is not without merit. To the palm he wrote:

> "Like me, thou art a stranger,
> Far from thy friends:
> Thou host grown up in a foreign soil
> Far from the land of thy birth."

STREET SCENE WITH GOATS, TOLEDO.

But his poetic instincts did not stand in the way of his prosaic care of himself and his throne. He kept power in his own hands, and required all officers in Spain to take their orders from him, and to obey him without debate. To execute his will he had forty thousand Berbers from Africa enrolled as a body-guard, and commanded by devoted officers. They did not speak the language of the Spaniards, and hated them. It was to them a joy to fall upon Spanish rebels with sword and lance, and to strew the field with their corpses.

Abderrahman himself was the hardest worker in his empire. He seemed to require neither rest nor sleep. He would work all night over the reports of his officers in the provinces, and at daybreak he would be found on his horse, reviewing his troops or leading them to battle.

A PATIO IN TOLEDO.

When he first made himself master of Spain he required the country to pay, him ten thousand ounces of gold, ten thousand pounds of silver, ten thousand horses, ten thousand mules, and one thousand cuirasses. Before him the governors of Spain had been called emirs, and had held their authority from the Caliph at Damascus. He now declared that he was the true Caliph, and the head of the Moslem Church, having the blood of Mahomet in his veins. And the Asiatic Caliph, who was in power at this time, removed from Damascus to Bagdad, and did not undertake to dispute his assumption with arms.

But if the successor of the Butcher let Abderrahman alone, his subjects in Spain were not disposed to be so submissive. They were perpetually plotting against him, and the plots did not cease, though the Caliph had a way of crucifying the plotters when he found them out. In the first years of his stay at Cordova he used to walk the streets alone and converse in a friendly way with any one he met. In his later years he never appeared without a powerful body-guard, armed to the teeth. He had several thousand soldiers to guard his palace and his person, and not one of them was a Spaniard. Woe befell any one whom he thought he had reason to suspect.

In his way he was pious. He would offer prayers over the bodies of the dead, and on Fridays he would get into the pulpit of the mosque and preach sermons. Having left the mosque, he would give orders for the execution of prisoners who were accused of disloyalty.

Abderrahman lived to be fifty-three, but his later years were years of misery. A tyrant may enforce submission, but he cannot command friendship. Everybody—relations, friends, comrades-in-arms, and even servants—deserted him, except at the hours when duty required them to attend his presence. They stood before him in silence, with bowed heads. He could not order them to execution because they would not talk to him, and yet it was galling to live a life of silence. Not one single person loved him. Every one looked forward eagerly to his death, and he knew it. Of the women who had laid their beautiful heads on his breast in his youth not one remained; they had died, I suppose—perhaps of broken hearts, for there was not a ray of tenderness in him. His son, who was an admirable young man, rarely saw his father, and could not have respected him. Not even one of those whom he had raised to high command was hypocrite enough to feign to like him.

This desolate old man, however, founded a dynasty which lasted three hundred, and an empire which lasted over seven hundred years. The race of which he was the leader ruled Spain for a period equal in length to that which separates us from the Crusades. They left a mark on that country which ignorance, intolerance, and bigotry have been unable to efface; and, by a strange fatality, the epoch of their expulsion coincides very nearly with the decline and fall of Spanish power and prosperity.

ABDERRAHMAN'S SUCCESSORS

A.D. 788-862

ARDERRAHMAN THE FIRST was succeeded by his son Hisham, who reigned eight years, and he by his son Hacam, who reigned twenty-six years.

The first was an excellent young man, who ruled his people justly and established schools all over the country. It had been foretold of him by an astrologer that he would reign eight years, and no more; and sure enough, in the eighth year of his reign he died. The people mourned him, for they had loved him as much as they had hated his father. He was famous for kind deeds; constantly visited the sick, sent food to the needy, and prayed with the devout who were confined to their houses by inclement weather or illness.

His son Hacam was a very different person. He loved nothing so much as pleasure—hunting, wine-drinking, gayety, and frolic. He counted some of the most beautiful women in Spain among his wives. When he died he left forty sons. His way of life gave offence to truly religious Moslems—the students of the college at Cordova, who were extremely devout, having been converted from Christianity, were especially incensed at the loose behavior of the head of the Church. It may give you some idea of the singular manners of the time to hear that these students followed the Caliph in the streets, jeering him and throwing stones at him.

Hacam only laughed at them; but when they concocted a plot for his overthrow, he showed that he was of the blood of Abderrahman. He swooped down upon the plotters at the head of his Mamelukes, caught the leaders, and crucified them. Three or four years afterwards, in 806, they formed another plot, and the plotters met the same fate. Then, after a time, the nobles of Toledo broke out in revolt, and declared that they would make an end of Hacam, as they had made an end of so many emirs before Abderrahman. They raised quite an army, and prepared to take the field against an unworthy follower of Mahomet.

Hacam sent his young son, whose name was Abderrahman, like his grandfather, and who was only fifteen years old, to deal with the rebels, giving him private instructions how to act. The boy got into the castle of Toledo—you can still see the ruins of its walls—and invited the nobles and chief people of the place, to the number of a thousand or more, to a banquet, at which he proposed to discuss with them the causes of their discontent. They came, and were directed to walk through the castle ditch round the main tower of the banquet hall. They were so numerous and made such a fine show that a crowd collected to see them enter the castle.

After a time the on-lookers were surprised that the banqueters did not come out of the castle. Some one said that they had doubtless gone out by the back door.

"Not so," said a physician, who was watching; "I have been at the back door for some time, and no one has gone out that way."

Next day it was discovered that the guests, as they walked through the ditch in narrow file, had been struck down by Mamelukes and their bodies thrown into a pit. The date of the massacre was long remembered in Toledo by the name of the Day of the Foss. It kept the Toledans quiet for many a long year.

Hacam's last years were spent in private. You will read in the histories that he was as melancholy and as wretched as his grandfather. But I notice that he wrote poetry, and was passionately fond of music, which seems to imply that he was not always sad. There are legends that he gloried in putting people to death in order to exult over their dying agonies. But this and other stories were probably started by fanatic Moslems, who hated him because he was not as bigoted as they. At the time of his death the Moors of Spain had got over the liberal toleration with which they began their empire. They had got the taste of persecution into their mouths.

The students of the college, who were crazy enthusiasts on religion, would have liked to crucify him. Once they roused the mob and attacked the palace with fury. Hacam, aroused by the noise, bade his page perfume his hair and beard with civet. When the page hesitated, in a moment of such peril, the Caliph cried:

THE MOORISH GATE, SEVILLE.

"Proceed, fellow! How shall the rebels identify my head among the rest except by its sweet odor?"

Then swiftly sending a force of cavalry by a round-about way to the quarter from which the mob had come, he ordered the houses set on fire. The rioters turning to rescue their belongings from the flames, the palace gates were opened and a swarm of Mamelukes poured forth, while the cavalry charged them under cover of the smoke. Thus caught between two foes the mob was crushed with frightful slaughter, and, by way of a lesson, Hacam burned down that part of the city in which they lived, and exiled the survivors to Africa. The students he spared. One of them, who was brought before him, was asked why he had rebelled against his sovereign.

"Because it was the will of God," said the fanatic.

"He who commands thee to hate me," said Hacam, "commands me to pardon thee. Go and live."

Hacam was succeeded by one of his forty sons, Abderrahman the Second. He came to the throne in 822, and reigned till 852. Throughout the thirty years religious feuds glowed and grew hotter and hotter. I will tell you of them in the next chapter. The king did not take much interest in them, and after the severe lesson his father Hacam had given the fanatics, they did not fly to arms as quickly as formerly.

Abderrahman spent his time in works of art and beauty. He built mosques and palaces and bridges; he laid out fine gardens, and watered them by means of aqueducts leading from mountain springs. His court was splendid. He gave handsome rewards to poets and musicians, and gathered the brightest of them round him. His wife Tarub is the first Moorish queen who figures in history. She seems to have been a woman of mind, though she did love necklaces and bags of silver, and was not particular how she got them.

Church affairs Abderrahman left to a bigoted priest named Tahya, who ruled the Moslems with a rod of iron, and punished neglect of religious duty severely. He does not seem to have troubled the Christians much unless they made themselves offensive; but whenever a Moslem omitted his daily prayers Tahya made an example of him.

Abderrahman's best friend and chief associate was a Persian named Ziriab, who was a musician and a singer. It was said that he knew a thousand songs by heart, and the king was so fond of hearing him sing them that he would spend all day by Ziriab's side, would share his meals with him, and was never tired of giving him houses and pensions and presents of value.

Ziriab was more than a musician; he was a wit and a wise observer of mankind. He gave his master advice which generally proved to be sound. He was also a man of taste, and he undertook to reform the manners of the Moors. He set new fashions in dress, and taught the Moorish nobles to cut their hair. He persuaded the court to cease drinking out of metal cups, and to use glasses instead. He abolished linen table-cloths, and covered dinner tables with leather cloths—which does not give me a high opinion of his notions of cleanliness. Linen sheets he declared to be an abomination, and advised people to sleep on leather instead. He invented fricassees and forcemeat; lie introduced asparagus into Spain. He did not rest till he had changed the fashions of the Moors in almost all their ways of living. And for these services the people admired him almost as much as the king did. Though he was the favorite, he did not inspire envy in his lifetime, and I think you can remember him with pleasure.

Abderrahman's thirty years' reign was a period of peace and comfort for the Spaniards. Taught by the king's example, the nobles in many places irrigated their land by bringing water to it in leaden pipes from great distances, and the consequence was improved harvests. They were stimulated to pursue this work by a drought which occurred in 846, and which of course was followed by famine and pestilence; those who had neglected their water supply starved in great numbers, while those who had aqueducts reaped the usual harvest.

In the year 852—the memorable year when the Danish or Norman sea rovers ravaged the coasts of England, France, and Germany, and captured the cities they could reach, including the City of London—King Abderrahman the Second ascended to the terrace of his palace to breathe the evening air. His eye was offended by a row of Christian corpses, mutilated, and swinging by the neck to a gibbet. He ordered them cut down and decently buried, and his cheek flushed as he thought of the bigotry of his fellow-believers. The flush rose and deepened till his whole face turned purple. He staggered and fell, and when the physicians came they declared that the king had died of apoplexy.

FLORA AND MARY

A.D. 840-859

WHILE Abderrahman the Second was Moorish King or Sultan—as the king was sometimes called—of Spain, there was born to an honest Moorish mechanic a daughter, whom he named Flora. Though her father was a Moslem, her mother was a Christian. Now the Moorish law was that children of Moors must be brought up in the Moorish faith; but in secret Flora's mother brought her up to be a Christian.

At that time Moors and Christians were living peaceably side by side. Moslemism was the religion of the country, but the Christians were not persecuted; they had their churches, their bishops, and their priests; nobody troubled them about their religion as long as they were decently respectful to the Moslem faith; but it chanced at that particular time that a wave of religious enthusiasm swept over Spain. In the gloom of their cloisters, monks let their minds dwell upon the history of the early martyrs until their beads were turned, and they could think of nothing but the joy of giving up one's life for religion's sake. They recalled the past glories of their Church, and they groaned in spirit when they remembered that it had been overthrown by infidels.

Such a one was Eulogius, who had spent years in fasting and prayer, till he had destroyed his constitution and upset his mind. Such another was Perfectus, who had worked himself up to such a pitch of frenzy that he went through the streets cursing Mahomet, and was duly arrested and executed for blasphemy, according to the Moorish law. Another such was a monk named Isaac, who went into court, reviled Mahomet in the presence of the cadi, or judge, was taken out and beheaded; whereupon the Christian Church enrolled him in the list of saints, together with others who proved their saintliness by insulting the faith of their fellow-countrymen.

Flora, who was a fanciful, high-strung girl, caught the exaltation of the priests and fled from her home, saying that she was a Christian. Her brother was a quiet Moslem; he was hurt at her conduct, brought her back, and reasoned with her; but as she would listen to nothing, he took her before the judge. According to the Moorish law she had forfeited her life by abandoning the faith of her father; but the judge shrank from sentencing one so young and so beautiful; he ordered that she be whipped, and he enjoined her brother to take better care of her thereafter. His back was no sooner turned than she ran away again, and this time hid herself with a Christian family, where she met Eulogius, the man who had prayed and fasted so long. He fell in love with her, and her Christian friends had to hide her from him as well as from the Moors.

By this time the religious enthusiasm had become a craze. Eulogius made a convert of one of the sultan's guards, who, to show his zeal, reviled Mahomet before his regiment. When he was taken out and beheaded six monks rushed to the court where the judge was sitting and roared at him:

"The guardsman was right! Now avenge your accursed prophet! Here we are, ready to die!"

They were promptly accommodated; and three more monks, who insisted on being beheaded, shared their fate. It looked as though the Christians had gone mad. I do not know what would have happened if the bishops had not called a halt, and proclaimed that suicide was not the road to heaven. Each bishop in his diocese preached against the folly and wickedness of the enthusiasts, and for a time the mania was checked.

But the mad priest Eulogius raved more loudly than ever, and confounded the bishops with extracts from the lives of the saints. He bawled and bellowed so furiously that the Moorish judge, not wishing to execute him if it could be avoided, locked him up in jail to stop his tongue. There he met Flora again, and with her another young and beautiful girl named Mary. Both of them had been imprisoned by the judge, who wanted to evade the duty of putting them to death. In the solitude of her cell Flora had had time to think, and she had seen the folly of insulting the faith which her father had professed and to which her brother belonged. She was ready, when her release came, to behave quietly, as became a young girl, and to keep her religious opinions to herself.

When the wild fanatic Eulogius met her, her good resolutions were quickly scattered to the winds. He overwhelmed her with his frantic fury. He besought her by the love he bore her not to let the opportunity of martyrdom escape. He entreated of her to show her true Christian spirit by reviling the Moors and their prophet. And the weak girl, probably loving him as he loved her, and believing him to be her best friend and adviser, did as he bade her. She and Mary went before the cadi and cursed Mahomet; whereupon the judge, whose patience was worn out, ordered them to execution; and their heads were severed from their bodies on November 34th, 851.

When she told Eulogius that he had convinced her, and that she was ready for martyrdom, he exulted and said:

"I sought to confirm her in her resolution by showing her the crown of glory. I worshipped her; I fell down before this angel, and besought her to remember me; then I returned less sad to my sombre cell."

When the Moors turned this maniac priest out of his sombre cell, the Christians of Toledo chose him to be their bishop. He had not been long preaching when another beautiful girl was missing. She also was traced to Eulogies who was training her for the glory of martyrdom. They were both arrested and taken before the judge. Eulogies, who had quite lost his head, burst forth with a storm of curses against Mahomet. Whereupon the judge sentenced him to die, as the law required; but before his execution a friend of the Sultan tried to save him, offering to get him a pardon if he would withdraw what he had said before the cadi. He stoutly refused, declaring that he had nothing to recant. Whereupon his bead was struck off, eight years after Flora, by his persuasion, had voluntarily given up her life.

I have no doubt that Eulogius was honest. But it is not enough to be honest, if the honesty be displayed in a way that will injure others. A blind teacher cannot escape blame for his teaching on the ground that his motives were pure. In the coming chapters of this history you will often be shocked by tales of religious persecution; I suspect that the fashion was set by the yearnings of Eulogius and his brethren for martyrdom.

ABDERRAHMAN THE THIRD

A.D. 850-961

THE second Abderrahman died before Eulogius, leaving Spain in disorder, through his weakness as a ruler. He was followed by his son Mohammed; he by his son Mundhir, who was assassinated; and he by his brother Abdallah, who reigned twenty-four years, and died in 912.

During all these reigns the power of the Caliph was gradually dissolving. Almost all Andalusia had risen in revolt and driven out the Caliph's officers. Seville declared its independence. Saragossa defied the Caliph. Jaen was in the bands of the Berbers. Granada was seized by Christians, who challenged the Moors to attack them. Toledo was up in arms again. All Marcia, Estremadura, Algarve, had thrown off the Moorish yoke. In the whole of the empire which had been ruled from Cordova, that city alone obeyed the orders of the Caliph, and there poverty reigned by his side. There was no money to pay troops, and the people had none to buy bread. Meanwhile the new chiefs of cities and provinces made incessant war on each other, and quite often raided the suburbs of Cordova. Matters were in this shocking condition when Abdallah died, and his throne fell to his grandson, Abderrahman the Third, a boy of twenty-one.

Young as he was, he was full of vigor. He called upon the rebels against his authority to lay down their arms, marched against those who hesitated, and beat them in the field. Town after town, district after district submitted. They had tried rebellion for fifty years, and as its chief result had been to hand over their vineyards and orchards and wheat-fields to bands of robbers, who destroyed more than they consumed, they concluded it did not pay. Even the Christians of Granada felt that no caliph could be as bad as the bandit chiefs, who, whenever their purses or their larders were empty, raided the nearest town for fresh supplies. The last place to submit was Toledo, which the young caliph beleaguered and starved into surrender.

Then Abderrahman returned to Cordova, prepared to reign in peace. It had taken him eighteen years to put the rebels down.

But he had other enemies on his hands whom he could not put down; these were the Christians of the North. Portions of the slopes of the Cantabrians, in Galicia, the Asturias, Leon, Old Castile, and Navarre had never been conquered outright by the Moors; here and there bands of Christians, feeding flocks in the mountains, had never surrendered their independence, and fought the Moors whenever they could get at them. They were rude and rough; they could neither read nor write; they gave no quarter in battle; but their courage was dauntless, and their perseverance inexhaustible.

One of these barbarians, whose name was Pelayo, shut himself up in the cleft of a steep mountain in the Asturias, and defied the Moors to take him. He had thirty men and ten women all told; they lived in a cave in the cleft, which could only be reached by a ladder of ninety steps. A Moorish general said:

"What are thirty barbarians perched on a rock? They must inevitably die."

They did die, of course, as all men must; but before they died they gathered round them armies of Christians from the rocky steeps of Northern Spain, poured down under old Pelayo into the valleys of Castile, and when they met the Moors in battle the Crescent was often routed and the Cross victorious. The war began before Abderrahman had been two years on his throne. It lasted, with some intervals of peace, till a few years before his death. It was a shocking and a cruel war. After some years of fighting—neither side asked nor gave quarter—and after each battle women and children were sold into slavery, simply on the ground of their religion. The generals who began the fifty years' fighting on both sides died in the course of nature; but other generals took their place, and the war went on. The net result was that before Abderrahman's death the Christians were masters of all Northern Spain, and had pushed the Moors south of the Guadarrama Mountains. The valleys of the Douro and of the upper Ebro, as well as the cities of Zamorra, Salamanca, Segovia, Tarazona, and Tudela were in their hands, and the great work of the expulsion of the Moors had begun.

I must now tell you something of the city of Cordova in the time of Abderrahman the Third. It was a fine city under Abderrahman the First. But it was the third caliph of the name who made it one of the wonders of the world. According to the ancient historians, it stretched ten miles along the river Guadalquiver, and for this distance the banks were lined with houses of white marble, mosques, and gardens, in which Eastern trees and plants grew luxuriantly, watered by irrigating ditches.

RESTORATION OF THE MOSQUE AT CORDOVA.

It is now a dead town, with about fifty thousand people in it, most of whom are poor and ignorant; it is the chief city of a miserable district. Then it was surrounded by a strong wall, on which square or octagonal towers rose at intervals; parts of the wall still endure, and you can overlook the country from the turf on their top. A thousand years ago, we are told, from the summit of these towers twelve thousand towns or villages could be counted in the valley of the Guadalquivir.

At that time the Arab writers say that Cordova contained a million people, two hundred thousand houses, six hundred mosques, nine hundred public baths, many thousand palaces of the nobility, and a number of royal palaces with poetic names, such as the Palace of Flowers, the Palace of Lovers, the Palace of Contentment. These palaces opened on gardens in front, and on the river in the rear; carpeted passages hung with jewelled lamps connected them with mosques, in which the Sultan and his family paid their devotions to God. The ceilings were supported by pillars of many-colored marble and porphyry, and the floors were mosaic.

The great mosque of Cordova, which devout Moslems from all parts of Asia and Africa came to pray in, was probably the grandest religious temple in the world. Its roof was light and elegant, and was supported by a forest of pillars of different colors. There were over twelve hundred of them, each with silver lamps kept constantly burning, and some with jewelled cornices. When the Catholics took possession of Cordova they pulled down many of the pillars and stripped the others of their lamps and ornaments. But enough remains to show what it was.

The finest of the palaces was built in honor of the Ca¬liph's pet wife, Ez-Zabra. The Arab writers say that Abderrahman kept ten thousand men and four thousand horses working on the building for twenty-five years. It contained fifteen thousand doors of brass or iron. In the centre of the Caliph's Hall was a lake of quicksilver, which was set in motion by a spring. When it moved it flashed rays of light like lightning, and dazzled the eye. To wait upon the queen in this palace we are told that there were thirteen thousand male servants and six thousand females. The terraces and balls and pavilions and flower-gardens were past numbering. Into one fish-pond it is said that twelve thousand loaves of bread were flung daily to feed the fish. In the main court-room stood a throne glittering with gold and gems. On the mosaic floors were Persian rugs, and silken portieres veiled the bronze doors. I am not sure that you can believe all these stories; but however this may be, you may feel sure that Cordova was the centre of art, science, and industry. It contained doctors who understood anatomy and medical science, astronomers who knew all that was known of the skies before Galileo and Kepler, learned botanists, profound philosophers, exquisite poets. Some of the poetry of the Cordova bards is delightful. In architecture and bronze work the Cordovans of the tenth century have not been surpassed to this day.

The working-men of Cordova were expert silk-weavers and skilled potters. They carved admirably on silver and bronze. They made a steel which was not surpassed at Toledo. In some of the museums in Europe you will see marvellous sword-hilts made at Cordova at a time when our ancestors fought with stone hatchets.

These various attractions drew travellers to Cordova from every part of the world. We hear of an ambassador who was taken by the Caliph to see the Ez-Zabra palace, and who fainted at the sight of such an accumulation of splendors. The great college was thronged with students from every country in Europe; they found professors there who could address each of them in his own language. It was indeed the only place in Europe w here a seeker after knowledge could obtain a good education.

Its glories did not last long. Fifty years after the death of Abderrahman the Third an army of Castilians and Berbers stormed Cordova, and pillaged it for several days. Thousands of magnificent buildings were burned, among others the palace of Ez-Zabra, which was thoroughly robbed before it was fired. Nothing was destroyed by the flames except that which could not be carried away. So one generation undid the work of a preceding generation, and after a century or more knowledge and civilization found themselves just where they had been at the beginning.

GARDEN OF THE ALCAZAR, CORDOVA.

If you wonder, as perhaps you may, at a nation which had made such progress in art and science being as bigoted in matters of religion as both Moors and Christians were in the time of Abderrahman the Third, you must remember that, in the country of your forefathers, in the very year that the Caliph was putting Christians to death in Northern Spain, an English priest dragged a young king from the altar at which he was being married to the lady of his love, and that this same lady, who was virtuous and beautiful, was shortly afterwards murdered by the order of an archbishop. The bigotry, you see, was not in the race, but in the times.

THE GREAT VIZIER

A.D. 961-1002

ABDERRAHMAN THE THIRD was succeeded as Caliph by his son Hacam, who was a scholar. He reigned fifteen years, but these years he devoted to study to the neglect of his empire; thus, though he collected a library of four, or, as some say, six hundred thousand manuscripts, at a time when other libraries were thought rich with five hundred; and though he established schools everywhere, so that every Andalusian could read and write, he was not a successful ruler. At his death his son, Hisham the Second, a boy of twelve, became caliph; and the real power passed into the hands of his mother, Aurora, and an exceedingly able minister of hers, who is known in history as Almanzor.

This was the son of a Cordova lawyer. He had studied at the college, and on graduating became a letter-writer for the court. Sultana Aurora took a fancy to him, and through her favor and his own address he rose from post to post until, at the age of thirty two or three, he was prefect of Cordova and general in the army. He had had no training in arms, but luck favored him, and he conducted two successful campaigns against the Christians of the North. On his return he was so strict in enforcing the law as prefect that when his own son committed a crime the stern father had him beaten to death with rods. It did not take him long to convince the Caliph that he would be far happier among the ladies of the harem than at the Council Board; and then Almanzor became ruler of Spain.

He was the most vigorous and unscrupulous ruler that country had had for many, many years. Those who stood in his way mysteriously died. He made himself friends with the high-church party by burning books which in the smallest degree questioned the Moslem faith. He kept the working-class quiet by giving them employment on new buildings. He endeared himself to the army by giving then full license to plunder the enemy; thus he always had full ranks, and many Christians served under his flag. He became popular with the people by winning victories and extending the empire. He conquered a large piece of Northern Africa, and during his time the

Christians of Northern Spain were pushed back again towards the Cantabrians and the Bay of Biscay.

THE ARCHWAY OF ST. MARY AT BURGOS.

Twice a year, spring and fall, he made war on the Christians. He took Leon, and pulled down its walls and towers. He captured Barcelona. He defeated the Christians at Castile and Navarre. He even seized Santiago in Galicia, where the famous shrine of St. James of Compostella was. When his army reached the shrine they found the church empty. Only a single monk was seen, kneeling.

"What dost thou here?" said a Moorish officer. "I pray," said the old monk.

And they spared him.

His soldiers had absolute trust in him. At a battle they were driven back, with the Christians at their heels; Almauzor leaped from the high seat he had occupied, and bending head to earth, covered his hair with dust, in token of shame and sorrow; at which sight the troops turned on the enemy, attacked them furiously, and routed them.

Another time the Christians cut off his retreat, and made sure of his surrender. He coolly collected lumber and farm tools, built houses, and began to plant seeds. When the Christians inquired what this meant, he told them that he intended to stay where he was, and to intrench, as the next campaign would begin in a few weeks. Upon which the men of the North, not being minded to encourage so uncongenial a neighbor, made haste to open the way for his retreat south.

The Christians learned to fear him. In the Kingdom of Navarre was a Moslem woman who was kept a prisoner. Almanzor sent word to the king that she must be given up, and instantly. The king did not lose a day in setting her free, with many apologies.

Almanzor was a man of iron nerve. When he was sitting at the council-chamber one day the councillors noticed the smell of burning flesh, and looked round inquiringly.

"It is nothing," said Almanzor; "my surgeon"—pointing to a man kneeling at his feet—"is cauterizing my leg with a red-hot iron."

If Almanzor had lived, and had been succeeded by men of his fibre, I am afraid that the Christians would have found the expulsion of the Moors more difficult than they did. He was a born soldier, and a statesman of genius; but such men do not often bequeath their qualities to their successors.

A day came when Almanzor was taken ill on one of his campaigns and died. A monk, who wrote the history of these times, disposed of the event in few words. He wrote: "In 1002, Almanzor died, and was buried in hell."

At his death a son of his took the title of Vizier, and tried to rule; then another son tried, in his turn, with no better success. The people, dreading the old troubles which racked Spain before Abderrahman the Third, dragged the Caliph Hisham out of his harem and insisted that he should exert his authority. He was no longer young, and had been living thirty years among women and eunuchs. He entreated them to let him alone, protesting that he knew nothing about government, and only wanted to lead a quiet life with his ladies and his books and his music. I am afraid that the poor old creature was roughly handled by some of his Moorish friends, who thought that vigorous measures might restore his energy; but it was all to no purpose. The caliph was like a baby.

He was allowed to return to his harem, where he remained several years, while caliph succeeded caliph, and each was murdered in turn. One of them, whose name was also Hisham, had a very sad fate. He was dragged from his throne by the guards and thrust into a dark dungeon under the mosque, with his wives and his only child. Sometimes the jailers forgot to bring him food. When the council of the chiefs had decided what was to be done with him, their messenger found him clasping his little child to his breast, with his wives all in rags and shivering with cold standing round him. At sight of the jailers he begged piteously for bread. Food was brought, and he was told that he was to be removed to a fortress in the mountains. He made no objection. "But I hope," he said, "that there will be a window, or at least a candle, in the prison. It is dreadful to he in the dark."

After many changes the people of Cordova remembered old Hisham the Second, and they pulled him out of his harem and told him he must be caliph once more. But the old man's mind was quite gone; he could only laugh in a half-witted way, and say he would do whatever they wanted. So they locked him up in a prison, and whether he died there or escaped, as one story says, and lived out his life in some friend's house, I do not know.

The Empire of Cordova ended with Abderrahman the Third and Almanzor. After them no Moor could control he quarrelsome chiefs, and the history of Spain for nearly live hundred years is an endless story of war.

THE CHRISTIANS OF NORTHERN SPAIN

A.D. 740-1065

IT is time that I should tell you something about the Christians who lived in Northern Spain and made unending war upon the Moors.

If you look at the map of Spain, you will see that the northern part is divided into five provinces, thus following each other from west to east—Galicia, Asturias, the Basque country, Navarre, and Catalonia—and that south of these the two provinces of Leon and Old Castile dovetail into them and are geographically part of them. This part of Spain is much broken by mountain ranges, and is cold and windy. It is not barren, for it grows wheat, barley, and flax in abundance, and on the mountain slopes the cork-tree flourishes. But the climate is harsher than in the valleys of the South, where the vine and the orange and the lemon and the fig luxuriate in an almost perpetual summer.

The Moors were never able to conquer this northern country. They made raids into it, fought battles, won victories, and built forts; but after the victories were won the natives were ready to fight again next year; and when the forts were finished they were often taken by the races against which they had been built. These native races were Christians, of a mixed Gothic and Spanish stock; with them were allied some Berbers, whom the Moors of Arab race had driven into Galicia from the fertile valleys of Andalusia, and who professed to be Christians, though at that time I do not think their Christianity was very deep.

You remember old Pelayo, who with thirty men and ten women took refuge in a cave in a cleft of the Asturian Mountains and defied the Moors. When this old warrior had driven the Moors out of his province he took the name of King of the Asturias, and the people round about agreed to accept him as their king. When he died his son became king after him, and reigned until a bear ate him. After him his son, who was named Alfonso the First, succeeded to the throne, and, being a famous warrior, extended his kingdom from Galicia to the borders of Navarre. This was about the year 750, just at the time when your ancestors in England were first enabled to read the Lord's Prayer, the Ten Commandments, and the Creed in their own language.

It was in the time of one of Pelayo's immediate successors that Bernardo, the champion of Spain, and one of the heroes of the Spanish legends, is said to have lived. He was the son of Sancho Diaz, Count of Saldaila; this count the king, from jealousy, had imprisoned and most cruelly maltreated. Bernardo, being unable to bear the tyranny of the king and the sight of his father's misery, fled to the woods, and at the head of a party of outlaws barricaded himself in a castle. The king besieged him there; but being unable to make a breach in the walls, he bethought himself of offering to Bernardo to set Don Sancho free if the castle were surrendered. The offer was accepted. The treacherous king forthwith had Sancho done to death in the prison. Bernardo came out of his castle, and cried:

"Where is my father, the Count of Saldana?"

"There he comes," said the king; and sure enough, in the distance a horse ridden by a knight in Don Sancho's armor was seen approaching.

Bernardo ran forward to seize his hand to kiss it; but the hand was cold, and the son perceived that his father was dead.

"What have I done?" cried he; "Don Sancho, in an it hour didst thou beget me!" For nearly a hundred years after that other kings reigned over the Asturias. Sometimes their dominions were large, and sometimes they were small; but whether they were large or small, the Asturians were always fighting, both with Moors and with their Christian neighbors. They must have been unpleasant fellows to live near.

About the year 942 there was a king named Ramiro, who was fierce and bold. He burned witches, and put out the eyes of robbers; but he swept the Moors out of his country, reclaimed the fields they had laid desert, rebuilt the churches they had pulled down, mended the forts they had wrecked. The old legend says of him:

> "A cry went through the mountains
> When the proud Moor drew near,

And trooping to Ramiro
Came every Christian spear;
The blessed San Iago
They called upon his name:
That day began our freedom,
And wiped away our shame."

He was king when the Moorish caliph demanded the payment of a tribute which the Christians had once, after a defeat, agreed to pay to Cordova. The tribute consisted of one hundred Christian maidens, the fairest of the Asturias. For an answer to the demand, Ramiro called out his fighting men, and went to meet the Moors near a village in Leon. The fight lasted two days, and the first day the Moors had the advantage. But in the night, says the legend, the blessed San Ingo appeared to the king and bade him be of good cheer, that he would be with him on the morrow. Sure enough, as the armies engaged, the saint appeared in a suit of white armor; on a milk-white steed, and scattered the Moors so that they threw their arms away in their flight. Thus the horrid tribute was abolished forever.

It was about these times that Fernando Gonzales was Count of Castile, and in love with Saneha, the daughter of Garcia, the King of Navarre. He was on his way to Navarre to court her when her father treacherously seized him and thrust him into a dungeon. A Norman knight heard of his capture, and the old ballad tells what happened:

"They have borne into Navarre
The great Count of Castile,
And they have bound him sorely
They have hound him hand and heel:
There is great joy and feasting
Because that lord is ta'en;
King Garcia in his dungeon
Holds the doughtiest lord in Spain,
The Moors may well be joyful,
But great should be our grief,
For Spain has lost her guardian,
When Castile lost her chief;
The Moorish host is pouring

Like a river o'er the land;
Curse on the Christian fetters
That hind Gonzales's hand."

CHURCH AT VALENCIA.

The knight bade Sancha try to set him free, for her love's sake.

> "The lady answered little,
> But at the dead of night,
> When all her maids are sleeping,
> She bath risen and ta'en her flight:
> She hath tempted the Alcayde
> With her jewels and her gold,
> And unto her his prisoner
> That jailer false bath sold."

Then she married her true love, and years afterwards, when he was made prisoner in the wars and again locked up in a dungeon, she prayed leave to visit him just once. The favor granted, she changed clothes with him. He escaped in the gown of a woman, and when the jailer came round he found the countess in the cuirass and boots of a knight.

Other kings followed Ramiro, but nothing happened in their reigns which you would care to hear. The provinces waged incessant war against each other; and in one of the wars the King of Leon, whose name was Garcias, overthrew the King of the Asturias, and annexed his kingdom. He and his descendants held the throne for a quarter of a century, and then the King of Navarre, Sancho Mayor, swooped down upon Leon and Asturias, conquered both, and extended his kingdom from the Pyrenees to the Atlantic. He left his dominions to his son Ferdinand, who in 1035 became monarch of all Northern Spain except Catalonia.

That fine province, which is separated from Aragon by the river Ebro, is one of the richest portions of Spain. It contains the City of Barcelona, which was a famous place of trade in the time of the Carthaginians, and is a lively seaport to-day. Eight hundred and fifty years ago it was ruled by a family named Berenguer, who called themselves counts, and were independent of Moor, Christian, Spaniard, and Frank. You hear much of them in the history of the Crusades. Two of them, father and son, both named Raymond Berenguer, went to the Crusades at the head of their fighting men, and both died in Palestine. One of them was a Knight Templar, whose exploits made much noise at the time. These counts set King

Ferdinand at defiance, and he did not care to molest them. So Catalonia was the only northern province of Spain which did not form part of the Christian league against the Moors.

Ferdinand, King of Northern Spain from 1035 to 1065, led a life of toil and strife; when he felt his end approaching he had himself carried to a church, where he prayed and confessed to the priests, took off his royal robes, put on the garment of repentance, and laid down and died.

Before we begin the long story of the death grapple between Moor and Christian, you may care to hear something of what was happening in other countries at that time.

In the year following the death of Ferdinand, William, Duke of Normandy, fought the battle of Hastings and conquered England, which was then a wild country, without learning, or wealth, or trade, or good roads, or fine buildings, except monasteries and churches. In France, about the same time, a Church decree forbade the marriage of priests, and this, among other things, caused the separation of the Catholic and the Greek Churches. In Italy a love for letters broke out, schools and colleges were founded, and interesting works were written; the courts of the Pope and of some of the nobility were polished, and were frequented by learned men. At this time the Empire of the East, of which Constantinople was the capital, began . to be molested by Moslem raids; the long fight between Moslem and Christian, which, after lasting four hundred years, was destined to end thirty-seven years before the same fight in Spain—though in a different way—had fairly begun.

And, finally, thirty-four years before Ferdinand became king, a Norman or Norwegian sea-rover named Leif, is said to have crossed the Atlantic and to have landed in Rhode Island. This story is legend, and you are not required to believe it if you think it improbable— though it may quite possibly be true.

THE CID CAMPEADOR

A.D. 1064-1099

AFTER some years of confusion the kingdom of Ferdinand fell into the hands of his son Alfonso. It was in his time that the Cid Campeador, or the "Lord Challenger," figured in the old history of Spain; and though his story reads like a fanciful legend, and some pundits have even doubted whether there ever was such a personage, he is too famous in Spain to be passed over.

We must suppose that he really lived, and that he was, at twenty, one of the class of men whom the troublous times called into being — a fighting adventurer, brave, strong, skilful, but ready to sell his services to any one who could pay for them. In those days, when two armies met, it was common for a knight to ride out of the ranks and challenge any knight on the opposite side to single combat, while the two armies looked on. This knight was called a challenger — in Spanish, campeador. Even while he was a mere boy the Cid became famous as a campeador; hardly a day passed that he did not fight some one. Once, when Castile and Navarre were at war, he challenged a huge knight of Navarre, and killed him. For this the King of Castile gave him high command.

But not long afterwards the king grew suspicious of him and banished him, declaring that any one who gave him food or shelter after ten days should lose their possessions and their eyes. The Cid rode away with a few friends, homeless, sad, and cheerless; but he took some comfort when at Bivar he saw a crow on his right hand, and at Burgos another crow on his left. At Burgos he tried to get food and a roof to shelter him; but every door was closed, and when he hammered with his spear, a little girl came out of a house and told him people were afraid to open to him, for the king had said that those that did so should lose their houses and their eyes. He rode on mournfully to San Pedro, where his wife and daughters were, and the good abbot of the monastery fed him and his men.

His wife wept bitterly at the parting, but he comforted her, saying,

"Please God, and Saint Mary, I shall live to give these daughters of mine in marriage, and to do my service to you, my honored wife."

From San Pedro he rode to Saragossa, which was ruled by the Moors, and he offered his sword to the Moorish prince, who quickly accepted it, and despatched him to raid the neighboring state of Aragon. He rode through Aragon like the wind, slaying every man he met, burning houses and trees, tearing up vines, and stealing what he could carry off. I hardly think that this was honorable work for one who relied on God and the Virgin Mary; but you must remember that the Cid was a soldier of fortune.

After a time he left the employ of the Prince of Saragossa, and took service with a Christian prince or count, to serve against the Moors. According to the story, he was the most terrible foe they had met. When the Moors saw him and his body-guard coming at full gallop on their fast horses, every man with his lance in rest and his shield covering his heart, they made a lane for them to pass, while the Cid shouted: "Smite them, knights, for the love of charity!" Queer ideas of charity they had in those days!

Then he went back into the service of the Moors, and the Prince of Saragossa gave him the city of Valencia to rule, and to be his own. From this city he raided the neighboring country, carrying off booty and prisoners for sale at Valencia. On one of these expeditions he strayed too far from home, and his old enemy Alfonso laid hands on Valencia. When he heard of it, the Cid turned furiously on Alfonso's Castilian towns in the valley of the Ebro, and with terrible hand he wasted and harried them, stripped them bare of their riches, and carried everything off that he could handle. But when he returned to Valencia he found the gates closed and the enemy in possession.

He sat down before the town and besieged it for nine months. There was no food to be bought in the place, and the people were in "the waves of death;" tender maidens and strong men were seen to drop of hunger in the streets. The Cid cut off the river Guadalaviar, so that the garrison had to battle with thirst as well as hunger. Valencia surrendered at last, and I am glad to say that the people were not butchered, as the custom of that day was. The Cid took their goods, and then forgave them; after which he proclaimed himself King of Valencia.

Here he kept his promise, sent for his daughters, and married them to two counts, whose name was Carrion. It was a fitting name, for the counts shamefully neglected their wives, beat them, whipped them publicly, and left them bleeding in a wood. I wish the Cid had punished the Carrion counts, but I cannot find that he did.

After a time a great Moorish army marched up against Valencia. The Cid had but a few men, but he was as undaunted as ever. He mustered his forces, such as they were, and at cock-crow they heard mass sung by a valiant bishop, whose name was Hieronymo. When the mass was over the bishop absolved the soldiers, and begged the privilege of leading the attack. It was so arranged; and when the gate was opened, the fighting bishop, on a powerful charger, led the van with a lance in his hand and a mace at his saddle-bow. Presently the voice of the Cid was heard shouting "God and Santiago!" the terrible bishop, who had broken his lance, was smashing a Moorish head with every blow of his heavy mace, and the Moors, scared by the appearance of a body of men whom the Cid had placed in ambush, broke in every direction and scattered.

But the Moors came on again, and this time they drove the Christians back into the city. In July, 1099, we are told in the story that the Cid died of grief for the defeat., That he died is sure; the accounts of his death-bed are hardly so certain. They say that for seven nights his father and his son, who were both dead, appeared to him and said:

"You have tarried long enough here, now come among the people who endure forever."

Then St. Peter appeared to him, and said he should live thirty days and no more. At the end of the thirty days he received the sacrament from the fighting bishop, and passed into his rest.

When he was stiff in death his wife, Dona Ximena, took his body and set it on his horse Barieca, and fastened his body on the saddle so that it should not fall. His sword Tizona was grasped in his hand, his eyes were open and strangely bright, and his long beard floated down his breast. A squire led his horse out of Valencia, five hundred knights rode as a body-guard; behind the body followed Dona Ximena and her attendants. The procession moved slowly and silently, and the Moors, not quite understanding it, made way for it to pass.

It halted at the church at San Pedro de Cardena, and there, under a canopy which bore the Cid's coat of arms, the body was set upright in an ivory chair, still sword in hand. For ten years, says the legend, the corpse forbore to decay; when the skin began to change color it was reverently taken out of the ivory chair and buried before the altar, by the side of the faithful Ximena. Just fifty years ago a coffin, which was said to contain the bones of the Cid Campeador, was dug out of the vault of the church of San Pedro de Cardena, and reburied in the town-hall of Burgos. You will thus perceive that good Spaniards believe that the Cid was a real personage, and that his body was really buried where the legend says. I think it will do you no harm to admit that his story was founded on fact.

A whole library of romance and poetry has been written about the Cid. Some of the poems which narrate his adventures are very fine indeed. One of the most beautiful stories of his life was written by the English poet Southey, and called the "Chronicle of the Cid." There is also in French a tragedy by Corneille, which is written in such pure French and such manly verse that boys read it in learning French at school. The Spaniards always think of the Cid as one of their early heroes.

THE BATTLE OF LAS NAVAS

A.D. 1002-1212

AFTER the fall of the great Vizier Almanzor all Moorish Spain went to pieces. The nobles declared themselves independent and absolute rulers over the country round their castles. They were continually warring with each other, and wasting the substance of the people who worked. Almost every year the Christians of Castile and Leon and Asturias, with the Berbers of Galicia, swooped down upon the Moorish cities, robbed them and murdered their inhabitants. In this way the beautiful city of Cordova was sacked, and most of its splendid monuments destroyed.

After enduring this misery for over half a century, the Moors resolved to call upon their friends in Africa for help. These friends were called Almoravides, or Marabouts, which means "the truly pious." They formed a powerful nation, which lived round the city of Morocco; their ruler was an old man named Yussef, who was tall and dark, with piercing eyes, a long beard, a powerful frame, and a pleasant voice. Like many of his people, he was ignorant, and could barely read and write; but his mind was broad, and his foresight clear.

When it was first proposed to invite this African to Spain some of the Andalusian chiefs objected, declaring,. that the fierce dwellers in the African desert were more like tigers than men. But it was answered that they could not be worse than the Christians, and that it would be better for an Andalusian to drive camels for Yussef than to herd swine for the dogs of Castile.

So Yussef came with an army, met Alfonso, who was then King of Castile, Leon, and the Asturias, at Zallaka, in October, 1086, and utterly defeated him. The Christian king had trouble to escape with his body-guard, and the Moorish chiefs, who for several years had been paying him tribute for the sake of peace, threw him over and welcomed Yussef to their cities.

They did not make much by the change. One of Yassef's first acts was to seize the chief who had invited him to Spain, and to banish him and all his family to Africa in chains. The Moslem went on board ship with unmoved face, saying to his children:

THE CATHEDRAL, SEVILLE

This is the will of Allah; let us bear it in patience." Then Yussef took Seville, Granada, and other cities, rich and splendid, and divided their treasures among his men. He put down robbery, because he intended to do all the robbing himself. He took the goods of Christians because they were Christians, the goods of Jews because they were Jews, and the goods of Moors because they were rich. His troops, who were never tired of comparing the fertile valleys of Andalusia with the parched sands of the desert where they had been brought up, turned brigands. He was laying a heavy hand on Spain, when he died, at the age of ninety-seven.

His power fell to a son, who died; then to a grandson, who one dark night rode over a precipice into the sea; and then to a boy, named Ibrahim. Now it befell that the city of Morocco, in Africa, where Ibrahim lived, was besieged by the son of a lamplighter, who said that he was more devout than the Marabouts themselves. Like the Arab chief who put General Gordon to death ten years ago, he called himself the Mahdi. The Mahdi's army took Morocco, and young Ibrahim on his knees begged his life from the conqueror, who hesitated, the boy was so young and so fair.

But a Mahdist cried:

"Would you spare the cub of the lion, who may some day devour us all?"

Which sealed the fate of Ibrahim and his followers.

It was this butcher who now took the command of the Moors in Spain, and declared he would tread in the footsteps of Yussef.

But Christian Spain was aroused. The Pope sent letters to the kings and counts, imploring them to save Spain from the power of the infidel, For a time they agreed to forget their quarrels. The kings and counts embraced, and swore they would stand shoulder to shoulder. Castile and Aragon, Navarre and Asturias, Catalonia and Galicia, all sent troops to serve under the banners of the King of Castile, who was another Alfonso; and many a good knight from France and Portugal rode to join the host. After a solemn fast, King Alfonso gave the signal, and the mighty army was set in motion. When it reached the great mountain range which divides New Castile from Central Spain they found the Moors in possession of all the mountain passes, and the king was for a moment puzzled. But a shepherd showed him a pass which the Moors had neglected, and by that pass the whole army gradually defiled into the southern plain.

A MOORISH CAMP

It was the July of 1212. In front of the Christian army which had camped at the mountain slope was the village of Tolosa, in a plain called Las Navas, on which the Moors were drawn in line of battle with the long thread of their spears shining in the sun from the blue horizon on one side to the purple mountain ridge on the other. At the trumpet call the Christians rolled down the slope like an avalanche and fell upon the enemy. They knew that if they were beaten the Cross in Spain would go down in blood, and the Crescent would rise, perhaps to stay. So every man tightened his waist-belt, called on Saint Jago, and struck his heaviest blows.

The sun had not set, though it was low down in the sky, the hot air still glowed on that sultry July afternoon, when an African led a swift mule to the Moorish chief, and gasped:

"Prince of the faithful, how long wilt thou remain here? Rost thou not see that thy Moslems flee? The will of Allah be done."

"Allah," gravely replied the Moor, "Allah alone is just and strong; the devil is false and wicked."

And he mounted the mule, drove his spurs into its sides, and was soon out of sight.

The victory of the Christians showed kings and counts what they could do when they were united. They did not all learn the lesson. Feuds still broke out among them, but after this they generally acted in concert against the Moors. In those old dark days, when there was no printing, there were few writers of history, and our accounts of events were meagre; but bits of stories have come down to us, which are sometimes pleasant and sometimes not.

One of the Alfonsos of Castile, sixth of the name, lost his son in a battle, and was nearly killed by his grief. The legend says that he paced the rooms of his court. crying:

"Oh, my son, joy of my heart, and light of my eyes, my mirror, in which I used to see myself! Oh, my dear! Cavaliers, what have you done with him? Counts, give me my son! Give me my son!"

Another Alfonso, who was King of Aragon, died without heirs. Being extraordinarily pious, he left his kingdom by will to a body of monks at Rome. But the people of Aragon had no idea of being willed away like a herd of cattle. They met as a Cortes, annulled the king's testament, and elected his brother to be their king. He was a monk by calling, but he made a very good king.

It was during this period of conflict between Moors and Christians that the Spanish people acquired their first liberties. Towns were generally built around castles, and the count of the castle ruled the town and the country round about, often cruelly and unjustly. I read of one of them who used to yoke his prisoners, and sometimes, when prisoners ran short, his own vassals, to the plough to till his lands;

when they complained of not having enough to eat, he bade them go fill themselves with grass.

When the king founded a city he gave it a charter, or Nero, which provided that the people should have certain rights that could not be taken from them. After a time the people of districts demanded charters from the counts who claimed to rule them, and in a great many cases, especially where the demand was made by a city which lent money to the count, the charters were granted. These not only provided for the punishment of crime, but likewise set limits to the power of the counts, declared that all men were equal before the law, forbade the persecution of Jews, fixed the amount of taxes which the count could collect, forbade his interference in households, and in several cases imposed penalties on bachelors who refused to marry. If the king or the count attempted to break these charters the people flew to arms to maintain them.

You will see, as we go on with this Child's History, that these fueros, or charters, were the nest of Spanish liberty, just as township self-government has been the nest of national liberty in this country. The Spaniard who lived in a town which had a fuero knew that he had rights which no king or count could trample on; it was a short step for him to learn that he had also rights as a member of the nation, and he would have learned the lesson, to his unending benefit, but for an influence of which I shall have to tell you in the remainder of this history.

SEVILLE

A.D. 1213-1284

BETWEEN the dates of the battle of Zallaka and the battle of Las Navas, all Spain, except a strip in the North, was in the hands of the Moors. They held the valley of the Guadalquivir, with Seville and Cordova, and the best portions of Andalusia; the province of Granada with the city of the same name; most of Murcia; the province of Valencia with its city; parts of Aragon, and the valley of the Ebro, with Saragossa; and in the centre of Spain the best part of Estremadura and New Castile, with the valley of the Tagus and the city of Toledo. The whole sea-coast, from the Cape of Gibraltar to the mouth of the Ebro, was theirs.

At this time the Christians held their own country in the North, spreading from the Bay of Biscay to the foot-hills of the Guadarrama Mountains, and comprising, in whole or in part, the provinces I have so often named—Galicia, the Asturias, the Basque Country, Leon, Old Castile, and Aragon. Navarre and Catalonia considered that they were independent, and not part of Spain.

After the battle of Las Navas the parts were reversed. One city after another, one kingdom, or principality, after another deserted the Moors, and declared itself on the side of the Christians. In 1236 Ferdinand of Castile occupied Cordova, and planted the flag of the Cross over the great mosque. Ten years later, after a long siege, he took Seville, which had been the Moorish capital after the Moors had been driven out of Cordova; two years afterwards he took Valencia. Malaga fell soon after. Thus, about the year 1250, the only part of Spain which the Moors still held was the City of Granada, the fertile country round it to the slopes of the snowy mountains, its seaport Almeria, and a strip of coast running towards Gibraltar. All the rest of Spain was in Christian hands, and was ruled by Ferdinand the Third, who had united Castile and Leon, and was recognized as the head of the Christian princes. He was a valiant soldier and a just ruler; but what made people think most of him was that he was in the habit of scourging himself frequently by way of penance for his sins.

A STREET CORNER, SEVILLE

When he died his body was embalmed and was placed in a silver coffin with glass sides, which stands in the royal chapel of the cathedral of Seville. He is in his royal robes, with his crown on his head. His hands are crossed over his breast. On one side of him lies his sceptre, on the other his sword. There were once jewels in the handles of both, but. they were long ago stolen, it is said, by later kings of Spain. On holidays the body is exhibited to the people.

When Ferdinand took Seville it was one of the largest and most beautiful cities of Spain, It is still marvellously beautiful, though it is not as large as it was five hundred years ago. It then contained as many people as Baltimore or San Francisco to-day. It only houses one-third as many in our time. The city stood in a plain on the banks of the Guadalquivir, and was surrounded by a wall with sixty-six towers and eighteen gates. Outside the wall were orange and olive groves, groups of palms, vineyards, and forests of graceful and fragrant trees from the East. The houses were of marble, and some of them were magnificent. The old Spaniards had a proverb: Who has not seen Seville has missed one of the wonders of the world,

It is one of the oldest cities we know. Twenty-three or twenty-four hundred years ago it was a Phoenician or Carthaginian town, and a place of active trade. The Carthaginians called it Sephela, and built there a temple to Astarte, their goddess of Love; the building has been successively a temple of Astarte, a temple to some Roman god, a Gothic church, a Moorish mosque, and a Catholic cathedral. It is a noble edifice, with a tower three hundred and fifty feet high, an immense organ, and a library which was founded by the son of Christopher Columbus. Other buildings carry you back, as you look at them, to very an¬cient times indeed, and remind you of the changes which the world has seen. There is a spot where the Cartha¬ginians used to light fires to Moloch and throw their children into them; it was afterwards a parade-ground for Roman legions; then a barrack was built on it for Moorish cavalry; and now it is covered with a bull-ring, in which eleven thousand people watch fights between bulls and matadors.

You can see a tall building which goes by the name of the Tower of Gold. This was built by the Romans. Patricians used to ascend to the top of it to enjoy the evening breeze and the sight of the silver

Guadalquivir winding through the orange-groves and the purple
vines. When Spanish galleons began to bring gold from America the
tower was turned into a treasure-house, and regiments of soldiers
camped round to guard it. It is a ruin now. And there is another
building, where three thousand women, chiefly from the Canary
Islands, make cigars and cigarettes. On its site there was once a
Moorish castle, where many a dark deed was done and many a
bright-eyed girl was stabbed to the heart by a jealous lover.

The Moors of Seville were as polished as the Moors of Cordova, and
they were gentle in disposition, though fierce fighters when they
were roused. Of the siege which led to its capture the ballad says:

> "King Ferdinand alone did stand
> One day upon the hill,
> Surveying all his leaguers
> And the ramparts of Seville.
> The sight was grand when Ferdinand
> By proud Seville was lying,
> O'er tower and tree far off to see
> The Christian banners flying."

A Christian knight who covered himself with glory at the siege of
Seville was Don Garcia de Vargas, of Toledo. He was a mighty man
of war, and never counted odds. Once he was attacked by seven
Moors together. The ballad tells us how he got out of the trouble:

> "That day the lord of Vargas
> Came to the camp alone,
> His scarf, his lady's largess,
> Around his heart was thrown;
> Bare was his head, his sword was red,
> And from its pummel strung
> Seven turbans green, sore hacked I ween,
> Before Don Garcia hung."

King Ferdinand of Castile and Leon died in 1252; his son and
successor, Alfonso the Learned, reigned from 1252 to 1284. As his
sobriquet indicates, he was a man of prodigious learning. He
understood music, astronomy, and mathematics. He drew a code of

laws. He wrote a history of Spain. He translated the Bible into Spanish. He wrote prose, discourses on politics and morals, and poetry on love and romance. He knew so much, and was so well aware of it, that be is said to have observed that if he could have been consulted when the world was created he might have made some useful suggestions.

A LANE IN SEVILLE

But, with all his learning and all his good heart—he was really a kindly monarch, though he had murdered his brother in the flush of youth—he was always in trouble. He forbade any interference with the Moors, who had gathered in Granada, and thus displeased the Christians, who were eager to persecute the Moslems, now they had got them down. He had two sons; they quarrelled with each other and with him about the succession, and both the Pope and the Ding of France took a hand in the quarrel; the former with bulls of excommunication, the latter with threats of war.

One of the Sons was named Sancho. He actually rebelled against his father, and took the field at the head of a body of fighting men. King Alfonso cursed him, and the Pope cursed him, and Sancho, who was a good deal broken up by so many curses, laid down his arms and took to his bed, declaring that he was going to die. At this the fond old father relented, and moaned and lamented till he also was taken ill of a fever. He was for taking back all his curses, but Sancho said it was no use, he was going to die, and a few curses more or less would not matter. At this the father bemoaned himself more piteously than ever, until he made himself so ill that, with the assistance of a few physicians, he presently died. On which occurrence Sancho got out of bed, shook off his illness, and began to rule the kingdom.

You may be interested to know that at the very time the Christians were crushing the Moors of Spain and taking cities which the latter never recovered, the same Moslem race were inflicting terrible defeats on the Christians, who for fifty years had been crusading to the East to rescue Jerusalem from the hands of the infidel. In the same year that the Spanish Moors were penned up in Granada, the knights and men-at-arms who, under the lead of Saint-Louis of France, had engaged in the Fifth Crusade, were slaughtered and driven into the sea by the Moslems in Egypt, and shortly afterwards the king himself was taken prisoner and held to ransom. Thus at one end of the Mediterranean the Cross was up and the Crescent down, while at the other end the followers of Mahomet were triumphant and the followers of Christ were plunged into overwhelming disaster.

THE GIRALDA TOWER, SEVILLE

CASTILE AND ARAGON

A.D. 1284-1469

KING SANCHO reigned over Castile for eleven years, and followed by Ferdinand the Fourth, Alfonso the Eleventh, and Peter the Cruel who became king in 1330. Of these three monarchs there is nothing to be said, except that the last named, Peter was a monster of cruelty.

He loved killing people for the mere pleasure of killing, and the closer of kin they were to him the more he enjoyed putting them to death. If he had lived longer he would have destroyed his whole family.

He married a sweet French girl, Blanche of Bourbon, but after the wedding he would not live with her, or even see her. His favorite was a black-hearted Spaniard, named Maria de Padilla. The queen had given him as a wedding-present a golden belt adorned with precious stones. Maria found a Jew who was said to be a magician; he contrived in some way to get the girdle off the king's waist and to put in its place a serpent. When the king saw it he was filled with horror; and Maria telling him that this was some of the queen's sorcery intended to injure him, he thrust poor Blanche into prison.

To hold her the more safely he sent her to Toledo. But the people of that city, were turbulent, as you remember and always did their own thinking, took the poor prisoner's side, turned out in arms, with the king's brother Fadrique at their head, and declared that no harm should come to Blanche. Cunning Peter answered them that he had never meant any harm to his dear Blanche; he only wanted to clasp her in his arms once more. Whereupon the people, not suspecting that the king would tell a lie, let him into the place, and showed him where Blanche was. He no sooner got her in his power than he shut her up in a strong dungeon, where he put her to death.

Then he turned on his brother Fadrique, who had taken Blanche's part. Him he invited to a tournament at Seville. When Fadrique came, the king appeared before him in the courtyard of the castle and ordered a man-at-arms to cut him down. When you go to Seville you will be shown the stains of his blood on the stones of the yard.

After he was dead Peter had his head cut off and laid before the fair Maria de Padilla.

Shortly afterwards another brother, Henry, rebelled against Peter and took the field against him at the head of an army. But Peter got Edward the Black Prince of England to help him, and won a victory over the rebels at Navarrete, on April 3rd, 1367. After the battle Peter began to murder his prisoners, which shocked the Black Prince, and caused him to remonstrate. Peter answered, simply:

"What's the good of your helping me, then? If I let them go they will join Henry, and all the work will have to be done over again."

This disgusted the Black Prince so much that he gathered his men and marched off home.

Then the war broke out again, and now that the terrible Englishman was gone, victory generally sided with Henry. The war ended, however, by a curious piece of treachery, which may give you some idea of the laws of honor which prevailed in that day.

Henry was in the tent of his ally, the gallant French general, Bertrand Du Guesclin, of whom you have read in the History of France, and who was looked upon as a type of chivalry. A message was sent to Peter, inviting him into the tent, which he accepted unsuspiciously. At first Henry did not recognize him, though he was his brother, they had been parted so long; but an attendant cried:

"There is your enemy!"

Henry shouted:

"Where is the Jew who calls himself King of Castile?"

"Here I stand," answered Peter, "the lawful king and heir of King Alfonso; 'tis thou that art a false pretender."

With that they grappled with each other, while the knights, including Du Guesclin, stood looking on. Henry stabbed Peter with his poniard in the face, but could not pierce his body, which was protected by a coat of mail. Peter was the stronger and threw his brother on a bench; but one of Henry's men, seizing Peter by the leg, threw him over on his back, and Henry stabbed him to death.

"Thus with mortal gasp and quiver,
While the blood in bubbles welled,
Fled the fiercest soul that ever
In a Christian bosom dwelled."

After Peter, there was another series of kings of Castile—two Henrys and two Johns—about whom there is nothing recorded that you would care to hear, unless it be an expression of the last John, who said he "wished he had been born in the hut of an obscure workman rather than on the throne of Castile." This John was father to the Isabella who became the wife of Ferdinand of Aragon, and Queen, not of Castile, but of Spain.

Of Aragon, I have told you little. There was, however, a long list of kings who reigned from the times when Cordova first became the Moorish capital until the times of Ferdinand. Most of them left no trace; there were a few who perhaps deserve to be remembered. One of these was Jayme the First, a poet, warrior, and statesman; a great, broad-shouldered, blue-eyed, fair-haired scion of the Goths, who won thirty pitched battles, founded two thousand churches, and died in 1276. Then there was his son, Peter the Third, a wise monarch, who added Catalonia and Valencia securely to Aragon, and gave to his people such a charter of liberty as at that time existed nowhere else in the world, not even in England. The motto of Aragon was: "Laws first, kings afterwards!" For nothing was an Aragonese so quick to draw the sword as for any breach of law committed by his sovereign. When a king was crowned, a noble addressed him:

"We, each of whom is as good as you, and who altogether are more powerful, make you our king, so long as you shall respect our charter, and no longer."

I am afraid that in securing their own rights against the king the nobles of Aragon did not pay as much attention as they might have done to the rights of their vassals against themselves; as the English barons at Runnymede did not include in their bill of rights any guarantees for poor men against oppression by King John or by themselves.

There was a king named Peter the Ceremonious, who was cold as a stone and pitiless as a tiger; be reigned fifty years, and did much to strengthen his kingdom by his calculating policy. And his son, John the Careless, who reigned from 1387 to 1395, made Aragon famous by keeping the most splendid court of Europe. It was under him that Barcelona and Valencia became rivals of Genoa and Venice for the commerce of the world. Their ships were to be seen in every ocean, and their storehouses were filled with rich goods from every part of the world. All the great islands of the Western Mediterranean belonged at this time to Aragon.

In the middle of the fifteenth century both Aragon and Castile were about to be plunged into civil wars over the crown. Both states had grown so rich that their thrones were prizes worth capturing, and it was evident to wise men that the only security for peace would be the union of the two kingdoms in one hand, strong enough to put down rebellion and to repel foreign attack. These wise men saw a chance of realizing their hopes when, on April 22nd, 1451, the heir to the throne of Castile proved to be a girl—Isabella; and on March 15th following an heir to the throne of Aragon was born, in the person of Ferdinand, who was afterwards known as Ferdinand the Catholic. Far-seeing people discerned that these two ought to marry.

They met when Isabella was eighteen and Ferdinand seventeen, fell in love at first sight, and the marriage contract was signed forthwith. Ferdinand was a good-looking boy, who could ride well, talk fluently, and say pleasant things to every one; his eyes were bright, his complexion fair. Isabella was blue-eyed, with chestnut hair; she was almost a beauty; her figure was perfect; her manner was gracious, and was marked by a modesty which is not always observed in queens. When the marriage was arranged Isabella went to live at Valladolid, on the Douro. Stories reached Ferdinand's ear that she ran some risk of being kidnapped by one of the many royal suitors who aspired to her hand; so without notice to any one he slipped away, with only six attendants, and rode breakneck to Valladolid, travelling under a feigned name. When he told his fears to his lady love, she fell on his breast, declaring she would not leave him again; and accordingly, on October 19th, 1469, in the palace of Don Juan de Vivero, and in the presence of a party of invited guests, the two children were married. It was not till five years later that the wedding celebration took place at Segovia, and that a herald, after blowing his trumpet, lustily proclaimed:

"Hear all ye people of Castile and Aragon, the King Don Ferdinand, and his wife, Dona Isabella, are proprietors-sovereign of these kingdoms!"

It is now time that I should tell you something about the Moors, who fill so large a place in the reign of Ferdinand and Isabella.

THE MOORS AT GRANADA

A.D. 1250-1476

WHEN the Moors were driven out of Andalusia,Valencia, and New Castile, they took refuge in Granada, and to that spot their countrymen flocked from all parts of Spain. They chose as their caliph, or emir, or sultan, or king—he is called indifferently by all these names—a chief from Seville, named Ibrahim Ben Akmar, who was known as the red-man, because his complexion was fair and his hair light. He was a bold warrior, but he could not hold his own against the Christians, and he thought it wiser to pay them tribute, rather than continue the war. So every year he sent twelve thousand gold ducats to Castile as the price of peace.

Granada, his capital, was a fine city when he made it his home, and he spent enormous sums in beautifying it. It lay on both banks of the little river Darro, in the heart of a vast plain which was surrounded by lofty mountains, so tall that they were generally capped with snow. The city, which was surrounded by a wall with twelve gates and one thousand and forty towers, was built on the sides of two hills, which sloped to the river; the houses, with gardens and courts, in which oranges, lemons, and pomegranates grew, rose one above another till the tops of the hills were reached. On the top of one hill stood a strong fort which commanded the city; on the other stood the famous Red Palace, or Alhambra, of which, I dare say, you have heard.

The palace of the Alhambra stood in an enclosure surrounded by a wall fifteen feet thick, and so high in places that from the terrace on the summit of the wall you can look down on the tops of tall trees growing in the valley beneath. The enclosure was large enough to have contained a small city, but it never enclosed anything but courts and halls, where the Moorish kings received ambassadors and transacted business, and splendid apartments where their wives and children lived. It is partly in ruin to-day, but enough remains to show you what it must have been in the days of its glory.

GIRLS DRAWING WATER AT THE FOUNTAIN, TOLEDO.

When you go to see it you will pass under a tall tower to a gate, which is called the Gate of Justice. Here the Caliphs of Granada used to sit, under a great stone key and a massive stone hand, to hear the complaints of their people, and render justice. Then you pass into the Court of Myrtles, whose walls used to be hidden by a myrtle hedge. Then comes another court, whose centre is a lake in which myriads of golden fish play; it is still, so still that you can almost hear yourself breathe. Then you come to the Hall of the Ambassadors, with its grand throne where the Caliph sat, its walls worked over with tracery, its white, blue, and gold cornices, its lofty dome with stars on it to imitate the vault of heaven. Under that dome some of the most famous people of Europe used to stand, before the days of Columbus, and for a long time after him.

In a building near by are the rooms where the ladies of the Moorish court lived. The rooms were thickly carpeted, and under the floor incense and perfumes were burned, so that the luxurious ladies should breathe sweet savors from an unseen source. There were a score of bathrooms, each with a bathtub cut out of a single block of marble, and on the floor were rugs of cloth-of-gold, on which the fair bather rested her pretty, bare feet. A fine metal tracery, representing stars and roses, let in light.

Another famous hall is the Hall of Lions, so called because the fountain in the centre is surrounded by marble lions, who, in the old days, poured water out of their mouths. The roof is a series of arches resting on groups of white marble pillars; it vaults from pillar to pillar with fantastic lightness. Yet another hall, also with a fountain and basin in its centre, is the Hall of the Abencerrages, of whom I will tell you presently.

To this marble building—under a balmy sky, breathing an atmosphere cooled by the snow-caps of the near-by mountains and scented by every sort of fragrant tree, plant, and flower, with no noise to disturb the ear except the soothing murmur of fountains, and with a picture for the eye of an endless garden, with the town of Granada in the foreground and the snowy range on the horizon—the caliphs returned from their toils to spend the evening with dark-eyed houris, and to listen to tender melodies and to the dreamy music of the lute. It must have been the life of a Moslem paradise.

You will not be surprised to hear that the Emperor Charles V., when he went over the Alhambra, exclaimed to his courtiers:

"Ill fated was the man who lost all this."

The whole of the wide plane of Granada had been turned into a garden by the skilful diversion of water of the Xenil and the Darro into thousands of irrigating ditches. The Moors were famous for knowing the uses of water; they did not allow a gallon of it to go to wast; every acre of their land bore bounteous crops of grapes, or figs, or oranges, or lemons, or citrons, or walnuts, or pomegranates; in rows of mulberry-trees silk-worms wove cocoons, which were reeled into the finest silk. In the city people worked industriously at making steel weapons and cloths, and beautiful objects in gold, silver, and bronze. It was a busier place than any of the Christian cities in Spain.

The Moorish nobles who lived there led lives of culture and splendor. Schools flourished, prose and poetry were written, music was played on lutes, science was studied. Both sexes dressed handsomely; the ladies wore bracelets and anklets of silver or gold, studded with emeralds and chrysolites; they braided their hair and fastened the braids with jewels. The men dressed in spotless white coats of linen, over which, in winter, they threw cloaks of wool or silk of the finest texture. The sheaths of their swords and daggers were inlaid and adorned with gems; their very horses' trappings were of green and crimson velvet, on which letters were traced with gold and silver thread. The masses of the people were kept busily employed on their farms or in their factories. But the noble Moors gave their whole time to love and war. They paid to young ladies a respectful devotion, which I find it difficult to explain in a people who locked their wives up in harems.

For over two hundred years the Moors lived in wealth and luxury at Granada, their only diversion from love-making being freebooting forays, generally directed from the town of Jaen against the Christian cities of the neighborhood. For all this long stretch of time we hear little of their history except a string of names and occasionally a story or two which reads like a legend. We are told that there were twenty-three caliphs of Granada, some of whom took the title of king, and nearly all of whom were named Mahomet.

One of the stories says that the governor of a Christian town near the border of Granada resolved to make a raid upon the Moorish country. Before putting his men in the field he sent secretly a party of horse to explore the road; they fell in with a Moorish courtier of fine appearance, whom they forthwith made prisoner and brought before the governor. The young man cried bitterly when he was examined, and the governor, disgusted at his want of manliness, reproached him, saying:

"You are no warrior, but a woman, for you weep like one. Are you such a coward as to fret for your capture?"

"It is not the loss of my liberty that I lament," said the Moor, "but I have long loved the daughter of an alcalde in our neighborhood. She loves me, and to-night. was to be our wedding night. Now she is awaiting me, and will think I have deserted her. She will die of despair."

"Noble cavalier," said the governor, "you touch my heart. Go and see your lady; I will take your word that you will return."

I need not tell you that the Moor rode fast and furious to the lady's house. When he told her the story, she said:

"You must keep your word. But I will go with you. I share your fate, bond or free. And see, here are jewels to buy your ransom."

Next morning the couple appeared before the governor, and offered him the jewels. But he would none of them from a cavalier so loyal and a maiden so true. He had the pair married by a priest, loaded them with presents, and sent them back under escort to the home of the groom.

Another story of these times was the legend of the Abencerrages. It is not certain that it is true, but the Spaniards believe it; when you go to Spain you will be shown the stains of the blood of the Abencerrages on the floor of the hall in the Alhambra which bears their name.

They were a noble and wealthy family of Moors, who were equally famous for their valor and for their mercy. They spent their money in ransoming Christian prisoners, and it was said of them that there had never been an Abencerrage who was a coward, or a false husband, or a faithless friend. Between these Abencerrages and another Moorish family, called the Zegris, a feud always raged. The Zegris were as brave as the Abencerrages and as skillful in war, but they had never been known to spare a prisoner's life, or to say a word of love to a woman.

Now the Sultan of Granada had married a Zegri girl. She was cold and cruel, like the men of her tribe, and the king, losing his love for her, married, as the law allowed, a Christian captive as his second wife. At this the first wife became furiously jealous, and called upon her kinsmen to avenge her wrong; and the Christian wife appealed to the Abencerrages to take her part, which they promptly did.

It chanced that a wedding in the nobility just then took place, and the usual games were given. At one of the games the object was for a rider on a galloping horse to pierce with the point of his lance a ring held in the mouth of a silver dove on the branch of a tree, new rings being supplied as fast as any were pierced. The young men of the Abencerrages entered the list in white tunics, embroidered with pearls and silver; they rode white horses, and carried a shield on which were a lion and a shepherdess, with the legend "Gentleness and Strength." The Zegris wore green tunics, with gold ornaments, on horses covered with gaudy velvet trappings. Their shield bore the device of a bloody cimeter, with the motto "This is my law"

At the first joust one of the Abencerrages won twenty-five rings, while the highest number won by any Zegri was five. The defeat drove the latter to fury, and they vowed revenge.

A young Abencerrage had loved a maiden named Zoroaide before the caliph's son had ordered her to become his wife. He did not cease to love her when she was taken from him, and she pined in secret for him on the splendid terraces of the Alhambra. One night, when he could not restrain himself, the young Abencerrage scaled the side of the castle, leaped on the terrace, and stood before his love.

She bade him go, telling him that his life depended on his flight, and promising him that every evening of her life she would come to that rose-tree and mourn for him.

He went; but it was too late. A Zegri had overheard his voice. Hastening to the caliph's son, the spy told what he had seen. The prince at once summoned all the chiefs of the Abencerrages to the palace. When they came they were dragged to the court of the Abencerrages—thirty-six in all—and the head of every one was cut off and thrown into the fountain. The prince himself struck off the head of his wife's lover. The rest of the broken-hearted family removed from Granada.

In the year 1476, when the King of Castile and Aragon sent a messenger to Granada to collect his annual tribute, the Caliph Muley Abul Hassan replied to the Castilian:

"Go, tell your master that the emirs who agreed to pay tribute are dead. The mints of Granada now coin nothing but sword-blades."

King Ferdinand pondered over the message. Then learning that the Moors of Granada occupied fourteen cities, ninety-seven fortified places, and castles without count, he said:

"I will pick out the seeds of this pomegranate one by one."

In Spanish the word Granada means pomegranate.

ZAHARA AND ALHAMA

A.D. 1481—1482

MULEY ABUL HASSAN, the fierce Moor who said that his mints coined nothing but sword-blades, did not wait for King Ferdinand to attack him. On a dark night, between Christmas and New-year, in a storm of rain and lightning and thunder, he suddenly loomed up at the head of a large force before the Christian town and fort of Zahara, not very far from the town of Malaga. Everybody in the place, including sentinels, was asleep. In a silence only broken by the patter of the rain and the roar of the thunder the Moors set their ladders against the walls and scaled town and castle.

The cry arose: "The Moor! The Moor!" But in the darkness the garrison could not find their arms nor their comrades. They were cut down by the savage Moors as fast as they groped their way out of their barracks. All—men, women, and children—were bidden to gather in the square, and wait for morning in their night-clothes in the cold rain. When day dawned they were marched to Granada under an escort of troops, and prodded with spear-points when they slackened their gait. Muley Abul Hassan followed after them with a string of mules laden with the plunder of Zahara.

But the conqueror was not received at his home with the welcome he expected. The Moors were a wise people; they foresaw that this raid on a Christian town boded trouble in the future. A dervish paced the streets, groaning aloud: "Woe to Granada! The hour of its destruction is at hand! The ruins of Zahara will fall on our heads!"

In Christian Spain the news of the Moorish capture of Zahara roused the people to fury. They clamored for war on the infidel. The first one to act was a valiant knight named Ponce de Leon, the Marquis of Cadiz. He gathered a body of fighting men and promised them that Zahara should be avenged. Not far from his chief castle was the Moorish fortified town of Albania, on the top of a hill, about twenty-five miles from Granada. It was the town which was shattered by an earthquake a few years ago. To spy out this place he sent a trusty officer, who walked round it at night, measured the walls, peered over the heights, counted the sentries. Then the marquis started out.

With four thousand foot and three thousand horse he set forth from his town of Marchena on a dark February night. The little army crept cautiously, lay hid all day, and lit no fires at night; so that a little after midnight of the third march they reached Alhama without having been seen by a single Moor. Ladders were quickly set against the citadel, and it was taken by storm before the garrison had any idea that an enemy was near. The Moors in the town resisted for a while, but so many of them were shot down from the citadel — gunpowder was then used for the first time in the Spanish wars — that the rest surrendered.

There is a story of the assault which will show you that the fighters of this period, fierce and cruel as they often were in battle, had still on occasion the instincts of gentlemen. In leading the attack on the castle the marquis broke into room after room, and found himself unexpectedly in the chamber where the Moorish governor's wife was in bed. She shrieked, wrapped the clothes round her, and begged for life.

"Madam," said the marquis, "fear nothing. You are in the hands of a Spanish gentleman,"

And when her maids came running in presently screaming, with half a dozen soldiers at their heels pursuing them, the marquis drove his men out at the point of the sword, and set a trusty guard at the door of the lady, with orders to cut down any one who attempted to enter.

Alhama was one of the richest and strongest towns in Spain. It was so strong a place that the Moors had used it as a storehouse. It contained quantities of gold and silver and gems and rich silks and grain and oil and honey, besides numbers of horses and cattle. All this was now given up to plunder by the Marquis of Cadiz, and the Moors — men, women, and children — were sold as slaves. Zahara was indeed avenged.

When the news reached Granada the people cursed the Caliph.

"Accursed be the day," they said, "that thou hast lit the flames of war. On thy head and on thy children's heads rest the sin of Zahara!"

The old ballad "Ay de mi Alhama," which Spanish girls sometimes sing to this day, tells the story:

"Letters to the monarch tell
How Albania's city fell;
In the fire the scroll he threw,
And the messenger he slew.
Woe is me, Alhama!"

But Muley Abul Hassan was not the man to content himself with groaning over disaster. He called the Moors to arms and marched swiftly to Alhama to retake the place. The garrison was ready for him, and beat his forces back with great loss. He sat down before the place raging with disappointment, and yet resolved to succeed.

Now the fort and town of Alhama had no water supply except what it got from a little stream running past the base of the hill. There were a few wells in the place, but they soon ran dry. And then the Moors diverted the water of the stream, so that the Christians could not get grater without passing through the Moorish camp. The throats of the soldiers dried till they could hardly speak; some died, others went mad from thirst.

Christian knights, among others Don Alfonso de Aguilar, tried to raise the siege, but they were beaten back by the Moors. Muley Abul Hassan stroked his beard, and feasted his hungry eyes with the sight of the Christians on the battlements, knowing they were doomed and must presently surrender. There was but one man who could save them; that was the Duke of Medina Sidonia, and be was at deadly feud with the Marquis of Cadiz, and was not. likely to help his enemy.

When the duke heard of the trouble in which his old foe stood he said it was no concern of his. But when the wife of the marquis fell at his feet, with tears flowing from her beautiful eyes, and besought him, in a voice broken by sobs, not to allow her noble husband to be butchered by the infidel, but to go to his aid, for the sake of his honor and of knightly chivalry, the duke, in a voice like thunder, commanded his horse to be saddled, and bade his squire blow the war bugle, and to keep on blowing it as long as he had a breath in his body. His people were quite ready to march. Every man of them felt that the day had come to settle the question whether Spain should be Christian or Moslem.

Messengers were sent to every town and fortress, east and west, and north and south, to send all the troops they could spare to Seville, and just as the marquis's men were reduced to such straits that they had to make sallies to get a little water, and paid for every drop of it with a drop of their blood, the duke marched out of Seville with fifty thousand fighting men and a long army of gallant. knights from every part of Andalusia.

King Ferdinand was in Castile when he heard of the siege of Alhama; the rode south on relays of horses, hardly taking time to sleep. When he reached Cordova he despatched messengers to Medina Sidonia, bidding him to await his coming. But the peril was too pressing. The duke's personal enemy was dying of thirst. He sent word to the king that he would not wait. He would march, and would not tarry an hour nor the tenth part of a minute by the way for king or devil.

When Muley heard of his coming he made one more attempt to storm the place. A band of picked Moorish warriors attacked it on a side thus far untried, and seventy of them actually got into the town. But they were quickly surrounded, and though they formed back-to-back, with the Moorish flag in the centre, and fought like heroes or demons, they were all killed, and their heads were thrown over the wall to their friends outside. Then Muley Abul Hassan, tearing his beard in his rage, and knowing that if he waited till Medina Sidonia calve up he would be caught between two fires, sullenly drew off his army and abandoned Alhama to the Christians forever. I need not tell you of the joy with which the duke was received by the garrison. Ponce de Leon fell upon his neck; and these two fierce warriors, who thought nothing of killing an enemy in battle, threw their arms round each other and cried like girls. Ever after that day they were brothers-in-arms.

BORDER WARFARE

A.D. 1453

EXULTING over his victory over the Moors, the Marquis of Cadiz pined for greater triumphs. He fixed his eye on Malaga, the great seaport on the Mediterranean, where the foreign trade of the Moors was carried on. This would be a nobler prize than Alhama.

Malaga was divided from Antequera, where the marquis mustered his force, by a ridge of lofty and rugged mountains, cut at intervals by rocky valleys and the beds of dead rivers, which were the only passes. On either side of these valleys and gulches cliffs rose, sometimes with very steep sides; from these cliffs great pieces of rock and bowlders, detached by storm or earthquake, had rolled down, par¬tially blocking the path at their base. It was over this difficult road that Ponce de Leon led his men to the attack of Malaga. It was a road almost impassable for cavalry.

He had hoped to get through the mountains and to reach the plain on which Malaga stands before the Moors discovered his purpose; but it seems they were informed of it before he set out; for on the second night, as his army in close file was slowly and painfully working its way through a narrow pass, man and horse stumbling over the rough stones, and sometimes tumbling into clefts by the road-side, lights flashed out on the top of the heights above the pass, and a shower of stones and darts rained upon the Christians. In a little while they found they could neither advance nor retreat, for the narrow pass was blocked in front of them and behind them with the bodies of the soldiers who had been killed by the stones and darts. When day dawned they found that they were caught in a trap. They were being slowly cut off by an enemy at whom they could not strike back.

A guide pretended to show them another pass through the range, but it was no better than the first. The Moors were still above them on the top of crags, pelting them with boulders and fragments of rock. After vainly trying to find a safe road in any direction, the army scattered, and every man sought safety for himself. Numbers of them were lost and perished miserably in the rocks; some fell over precipices, some were killed, others made prisoners by the Moors. And so ended the wretched expedition against Malaga.

But though the Moors won the day, they had cares enough from another source to prevent their being extravagantly happy. Muley Abul Hassan had two wives. One, Ayesha, was of his own kin, and was the wife of his youth. She had a son named Boabdil, who at the time of the rupture with the Christians was grown up. The other wife, Zoraya, had been a Christian, taken prisoner in battle; she was surpassingly beautiful, and became the sultan's favorite. She had two sons, who were babies; but she hoped they would grow up to succeed their father, while Ayesha, who was jealous of Zoraya, determined that her son Boabdil should succeed.

When Muley Abul Hassan returned baffled from Albama, he was received at Granada with groans and curses. The old dervish went round predicting disaster more shriekingly than ever. The king, wearied with the clamor, went with Zoraya to a country-house in search of peace. He had only spent a few hours there when, just at nightfall, he heard a strange sound rising from Granada like the gathering of a storm. Presently a messenger, who had ridden at wild speed, told him that a rebellion had broken out in the city, and that the people had proclaimed his son, Boabdil, king in his stead.

As full of fight as ever, the king put himself at the head of his guards, and with his vizier, Abul Cacim, tried to break into the Alhambra, but was driven back and chased out of the city.

"God is great," said he; "let us bow to what is written in the book of fate."

So he rode off to a castle where he had friends, and left his son on the throne at Granada. Just to show that he was not dead, he headed a foray into the territory of the Duke of Medina Sidonia, and carried off booty and cattle.

This set the Granadans to murmuring at the sloth of their new king, Boabdil, whom they called The Little; and the king's mother, Ayesha, who had spurred him to seize his father's throne, joining in reproaching him for his sluggishness, he resolved to do something for glory. He called his men to arms, nine thousand of them in all, and among them the flower of the Moorish chivalry. His mother girded on his cimeter with her own hands, and when his wife cried at the parting, the fierce old woman rebuked her:

"Why dost thou weep? These tears become not the daughter of a warrior, nor the wife of a king. Believe me, there often lurks more danger for a monarch within the strong walls of a palace than within the frail curtains of a tent."

Boabdil sallied forth from Granada in grand array. His horse was black and white; on his breast he wore a steel corselet with gold nails, and on his head a steel casque richly engraved. On his back he bore a shield; over his saddle hung a cimeter of Damascus, and in his hand he carried a long lance. But the troops, who admired his fine appearance, were rather taken aback when a fox ran out of a thicket and scurried through the ranks of the army, pressing close to the king without being touched by any of the missiles which were thrown at it. Like the Spaniards, the Moors were superstitious. They marched swiftly, however, and presently, having been reinforced by Ali Atar, Boabdil's father-in-law, a veteran of nearly ninety, who had spent his life in fighting the Christians, they came to a stand over against the Christian town of Lucena.

They had been seen coming. On the night of April 20th, 1483, as Don Diego de Cordova, Count of Cabra, was going to bed, his watchman brought him word that the beacon-fires were lit on the mountain-tops. He knew what this meant. There was no rest that night in his castle of Vaena, or in the town adjoining. By daylight the count marched forth at the head of fifteen hundred men, taking the direction of the frontier. Word soon reached him that Lucena was the place threatened, and he made for it with all speed. When he got there he found the Moors gone. They had collected such a quantity of plun¬der that they had started homeward to divide it. Ninety-year-old Ali wanted to burn Lucena and slay all the people; but the soldiers preferred saving their booty to fighting.

The Count of Cabra, not paying the least heed to those who warned him that the Moors were six or seven times as numerous as his force, and who wanted him to wait for reinforcements, spurred after them. He found them in a valley near a little stream which the heavy rain had swollen into a torrent. They were eating their dinner with great content.

"By Santiago," said the count, "if we had waited for reinforcements the Moors would have escaped us."

And he flung his cavaliers on the enemy. It is not easy to understand the battle, or how fifteen hundred Christians could overcome nine thousand Moors. I suppose the latter were badly handled, and that Boabdil did not understand the business of war. Many of the Moors thought they had got what they wanted, and that the best thing was to go home. As the battle began a dense fog settled on the field, and it seems to have confused the Moors more than the Christians. The former fought with their backs to the torrent I have mentioned; when they were pushed they backed into the torrent, lost their footing, and many were drowned. In this and other ways the battle was lost.

King Boabdil fell back with the others; his horse being shot, he was on foot. Afraid that his grand costume would attract shots or arrows, he hid in a clump of willows, where he remained until a Spanish cavalier detected him. He cried for quarter, saying that he was a man of family and would pay a rich ransom. A quarrel then arose between the soldiers as to whose prisoner he was; but the Count of Cabra happening to ride up, the king surrendered to him, without, however, saying who he was. The count accepted him, put a red band round his neck to signify that he was a prisoner, and sent him off under escort to his quarters. It was not till three days afterwards that the count knew that his prisoner was the King of Granada.

On the day after the battle the Moorish people of Loxa, who had been straining their eyes all day for the return of the king and his army, saw one horseman approaching on the borders of the Xenil. When he reached the city his horse, which had carried him swiftly so far, fell dead. The rider's face was so sad that at first no one dared accost him. At last an old man asked:

"How fares it with the king and the army?"

"There they lie!" answered the horseman, pointing to the hills. "All lost! all dead!"

And he mounted another horse, while the people wailed; he shook his head and rode on and on to Granada. There he told his wretched story to the people; and still riding on and on, he did not draw rein till he stood at the Gate of Justice, in the Alhambra.

The wife of Boabdil flung herself on the ground, weeping, and had to be carried to her apartments; but the stern old mother shed never a tear. She only said:

"It is the will of Allah."

The minstrels came with their lutes to sing and play for the harem, but their song was attuned to the sorrows of the hour. They sang:

"Beautiful Granada! Why is the Alhambra so lorn and desolate? The orange and myrtle still breathe their perfumes into its silken chambers; the nightingale still sings within its groves; its marble halls are still refreshed with the plash of fountains and the gush of liquid rills. Alas! alas! The countenance of the king no longer shines within these halls. The light of the Alhambra is set forever."

THE FALL OF MALAGA

A.D. 1483—1488

WHEN King Ferdinand learned that the Moorish king was a prisoner he was puzzled to know what to do with him. Happily he had at his right hand one who was wiser and stronger-minded than he. This was his wife, Isabella. For some time she had been residing at Seville, and though she was barely thirty, she had presided over the royal court of justice there, had heard cases, and decided them wisely. The king had learned to lean upon her judgment for counsel. She now advised that Boabdil be released, on condition of his paying the old tribute to the King of Castile, and of setting free a certain number of captives. The prisoner readily agreed to these terms, and started for Granada.

But Boabdil had not heard the news from his capital. No sooner had his capture by the Christians become known there than his fiery old father dashed into the place at the head of his troopers, proclaimed that he was king once more, and camped in the Alhambra. Boabdil's mother, Ayesha, he drove out of the palace, and bade her find lodgings in the quarter where the workmen lived. She, who was as fierce as her husband, barricaded herself in the quarter which had been assigned her, seized one of the gates of the city, and bade defiance to Muley. When Boabdil, who had left Granada in such glory and splendor, came creeping back under cover of night, cowering and quaking from fear of his terrible father, she let him in, flung herself on his neck, called the workmen to his support, and told him:

"It depends on thyself whether thou wilt remain here a king or a captive."

When day dawned and old Muley Abul Hassan heard that his son was back he foamed with rage and summoned his fighting men. Ayesha summoned hers, and the two parties—father against son—fought all day in the streets. When night came Boabdil cried "Enough!" and ran away to live at Almeria, his mother taunting him as he went with the jibe that a man was not worthy of being called a king who could not hold his own capital city.

King Ferdinand's hope for peace and a revival of tribute were ended when Boabdil was overthrown; so he began again to raid the Moorish country, to carry off booty, and to make slaves of the Moors. At first Muley Abul Hassan watched him from the highest tower of the Alhambra, growling like a tiger and grinding his teeth, because he could not trust his troops; but at last a body of them were collected who were willing to follow the Christian example of fighting for plunder, and they raided Andalusia, while Ferdinand raided the plain or vega of Granada. I do not think that you can feel much sympathy for either. There was very little fighting done in comparison with the amount of robbing. The chief sufferers by the war were the poor peasants and residents of small towns and villages, who lost everything they had, and saw their children carried off to be sold as slaves, Moors by Christians, Christians by Moors. It could not have mattered much to them whether they were despoiled by Moslems or Christians. Whichever race it was, the peasant lost his wheat crop, his vines, his orchard, his orange and olive grove, and his sons and daughters.

But the Christians had the advantage in this border warfare. King Ferdinand took town after town, castle after castle, village after village, and what he took he kept. Muley Abut Hassan took few places, and those he did take were quickly wrenched out of his grasp. During the whole of the year 1484 the Moorish territory was gradually growing narrower and the Spanish territory wider.

Moreover, from repeated defeat, the Moors were losing heart. The old king, who had spent such a life of toil and battle, became blind and bedridden. His son Boabdil, who was always conspiring against him, was chased out of the kingdom by his uncle, El Zagal, and forced to take refuge, like an outcast, with the Christians at Cordova. When El Zagal appeared at Almeria to seize him, Queen Ayesha intrepidly faced him, and called him a perfidious traitor. So El Zagal thrust her into prison, and made an end of her for the time.

Meanwhile, May, 1486, King Ferdinand assembled at Cordova an army of twelve thousand horse, forty thousand foot soldiers armed with cross-bows, lances, and arquebuses, and a park of heavy cannon, which were then called Lombards. With these he marched down against the Moorish strongholds in Southern Spain lying back of Malaga. He took them all, one after the other—Loxa, Elora, Moclin, and others; thus gradually, by slow degrees, he encircled Malaga in his grip.

Malaga lies on the shore of the Mediterranean, and is backed up against a range of sloping mountains, whose sides are clothed with the vines bearing Malaga grapes, which I dare say you have eaten, and with fragrant plantations of oranges, lemons, olives, and pomegranates. Five hundred years ago two of the heights behind the city were crowned, the one with the citadel and the other with a fort called the Gibralfaro. The latter, which was a strong work, was commanded by a dark and fierce-eyed Moor, who was known as Hamet el Zegri, and garrisoned with Moors fresh from Africa. Round the town itself ran a high wall with tall towers at intervals.

Ferdinand fired his heavy guns at the towers, and presently made a breach through one of them by which some of his troops entered; but the Moors attacked them with heavy stones and boiling pitch, and undermined the tower which the Christians had taken, so that it fell in. Then the Marquis of Cadiz massed his men to storm Gibralfaro, but the Moors sallied forth at night, swooped upon the enemy with such fury and threw so many down the cliff-side that the stormers drew off with sore heads. Then the Christians undertook to undermine the walls. Hamet found it out and dug countermines, so that sometimes one tunnel would run into another, and Christian and Moor would engage in a death-grapple under the ground.

Ferdinand held the sea, and Malaga could get no food from outside. Hamet had seized all the food in the city for the use of his soldiers, doling out to them a quarter of a pound of bread in the morning, and half as much at night. Women and children ate what they could get—the flesh of horses and stray remains of dried fruits. And all the while they saw ships arriving with grain for the Chris¬tians, and droves of cattle slowly winding over the hills. Queen Isabella, who had joined her husband in camp, was touched by the stories of suffering in Malaga, and sent word that the most liberal terms would be granted in case of surrender. But Hamet el Zegri replied that he had only begun the fight, and that the sooner King. Ferdinand raised the siege the better it would be for him. Numbers of citizens were ready to surrender, but Hamet threatened then with death if they spoke.

After a time the fathers of starving families climbed up the rock of Gibralfaro, and besought the Moorish chief not to doom so many to die of hunger. He replied that the day of deliverance was at hand. All he asked was a little patience. It seems he had on his staff a crazy dervish, who pretended to be an astrologer; this astrologer said that it had been revealed to him by the stars that an attack made upon the Christians on a certain day, he leading the Moors with a certain white flag in his hand, was certain to make an end of the Spanish army.

Accordingly, on the day set, the dervish led the way with his white flag, and the whole Moslem army in brave array sallied forth and fell upon the Spaniards. It was a foolhardy enterprise. The Christians were at first taken by surprise, but they recovered their wits, and attacked the Moors with such fury that hundreds of them were slain and the rest driven back, wounded and bruised, into Malaga. The crazy dervish had his poor sick brains knocked out by a stone.

The city of Malaga then surrendered, and the starving people were abundantly supplied with food from King Ferdinand's stores. Hamet el Zegri shut himself up in his castle of Gibralfaro. But the Africans had suffered so dreadfully from battle, hunger, and fatigue that there was a dangerous light in their eyes; and when they bade Hamet ask terms of surrender, he did not keep them waiting. He wanted to make special terms for himself and his men; but Ferdinand, like some one else whom you will remember, answered that the only terms he would accept were unconditional surrender. And those were the terms settled. Hamet was imprisoned for life. His Moors were all sold as slaves but one.

That one was Ibraham Zenete. I must close this chapter with the reason why, of all that band, Zenete alone was spared.

When Hamet el Zegri made his great sortie from Malaga, under the guidance of the crazy dervish, Zenete led the advance. In leading the van, he broke into a house which was occupied by Spanish officers, and in a room in that house he found three Spanish boys in a bed sleeping. lie struck them sharply with the flat of his sword, and cried:

"Away to your mothers, brats!"

"Why," said a Moorish officer, "do you not kill the Christian dogs?"

"Because," replied Zenete, "I see no beards on their faces."

This was accounted so chivalrous an act that King Ferdinand declared a Castilian hidalgo could not have been more high-minded; and this was why, when all his comrades were sold into slavery, Zenete was forgiven and set at liberty.

Malaga fell in the year 1488; and when it fell, as the Moorish saying went, the eye of Granada was plucked out.

THE FALL OF GRANADA

A.D. 1488-1492

KING FERDINAND found ill Malaga, after the surrender, sixteen hundred Christians, men and women, many of whom had been years in captivity;, some with shackles on their legs, with long hair matted and uncombed, with haggard, pale faces, and figures gaunt from famine. They were set at liberty, fed, and clothed, and sent to their homes. Among the Moorish captives were four hundred Jews, chiefly women, who were ransomed by a wealthy Jew of Castile. The others were held for ransom; but whatever they had was taken to the king, and accounted as part of the ransom. Each person—man, woman, and child—stepped singly out of their house, bearing their money, jewels, bracelets, anklets, and whatever they had of value. These were taken and valued. If they amounted to less than the ransom fixed, the owner was confined in an enclosure to be sold as a slave. Some of the most beautiful girls were allotted to Queen Isabella, who gave them as presents to her sister-in-law, the Queen of Naples, or to the ladies of her court.

Meanwhile a bishop was appointed over the chief mosque, which was turned into a cathedral, and the king and queen, with the officers of the army, heard mass in it. While the plain-chant of the mass rose to heaven, the Moors, with their hands bound, chanted outside:

"Oh, Malaga, city so famous and beautiful! Where is now the strength of thy castle? Behold thy children driven from their pleasant abodes to drag a life of bondage in a foreign land, and to die far from the home of their childhood! What will become of the old men and matrons when their gray hairs will no longer be revered? What will become of thy tender and delicate maidens, when reduced to hard and menial servitude? Oh, Malaga, city of our birth! who can behold thy desolation and not shed tears of bitter grief?"

Ferdinand spent the winter in preparing for the final conquest of the Moors, and gave his army a rest. It was not till the end of May, 1489, that he moved from the fortress of Jaen into the Granada country. He had to make sure of several castles, and especially of the fortified town of Baza, before he could venture to attack Granada. Granada was in the hands of Boabdil, who acted like a mean hypocrite. His heart was always with his people; but when Malaga fell he sent congratulations and presents to Ferdinand, and assured him of his fidelity and of his intention to pay tribute. Ferdinand received his messenger in grim silence. He knew that the real ruler of the Moorish empire was Boabdil's uncle, old Muley el Zagal, who was at Almeria, at the head of a considerable force. Ferdinand left him there while he laid siege to Baza.

THE SURRENDER OF GRANDA.

Baza was so strong a place, and was so stanchly defended by the Moors, that the Spaniards beleaguered it for six months before they could reduce it. They would have had to raise the siege for want of food had it not been for the energy of Queen Isabella. The country round the town had been laid bare by the raiders on both sides. It contained nothing to eat. There were no wagons to be had, and no roads to drive them over if there had been. The army was on the point of starving, when long convoys of loaded mules were seen winding down the hill-side, and bearing relief. Isabella had bought all the corn in Andalusia, and all the mules. She loaded each mule with as much corn as it could carry, and day after day started off droves of two hundred mules each to the camp. Her husband and his troops were thus saved by her vigor and foresight.

Not content with victualling the army, the queen resolved to join it, in order to give heart to her husband, and to see personally to the establishment of field hospitals, which were always very near her heart. She journeyed from Jaen with a cavalcade of troopers and attendants, and rode slowly past the Moorish city with gay banners and pennons, and a splendid retinue of cavaliers, as if she were going to make a holiday. When the Moors saw her pass, they knew that the king was there to stay until the city fell, and the commanding officer sent a messenger to old El Zagal.

The white-bearded veteran sat with a scowl on his brow, and said: "How fares it with Baza?"

The messenger handed him a letter, which he read with bowed head.

"There is but one God," said he, "and Mahomet is his prophet; the people of Baza must submit to the decree of fate."

So the city surrendered, and largely through the intercession of Isabella no one was sold as a slave, no one lost his property, and the Moors were allowed to go on praying in their old fashion.

Then other forts surrendered. One of them was commanded by an old soldier, who said that his men refused to stand by him, and therefore he could not hold out. Ferdinand offered him gold, but he refused it, saying:

"I came not to sell what is not mine, but to yield what fortune has made yours."

"But," said Queen Isabella, "can we do nothing for you?"

"You can," said the Moor; "you can give me your royal word that my unhappy countrymen, with their wives and children, shall be protected in the peaceable enjoyment of their homes and their religion."

"We promise it," said the queen.

And the high-minded old warrior took the road to Africa.

Then Almeria fell, the second city in the Empire of Granada, and El Zagal was taken prisoner. He was set free, and given an estate to live on. But he thought he would be happier in Africa, and went there.

Unhappily he fell into the clutches of the Sultan of Fez, whose executioner held a basin of molten copper before his eyes; and blinded him. He spent his last years groping about Fez, in rags and penniless.

Then all that remained of the Moorish Empire was the city and plain, or vega, of Granada. Boabdil was there, in the Alhambra, writing cringing letters to Ferdinand—who answered none of them—hated and cursed by his people as a traitor. Suddenly, in the summer of 1490, a Spanish army appeared in the vega of Granada, which was clothed with a rich crop of fruit and grain. The soldiers ravaged it after their fashion: reaped the wheat, and put the grain in their stores, cut down the fruit-trees, and tore up the vines. The bad work done, Ferdinand summoned Granada to surrender. Boabdil tried to argue with him; Ferdinand would not listen to him or deal with him, but wrote to the officers in command at Granada, demanding the surrender of their arms. With one voice they refused. An officer named Muza spoke for them, and said they were ready to die, but they would not surrender. Boabdil, who then once more recovered courage, and said he was loyal to his race, begged to be allowed to lead them against the Spaniards, and they took him into favor once again.

The siege lasted over a year, and though there was no general battle, single combats and feats of daring were of daily occurrence. Between the advanced line of the Christians and the walls was an open space. Almost every day some Christian knight or Moorish warrior rode into this space and challenged any horseman on the other side to meet him in a joust of arms. When these duels took place the two armies looked on; it was esteemed unknightly to interfere.

One of the Moorish warriors, named Tarfe, was famous for his personal exploits. In open day he rode so near to the Spanish lines that he flung his lance almost into the royal tent; when it was pulled quivering out of the ground it was found to bear a card with the queen's name on it. Yet Tarfe rode safely back to Granada. A Spanish cavalier, named Hernan del Pulgar, with a handful of horsemen, rode stealthily at night into the city of Granada, nailed on the door of the chief mosque a placard bearing the words Ave Maria (" Hail, Mary"), galloped furiously through the crowd which tried to stop him, and got safely away. Next day a Moorish warrior of gigantic size appeared before the walls with this very placard tied to his horse's tail. He taunted and jeered the Spaniards till a young hidalgo rode out to meet him. The two cavaliers met with such a shock that their lances were shivered to pieces, and both rolled into the dust. Then the Moor, who was a giant, turned his adversary over on the ground, and drew his poignard to stab him in the throat; but the young hidalgo, shortening his sword, thrust it through a chink in the Moor's armor straight into his heart.

These encounters did not drive the Spaniards away from Granada, and the Moors saw that it was a mere question of time when they must yield from hunger, now that their fields were laid waste. So, after much strife among themselves, they agreed on terms of surrender in November, 1491, and on January 2nd, 1492, the Spaniards marched into the place.

Boabdil met the advance party with a face pinched by grief, and handed them the keys of the city. As he turned to look at his walls he burst into tears, and said:

"God is great!"

His old mother, Ayesha, who had somehow got out of her dungeon, and was spiteful to the last, exclaimed.

"You may well weep like a woman for what you could not defend like a man."

The Spanish advance-guard quickly raised the banner of the Cross and the flag of Castile and Aragon over the Alhambra, and in the open street the king and queen fell on their knees to thank God for their victory. The old ballad draws the scene so that you can almost see it:

> "There was crying in Granada
> When the sun was going down;
> Some calling on the Trinity
> Some calling on Mahoun.
> Here passed away the Koran
> There in the Cross was borne
> And here was heard the Christian bell,

And there the Moorish horn.
Here gallants held it little
For ladies' sake to die,
Or for the prophet's honor,
And pride of Soldanry;
For here did valor flourish,
And deeds of warlike might
Ennobled lordly palaces,
In which was our delight.
The gardens of thy vega!
Its fields and blooming bowers!
Woe! woe! I see their beauty gone,
And scattered all their flowers.
No reverence can claim the king
That such a land bath lost;
On charger never can he ride,
Nor be heard among the host;
But in some dark and dismal place,
Where none his face can see,
There, weeping and lamenting,
Alone that king should be."

Ferdinand promised that the Moors should continue to pray as they chose in their mosques; that their property should not be taken from them; that they should not be taxed more than they had been under their own kings.

We shall see how these promises were kept.

Boabdil was given a sum of money and a castle. But he was restless. He sold his property and went to Africa. There he was robbed by the sultans, and his children lived to beg their bread.

THE LAST OF THE MOORS

A.D. 1492-1375

THE Moors of Granada, who were a common-sense people, made no objections to the rule of the Spaniards so long as their religion was not interfered with, and they were allowed to pursue their several callings in peace. I dare say they were not sorry to exchange the turbulence of the old Moorish times of strife for the quiet of a government which was strong enough to keep order.

But now came to the front in Spain an influence which was destined to work untold mischief—the influence of the Church.

Three months had not elapsed from the surrender of Granada when Torquemada, the Grand Inquisitor of the Papal Church, terrified King Ferdinand into signing a decree for the expulsion of the Jews from Spain. The Jews were among the most useful and the richest of the people. They were skilful artificers, enterprising merchants, and liberal citizens. But because they were not Christians the priests insisted on their banishment. The Jews offered the king a bribe of thirty thousand ducats to let them alone. While the king and queen were considering it, Torquemada burst in upon them with a crucifix in his hand, and cried:

"Judas Iscariot sold his master for thirty pieces of silver. You would sell him for thirty thousand. Here he is! Sell him!"

And he flung the crucifix on the table.

The king and queen yielded, and several hundred thousand Jews, some of them old and infirm, some of them delicate women and children, were driven out of their homes and along the highways by brutal soldiers, to starve in a foreign land—just as the Russian Jews have been in our day. They were not allowed to take silver or gold with them. Those who were rich were as badly off as those who were poor. If they halted on the journey, from fatigue or illness, the soldiers prodded them with their sword-points. So they scattered to Africa, to Portugal, to Italy, to Holland, and Germany and England, and to this day you can meet descendants of theirs who cherish a tender memory of their ancient home.

111

IN THE DUSK AT GRANDA.

You can imagine that priests who thus persecuted the Jews were not inclined to be tolerant to the Moors. Ferdinand, as you remember, had promised the latter that they should be free to pray in their mosques after their fashion. Cardinal Ximenes now told the Moors of Granada that infidels could not be suffered to live in Spain. They must be baptized or go. Numbers of them had nowhere to go to, and had trades at their homes. They submitted to be baptized, and consoled themselves by washing off the mark of the holy water when they got back to their houses. Some fled to a mountain range near Granada, and barricaded the passes. There they stood a siege, but could not long hold out against the power of Spain; they surrendered, agreeing to be baptized or to go into exile, not, however, until they had killed the Spanish leader, Aguilar, in battle.

Of him and of this expedition of his there is a ballad which says:

"Beyond the sands, between the rocks,
where the old cork-tree grows,
The path is rough, and mounted men
Must singly march and slow;
There o'er the path the heathen range
Their ambuscade's line,
High up they wait for Aguilar
As the day begins to shine.

Nor knightly valor there avails,
Nor skill of horse or spear,
For rock on rock comes tumbling down
From cliff and cavern drear;
Down, down, like driving hail they come,
And horse and horsemen die,
Like cattle whose despair is dumb
When the fierce lightnings fly.

"A hundred and a hundred darts
Hiss round Aguilar's head;
Had Aguilar a thousand hearts,
Their blood had all been shed.
Faint and more faint he staggers

Upon the slippery sod;
At last his back is to the earth,
He gives his soul to God.

"Upon the village green he lay
As the moon was shining clear.
And all the village damsels
To look on him drew near;
They stood around him all agate,
Beside the big oak-tree;
And much his beauty they did praise,
Though mangled sore was he."

Then the Moors of Granada submitted in patience. Cardinal Ximenes burned their splendid library of Arabic manuscripts, as the Church was afraid of learning, and shut up the mosques. A number of Moors who refused to repudiate their religion were burned at the stake by the Holy Inquisition. And a few years later successors of Ximenes resolved to make life intolerable to the Moriscoes, as the Moors began to be called.

They forbade the Moors speaking their own language, and ordered them to speak nothing but Spanish. They forbade their bathing, as that cleanly people were in the habit of doing, and required them to be as dirty as the Spaniards. In order to make sure of this they tore down the baths. These oppressions again aroused the Moors to rebellion, and once more they took to the mountains, where the land, broken by many a torrent bed and many a dry gulch, slopes from the heights where the cattle browse under the shade of pine-trees to the narrow vega, spotted with cornfields and olive groves and vineyards, and again down to the tropical valleys, where the sugar-cane flourishes and the air is scented by the pine-apple. Here for two years the Moors held out. The war was one long string of murders and outrages, first on one side and then on the other.

How fiercely Moor and Christian hated each other you may guess from what happened in the prison of the Albencin. There were a couple of hundred Christian prisoners confined there for various offences. One hundred and ten Moors, made captive in battle, were thrust into the jail. Instantly, with fists and feet and teeth and pocket-knives, the two sets of prisoners fell upon one another. To separate them the governor of the place marched in the guard. But the jailer stopped the guard, saying:

"You are not needed. The prison is quiet. All the Moriscoes are dead."

The warfare did not cease until the king put his army under the command of lion Juan of Austria, a young plan of twenty-two, of whom you will presently hear more. He bade his soldiers give no quarter; and so, in course of time, the rebellious Moors were wiped out. Most of them were killed; the rest were banished. In the words of the old Arab historian:

"The Almighty was not pleased to grant our people victory. They were overcome and slain on all sides, till at last they were driven forth from the land of Andalusia, the which calamity came to pass in our own days. Verily to God belongs land and dominions, and He giveth to whom He cloth will."

It is said in larger histories than this that three million Moors were driven into exile between 1492 and 1610, when the last of them were sent out of the country. I suppose that this was about one-fifth or one-fourth the entire population of Spain. And it embraced the most industrious workmen, the most skilled artisans, the best farmers, and the most refined, polished, and learned people in the country.

At the time of their banishment Granada produced the finest cloths—of wool, silk, and linen—that were made in Spain; highly-tempered steel; perfect work in leather, bronze, and copper; elegant designs in embroidery and tracery; and at the same time the farmers of the vega had brought to such perfection the science of fertilizing land, and of developing the uses of water, that their performance has not been surpassed, if it has been equaled, to-day.

At this same time the Christians of Spain, with the exception of those who had learned from the Moors, were unable to make a fine sword-blade, or a rich silk, or a glowing dye, or a carved object in metal. Their farming was as rude as that of the Goths. They had a noble country with a fertile soil and a glorious climate. But they did not know how to turn either to account; the only occupation of which they really knew anything was fighting.

Yet the Moors were turned out for the sake of the Christians. The Cross took the place of the Crescent. But at the same time ignorance took the place of learning. Deserts gradually succeeded to smiling cornfields and purple vine-yards. A polite and refined people made way for a race of stupid peasants, who could neither be taught nor made to work. A people who were the leaders of civilization were banished from their homes to make room for a people steeped in sloth and superstition, and who to this day, in the opinion of their leading men, are unfit to be trusted with self-government.

THE CONDITION OF SPAIN

A.D. 1450-1500

WHEN Ferdinand and Isabella became King and Queen of Spain that country was divided into four States: Castile, which included the old provinces of the North, Galicia, the Asturias and the Basque country, Leon, Old and New Castile, Estremadura, Andalusia, and Murcia; Aragon, which included Catalonia and Valencia; the Moorish kingdom of Granada; and the independent kingdom of Navarre. You have heard how Ferdinand conquered Granada. Soon afterwards he annexed Navarre. Castile and Aragon being firmly united, the four States were merged into the kingdom of Spain. It was the home of many races, but thenceforth it constituted but one nationality.

The people of Spain were divided into four classes: 1. The nobles, who were of various ranks and grades; 2. The clergy; 3. The burghers of cities which held fueros, or charters, from the kings; and 4. The common people. In some provinces there was a fifth class, consisting of slaves—prisoners taken in war, captives bought from roaming slave-traders, or peasants belonging to the land they tilled. But the slavery of whites gradually died out, except on war-galleys, which were rowed by slaves a long time after Ferdinand and Isabella.

In those days the nobles—the highest among whom were called Grandees of Spain—possessed vast estates and enormous incomes. They lived in castles, with their retainers in towns and villages round them. Some of them were as powerful as kings. The Duke of Infantado could put thirty thousand men into the field. The Duke of Alva had an income of half a million a year of our money, which would buy as much goods or labor as several millions to-day. The income of the Duke of Medina Sidonia, of whom you have heard, was still larger. The family of Gonsalvo de Cordova, of whom you will hear presently, was nearly as rich, and so were a dozen others. All these nobles called themselves subjects of the king; but on their own estates they were monarchs of all they surveyed. They paid no taxes, but were bound to lead their fighting men to the king's wars.

The clergy were a large and powerful body, with the Archbishop of Toledo, who was called Primate of Spain, at their head. They also paid no taxes, and broad estates were assigned for the support of the several cardinals and archbishops and bishops. The Archbishop of Toledo had three-quarters of a million a year of our money, which was as much as five millions to-day. Many of the priests could afford to live in palaces; some of them had armies of retainers, whom they led to the wars. It became the fashion under Ferdinand and Isabella for the head of the Church to be likewise head of the government; thus Cardinal Ximenes ruled Spain in Ferdinand's later years. We should not think it a wise plan to put a bishop or archbishop at the head of the Cabinet in Washington; but four hundred years ago in Spain people looked at the thing in a different light.

The cities which had fueros or charters had a right to elect members to a Congress or Cortes, which made laws for the cities and the country round about them. I do not find that these laws were binding upon king, nobles, or clergy. But as the burghers had a way of their own of resenting invasions of their liberties by rising in arms, and as, moreover, the men in the cities had enrolled themselves in a brotherhood for mutual defence, I find that, so long as the Cortes continued to meet, neither king nor nobles cared to quarrel with them. After a time they fell into disuse, and their meetings ceased.

The common people of Spain—muleteers, shepherds, farm laborers, ploughmen, vine-dressers, and the like, in the country, and shoemakers, tailors, blacksmiths, masons, carpenters, servants, and the like, in the cities—do not seen to have enjoyed any rights worth mentioning, except the right of living, when they did not incur the wrath of the Church. They were often robbed by the nobles, and driven into the armies against their will. But when the nobles were not busy robbing people, and there was no war raging, and they did not quarrel with the Church, the common people appear to have led fairly cheerful lives, and to have danced merry boleros and sung tuneful romances on summer evenings.

Since the Moorish conquest Spain had made progress. Christians had learned from the Moors their methods of agriculture. They tilled every field that was covered with soil, and watered it from the near-by rivers. Thus all the land was made to yield its increase, and Spain had quantities of fruit and oil and wine to send abroad in exchange for foreign goods. The forbidding and sunburnt desert over which you will now travel if you go from Madrid to Toledo was then a garden, fed with water from the Tagus. The Moors were as expert breeders of cattle and sheep as they were good farmers. They raised fleet mules which were preferred to horses, and a breed of sheep, called Merinos, which yielded the softest and brightest wool in the world. You will see on some of our pastures sheep of that same Merino breed to-day. I have told you in former chapters of the products of the Moorish looms and factories and foundries. They also were copied by the Christians.

Thus at the close of the reign of Ferdinand and Isabella the cities of Spain were numerous and rich. You have heard of Cordova and Seville and Malaga and Granada.. Toledo, with its turbulent people, was at the end of the fifteenth century as splendid and bustling as any. Valladolid, in Castile, which is now a small place of ten thousand population, could put thirty thousand soldiers in the field. Saragossa was the centre of so rich a country that it was called "the abundant." Barcelona was a great seaport, whose flag was seen in all harbors. Valencia was its rival for the trade of Africa. Salamanca, the home of learning, was crowded with students from all parts of Europe. Burgos was a hive of industry.

At that time the Spanish hidalgos were cultured and accomplished gentlemen, as well as valiant warriors. In comparison with Spain, England was a poor, weak, obscure country, peopled by an ignorant race, which at this time was busied in hanging witches, and among whom laborers worked for fourpence a day—a country where Jack Cade thought to better matters by turning everything topsy-turvy, and Parliament had nothing better to do than to prohibit the importation of flour until it reached a price when it was too dear for the poor to afford it.

The increase of wealth and the splendid example of the Moors led to much extravagance in living in the cities of Spain. People lived in houses with mosaic floors, fretted arches by way of ceilings, delicately carved windows. They wore clothes of cloth-of-gold and silver, and of silk richly embroidered. Ladies carried priceless gems round their necks and in their hair. The queen herself was not fond of show. When not engaged in affairs of government she spent her time in embroidery and fancy needle-work. A law was passed that no one but nobles should wear silk; but it was not obeyed. The rich burghers in the cities, like the nobles, gave grand feasts, at which rich food was served on gold and silver plates; after the banquet the ladies danced in gowns which were worth a fortune, and which were as stiff as if they were made of boards. When a man died another fortune was spent on his funeral. Ferdinand tried to stop this by law, but the priests said he was trying to take the bread out of their mouths, and he gave up his attempt.

"REMEMBER THAT THOU TOO MUST DIE!"

The king and queen led frugal lives. Isabella never used a carriage; she travelled on horseback. Both wore plain clothes and ate plain food. Isabella rarely touched wine. But the court did not follow her example. In one thing, however, she was extravagant. Printing had lately been invented. She sent for all the printing-presses and all the printers she could get; so that it is said there were more books printed in Spain during the century which followed the invention of printing than in all the rest of Europe put together.

One popular Spanish pastime she could not endure. That was the custom of bull-fighting, which lasts to the present day. In her youthful days she was taken to a bull-fight, and she saw horses gored to death, and the poor bull, after being teased by the cruel picadors, finally stabbed to death by the keen blade of the matador. As she came out she said she would never see such a spectacle again. She kept her word; but in this, as in the other case, her people did not imitate her.

In one more instance this admirable woman failed to carry her point. When the priests of Castile begged to be allowed to establish the Inquisition to crush the Jews, she objected, though she was a devout Catholic; but afterwards she yielded to the bullying of her confessors and her bishops, and assented to the introduction of the Holy Office in Spain, on the condition that it should be mercifully administered.

I wish I could tell you that it was; but I cannot. On the contrary, the cruelties which were practised upon heretics, or persons suspected of being heretics, by the priests of the Inquisition were so horrible that I will not undertake to describe them. You will find them set forth in larger books than this. It is enough here to say that during the reign of Ferdinand and Isabella several thousand persons were burned to death after being tortured in the dungeons of the Inquisition, and that probably a still larger number of persons were despoiled of their property in favor of the Church under threats that they would be accused of heresy.

COLUMBUS

A. D. 1484-1492

WHILE Ferdinand was fixing his mind on the foolish enterprise of crushing the Moors, a poor sailor was spending his time in trying to attract his attention to a far more sensible undertaking.

This was Christopher Columbus. He was a native of Genoa, the son of a wool-carder; at this time about fifty years old, quite gray and bronzed, as seafaring men are, though his blue eye was still clear, and his skin was fair and ruddy. He had spent all his life at sea, from the time he left the college at Pavia, at the age of fourteen. More than once he had been shipwrecked; once off the coast of Portugal his ship foundered in battle; he leaped into the waves and caught an oar, with the help of which he swam to shore, which was five or six miles distant. But the danger did not prevent his going to sea again as soon as lie could get a ship.

At that time there was a craze for adventure at sea. Within a short period the mariner's compass and the astrolabe, which took the place of our quadrant and sextant, had been invented, and with their help seamen were enabled to make voyages far from land. Thus the coasts of Europe, Africa, and parts of Asia had been explored. But nothing was known of America. Some people supposed that Asia spread over the greater part of the world, and that it was not very far by sea from China and Tartary to Spain. Many mariners believed that by taking ship at any Western port in Europe, and sailing due westward, the eastern shore of Asia could be reached. This was the notion of Christopher Columbus, and he had confirmed himself in the belief by studying the maps of the period, which were drawn chiefly from fancy.

Columbus was in this mind when he settled at Lisbon, in Portugal, and married. For a whole quarter of a century he made voyages of exploration, one after another—sometimes sailing to the Northern Seas, where the ice never melts, and sometimes down to the gold coast of Africa, where snow never falls—all the time keeping wary watch of the tides and currents and winds, of the flight of birds, of the drift of weeds, and of the course of fishes, so as to learn the secrets of the great ocean. To the beautiful islands lying off the coast of Spain and Portugal, Madeira, the Azores, and the Canary Islands, he made many voyages, studying their shores and their waters, and whenever he found a mariner who had sailed out beyond them into the dark blue sea where the sea-weed grows on the top of the water, and blocks the way for ships, he was never tired of questioning hint about what he had seen.

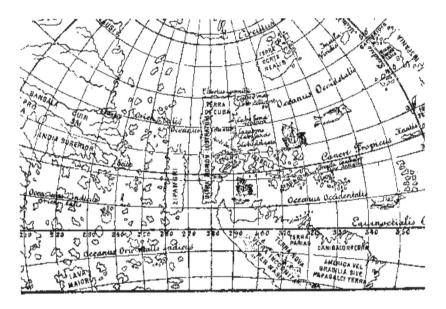

THE WORLD AS IT WAS KNOWN IN COLUMBUS'S TIME.

At last he made up his mind, and asked King John, of Portugal, to give hire a vessel or two to, discover the western road to Asia. The king hesitated, consulted his ministers, studied over the maps; then resolving that if there was any discovery to be made he would make it himself, and would leave none of the glory of it for Columbus, he despatched a fleet westward. But the ships presently came back, the captains declaring that they had sailed as far as they dared westward, and had found no land. Columbus heard their report; and, understanding its meaning, slipped privately out of Portugal and took refuge in Spain.

He had no money and no friends. But a good priest, Juan Perez de Marchena, took him up, fed and clothed him, listened to his plans, and gave him a few coins and a letter to the queen's confessor. The confessor was of opinion that Columbus was crazy. The Duke of Medina Sidonia was like-minded; so were other great men at court. Many priests were inclined to suspect that any such discovery as Columbus planned was contrary to the Bible. Still, as the poor, battered old sailor stuck to his plans, and kept pressing them on the court, the king finally appointed a committee of learned men to consider them, and report to him at their leisure. The committee met at Salamanca.

It seems that the committee took six years to make up its mind on the subject. During all this time Columbus—who had with him his little son Diego—was strained to find bread. Sometimes he served as a soldier in the Spanish armies against the Moors. Sometimes he drew maps, at which business he was skilful, and sold them for a few cents. For two years he kept a book-store at Seville, and young men eager for adventures used to gather there to hear him talk of the rolling sea., of the dangers which beset those who go down to the deep in ships, and of the gold and gems which were to be gathered in the dirt of the distant countries where the savages lived.

At last, in 1491, the committee reported that Columbus's scheme was vain and impracticable. The king thought so too; so did most of his ministers; the queen hesitated; only Cardinal Mendoza, of whore you will hear more presently, and one or two other intelligent priests, thought that Columbus should have a chance to try his experiment. For nearly a year, while King Ferdinand with his army lay before the city of Granada, the debate went on, and the big heart of Columbus almost broke from disappointment and delay. At last, just as Granada surrendered, he gave up hope, and, mounting a horse, he rode slowly away from the camp.

He had not gone far when he was overtaken by a messenger from the queen's household, who bade him return. As soon as it became known that he as gone, Queen Isabella called a council, and declared that she was for granting the prayer of Columbus. When she was told that it would cost a great deal of money, and that the royal treasury had been emptied by the Moorish war, this glorious woman replied:

"I will assume the undertaking for my own Crown of Castile; if there is not money enough in the treasury to meet the expense, I will pawn my jewels."

I think you will understand the feelings with which Columbus wrote of this turning-point in his fortunes:

"In the midst of general unbelief, God infused into the Queen, my lady, the spirit of intelligence and energy; while every one else in his ignorance was thinking of the trouble and cost, she approved it and gave it all the help in her power."

In a sheltered cove on the shore of the Mediterranean, near the mouth of the River Tinto, is the little village of Palos, which four hundred years ago was larger than it is now. For some misconduct it had been condemned to furnish two ships for two years to the government service. These two ships were now placed at the service of Columbus; a third his friends agreed to supply. An order from the queen required the merchants of Andalusia to outfit these vessels at cost. To man them, one hundred and twenty men were needed. Adventurous young men from every part of Spain came forward; but to make up the full number of the crew, the government had to exempt volun¬teers from arrest for crime for two months after their return from. the voyage.

In this way the little fleet was manned.

It consisted of three vessels the *Santa Maria*, which was a large vessel for those days, and was the flag-ship, with Columbus himself in command, and the *Pinta* and *Nina*, smaller vessels, but well prepared for the voyage by two ship-builders named Pinzon, who commanded them. The *Santa Maria* carried sixty-six men, the *Pinta* thirty, and the *Nina* twenty-four. All three were provisioned for a year, and were supplied with fire-arms and a large stock of ammunition. Models of these ships, as large as the originals, were at the World's Fair at Chicago.

There was only a glimmer of dawn in the eastern sky when, at three o'clock in the morning of August 3rd, 1492, the fleet weighed anchor and spread sail to a fair wind. The people of Palos were out of bed, watching the sailing of the ships, and at the window of the convent where Columbus had found shelter and hospitality eight years before, his good friend the priest Perez de Marchena stood, with tears streaming down his cheeks, asking a blessing on the enterprise, and waving a white flag.

THE DISCOVERY OF AMERICA

A.D. 1492-1493

IN six days the little fleet reached the Canary Islands, and there it spent nearly a month in refitting. The rudder of the *Pinta* required mending, and the sails of the *Nina* were too large. On September 6th the repairs were finished, and the ships sailed westward on the unknown deep.

The crew soon began to see wonders. They sailed into a sea which was full of orange sea-weed floating on the surface, with crabs swimming in the branches. In the air were flocks of boobies, gulls, and petrels. Strange visions appeared before the excited fancy of the sailors, and they began to long to be at home. They became quite discontented after September 23rd, when Martin Pinzon fancied he saw land, and it turned out to be a cloud on the horizon. Columbus never allowed himself to be discouraged, and he kept up the spirit of his men by praying to the saints, and telling stories of the vast treasures the crew would reap when they reached the dominions of the Khan of Tartary. Martin Pinzon was for steering south, where he believed he would find a rich island which he called Cipango, but Columbus insisted on sailing due west, in order to strike the continent of Cathay. Both were kept up by dreams of land which only existed in their imagination.

Early in October objects came floating by which no one could mistake. A branch of a rose-bush with rose-buds on it passed close to the *Nina*. Then a stick with carving on it was seen. Land could not be far off. A reward of thirty-six dollars in money—to which Columbus added his velvet coat—was offered to him who first saw the shore.

At ten o'clock in the evening of October 11th Columbus thought he saw a light bobbing and flickering in the west, and four hours later a gun was fired from the *Pinta*, to signify that land was iii sight. The crews could hardly contain themselves till morning. When the sun rose they saw that they had found land in reality—a white sandy beach with clumps of palms and other trees in the back-ground, very refreshing to the eye of the tired sailors. Columbus and his officers landed in their most gorgeous apparel, and after returning thanks to

God on their bended knees, planted the cross and the flag of Spain on the beach, to signify that these regions henceforth belonged to the Spanish king.

A number of natives, wearing no clothes, came down to meet them, and said that the island was called Guanahani. Columbus called it San Salvador. For a long time it was supposed to be the island which is marked as Cat Island on the maps. But now it is believed to be Watling Island, one of the Bahamas, a coral rock on which the winds have deposited a little soil, and trees have grown from seeds blown from other islands. Columbus stayed there several days, exchanging glass beads for balls of cotton, rolls of tobacco, and little rings of gold, which the natives wore in their noses. Then he sailed to other islands near by, sonic of which were more beautiful than San Salvador in their rich tropical foliage and their bright clear waters.

On their shores he found curious fish, pink, and silver, and striped, with yellow fins, hog-fish, purple and scarlet fish, flying fish, and whales; strange monstrous crabs, queer lizards and iguanas, with rows of white teeth and sharp claws; and in the woods a variety of parrots and birds of brilliant plumage, flying and singing over meadows in which flowers and fruit perfumed the air, He found one thing which was worth more than all the rest—the potato. But Columbus had not sailed across the ocean to see pretty birds, or strange fish, or green lizards, or flowers, or even potatoes. He wanted gold, and that he had not found. The natives told him that there was an abundance of gold and pearls too in the island of Cuba; therefore he weighed anchor, and to Cuba he went.

This island, again, he said, was the fairest ever seen by the eye of man, with great tall palms and giant trees full of singing birds, and fields planted with corn and sweet-potatoes. Ile found here guinea-pigs and musk-deer and a queer fish, called a coffer-fish, which wore a coat of mail from its head to its tail; likewise sugar-cane, bananas, cocoanuts, and cassava, out of which they made bread. But no gold.

The natives said he must go farther on—to the island which Columbus called Hispaniola, his successors named San Domingo, and of which one end is now called Hayti, and the other end Dominica.

VISION ON THE VOYAGE.

Here again he found a lovely country, spreading trees, in which nightingales sang, and a great abundance of fish in the waters round the island. He also bought from the natives, in exchange for beads and cloth, a few plates of gold, not many nor large of their kind. But the native chief told Columbus that if it was gold he wanted he could show him a place where he could load his ships with it, only it was a little farther on. There were whole mountains of gold a few days' sail farther west. Columbus said he would see those mountains.

But on Christmas Eve, as the *Santa Maria* was sailing round an island, Columbus and his helmsman fell asleep, and their vessel ran on a sand bank, where the cruel waves battered the life out of her on the bottom. The *Pinta* was cruising on her own account; and nothing remained of the fleet but the little *Nina*. With her Columbus tried to find his way to the islands with the mountains of gold. But his men were anxious to see their homes, and to tell of the new world they had found. Forty-two of them, who were willing to stay in the new country, Columbus planted in a fort which he built at a place he christened Navidad, in Hispaniola; with the rest, and a few natives who were anxious to see the world, on January 4th, 1493, he started homeward in the *Nina*.

THE LANDING OF COLUMBUS.

It was a dreadful voyage. After the expedition had been a fortnight at sea the provisions gave out, and the crew had to live on the flesh of tunnies and sharks which they caught. Then a storm overtook them, and though Columbus on his knees agreed to carry a candle to our Lady of Guadaloupe, and to undertake a pilgrimage to Saint Clara's shrine; though the entire crew vowed to walk barefoot and in their shirts to offer thanks for their rescue at the first church they found — if they ever found a church again — the little *Nina* nevertheless came very near foundering with all on board.

Columbus wrote to Ferdinand and Isabella a touching account of his distress:

"Above all," he said, "my sorrows were multiplied when I thought of my two sons at Cordova, at school, left destitute of friends in a strange land before I was known to have performed such service that your Majesties might be inclined to relieve them."

Happily the wind moderated, and after much further buffeting by the waves the *Nina* managed to cast anchor off the Portuguese island of *Santa Maria*, and to land her men to fulfil their vow. The Portuguese governor was for holding them as prisoners, on the ground that they had made discoveries which should by right have been made by King John of Portugal. But Columbus swore a great oath that if one of the *Nina's* crew was touched he would sweep every living creature off the island, and the *Nina* sailed without further interference.

Her troubles were not ended, however; for no sooner had she got fairly to sea again than the tempest rose once more, her sails were torn from the masts, and the little craft, helpless as a cork on the top of the waves, was dashed hither and thither in a mighty sea, with high winds, a deluge of rain, and constant thunder and lightning. Once more Columbus vowed to go on a pilgrimage to our Lady of La Cinta in his shirt and barefoot, and he had hardly taken the vow when the land appeared over the weather bow, and a tremendous succession of high seas carried the *Nina* into the mouth of the river Tagus.

King John's first idea was to lock up Columbus in prison. He could not forgive himself for having been so stupid as to let the glory of the discovery slip through his fingers and go to Ferdinand and Isabella. But by this time the discoverer had landed, the people of Lisbon had seen the Indians and the gold, everybody was in the wildest excitement, Columbus was the hero of the hour, and there would have been trouble if he had been molested. So King John put the best face on the matter, smothered his disappointment, invited Columbus to court, and bade him sit by his side with his hat on his head.

When a man was allowed to sit by King John with his hat on his head people understood that he was somebody quite out of the common run. But when the great lords of Portugal heard the story which Columbus had to tell, and his account of the splendid countries he had seized for Spain, and when they remembered that the Pope had given all these countries to Portugal, they declared that such things could not be endured, Columbus must be killed, and a fleet sent out to rediscover the islands on which he had landed.

THE SECOND VOYAGE

A.D. 1493-1498

ON reflection, King John of Portugal refrained from killing Columbus, and he sailed to Palos, where the people, as you may imagine, were very glad to see him again, and his good old friend, the priest Perez, fell on his neck for joy.

The king and queen were at Barcelona, and thither Columbus proceeded to meet them, making a triumphant march through Spain, like a conqueror. In every city he passed through the people turned out to welcome him with shouts and flowers and music. At Barcelona the city made a grand holiday of his reception. A squadron of cavaliers, splendidly mounted and bearing banners, rode out to escort him into the city. Houses were decorated with flags, streets were densely crowded, and the house-tops covered with spectators, who waved handkerchiefs. A procession was formed. Columbus rode in the middle, leading six Indians in plumes and gaudy costume; the members of his crew followed in their best clothes, bearing products of the islands they had seen.

Trumpets blew blasts of welcome as high court officials, bowing to the ground, led the discoverer, or the Admiral, as be was called, to the throne-room where Ferdinand and Isabella sat side by side in solemn state. He knelt to kiss their hands, but they raised him and bade him sit in an arm-chair opposite them, while he told them the story of his voyage. The courtiers' jaws dropped when they saw a common man sitting in the presence of majesty; they lifted up their eyes as if to say, What is the world coming to? To them the finding of a New World was far less important than the seating of a commoner in the presence of royalty. The monarch treated Columbus like an equal. Isabella invited him to her parlor, and was never tired of hearing him talk about the New World, and Ferdinand took him out riding, as if he had been a lord of high degree.

Most of the nobles made much of him. One of them was captious, and sneeringly said at a public banquet that if Columbus had not discovered the Islands of the West, some one else would have done so. It was then that Columbus asked the party whether any of then could make an egg stand on end. As none of them could, he seized the egg, brought it down with such force on the table that the shell broke, and the egg easily stood upright on the broken end. "Any one could do that," said the noble. "Yes," replied Columbus; "so any one could have discovered the New World if he had known how to do it."

THE BRADLEY PORTRAIT OF COLUMBUS.

A new expedition of seventeen vessels was fitted out at Cadiz, and the command given to Columbus. But what will surprise you, the general direction of the whole business was intrusted to an archdeacon named Fonseca. It may puzzle you to figure out what archdeacons had to do with naval expeditions. Another thing at which you may be astonished is, that a dispute arising between Spain and Portugal about the ownership of the new countries, the Pope decided that all strange countries which were not inhabited by Christians should be divided between Spain and Portugal, Spain taking those which were west of the Canaries, and Portugal those which were east. It was hard enough on the people of Asia and Africa and America not to have had a chance of being Christians; to lose their lands as well was especially severe; don't you think so?

The fleet sailed on September 25th, 1493, and taking a more southerly course than the first expedition, it first sighted Dominica, and then in turn visited Guadaloupe, Montserrat, Nevis, Santa Cruz, and other islands, which Columbus christened. One of them he called after his flag-ship, the *Marie Galante*—a name which it bears to this day. Sailors who landed on these islands lost themselves in the dense thickets of the interior. Plants grow so thickly in that luxuriant soil that to this day a traveller has to cut his way through the underbrush with a sword-knife.

On these islands Columbus found a race of natives different from the kind, gentle, timid creatures he had met on the Bahamas and in Hispaniola. He called them Caribs. They were fighters and cannibals, men and women alike. They fought with spears, hatchets, and bows and arrows, and sometimes their arrows were poisoned. They ate dogs, lizards, snakes, wild birds, fish, with corn, cassava, and pine-apples. They were the most vigorous Indians Columbus had met. Some of them wore clothes, and they had a system of laws. But they were always at war with their neighbors, and after a battle they ate their prisoners.

Columbus was not sorry to leave these savages; his fleet sailed to the place in Hispaniola where he had left forty-two men of his first expedition to hold the fort he had built. He was greatly shocked when he got there to find that the fort was gone, and the men gone too. After long search he found a few skulls and some bones. It turned out that the men had quarrelled among themselves over booty, had robbed the Indians, and had behaved infamously to the Indian women; whereupon a tribe of Caribs landed on Hispaniola and murdered them all.

A SPANISH CARAVEL
EXACT REPRODUCTION OF THE SHIP IN WHICH COLUMBUS
SAILED ON HIS VOYAGE TO AMERICA. SENT TO THE
COLUMBIAN WORLD'S FAIR BY THE SPANISH GOVERNMENT.

This was a bad beginning for the conquest. But Columbus plucked up spirit, built him a new fort, which he called Isabella, put a garrison into it, and with the rest of his force explored the coasts of Cuba, Jamaica, and Hispaniola. In the two latter he found rivers with gold in the sand and gravel, and he was beginning to hope that he was going to realize his old visions, when he was taken ill and lay five months in his bed in a fever which deprived him of speech, hearing, sense, and memory. Many of his men took the fever; it was probably while it was raging that one of them saw a fish as big as a whale, with a shell like a turtle, two fins like wings, and a head sticking out of the water as large as a wine-cask.

When he got better Columbus led his men on one expedition after another, partly in the hope of finding gold, and partly to divert their minds. But the fever kept spreading, and with it other new and strange diseases which the doctors could not cure. And as many of the men whom Columbus had led across the ocean were idle, and would not work in the hot sun, provisions began to grow scarce. At the same time parties of Spaniards who roamed the island in search of gold behaved so badly that even the meekest Indians turned upon them and attacked them. This was a dark time for the discoverers of the New World.

Driven beyond bearing by the misconduct of the Spaniards, the Indians gathered all their fighting men into an army, and marched down to chive the strangers into the sea. But the poor naked creatures could do little against soldiers who wore coats of mail, and fought with arquebuses. The battle ended in a rout,, and so many of the Indians were killed that the survivors submitted to their fate, bowed their heads meekly, and bore whatever their cruel conquerors chose to inflict.

I am sorry to say that at this time Columbus, who was very much concerned about the salvation of the Indians' souls, proposed to Ferdinand and Isabella to make slaves of them, as the best way of converting them to Christianity, and I am not surprised that the pure and noble woman who was queen wrote on the margin of his letter:

"This should not be done till every other way of converting them has been tried."

But new troubles were in store for the discoverer.

Away across the ocean, in the city of Seville, Archdeacon Fonseca was jealous and spiteful; he intrigued against Columbus, while sailors who had sailed under the Admiral and had been sent home told false stories of his doings in the islands. Spaniards began to complain that he was not sending much gold home, and it was whispered that he was keeping it for himself. People went about saying that Columbus was not the man for the place, that if others whom they could name had been put in command, things would have turned out differently.

Rumors of this spite-work reached the ears of Columbus, and he resolved to go home to face his enemies. He filled a ship with Indian slaves, embarked for Europe, and after dangers from storm and perils from hunger—at one time the ship ran out of provisions and the sailors could hardly be kept from eating the Indian slaves—he landed in Spain in May, 1496. The king and queen received him well, but the Spanish people were tired of him. They had heard stories of the sufferings of the adventurers in Hispaniola. They had been disappointed at the small amount of gold which had come from the New World. Like other races, the Spaniards were fickle; the very people who had roared themselves hoarse three years before, when Columbus first arrived from the Indies, now turned their backs on him, and growled that the archdeacon was probably right after all, and that Columbus was nothing but a crank. King Ferdinand grew cool to him. Queen Isabella alone stood by him, and still cherished faith in his honor and his wisdom.

He had offended her when he brought home a ship-load of Indians, and wanted to sell them as slaves in the market-place of Seville—the money they brought to go to the queen. She would have no such slave sales in her kingdom, nor any blood-money in her pocket. Such Indians as wished to stay in Spain she bade the guards set free; the others she ordered Columbus to take back to their own country. And as Columbus, after all his discoveries, was so poor that he could hardly buy himself clothes, and could not charter a ship to return to the islands he had found, she bought for him two vessels, which he tried to man with volunteers. But the time had passed when young men of ambition craved to sail on voyages of discovery. Nobody was willing to take service under Columbus. To fit out his vessels he had to man them with the worst convicts from the prisons, with which sorry crew he embarked from Spain on his third voyage in May, 1498.

THE DEATH OF COLUMBUS

A.D. 1498-1506

AGAIN, in 1498, Columbus crossed the Atlantic, having found places for his two soils as pages of Queen Isabella. This time he first sighted a three-pronged island, to which he gave the name of Trinidad; he sailed along the coast of the country we call Venezuela, which forms part of the continent of South America; likewise the shore of Central America, where he found gold mines, from which he got nuggets. One of the places he saw was so beautiful that he felt sure that it was the garden of Paradise, where Adam and Eve lived.

In these voyages and travels he collected gold and pearls, which he set aside for his good friend Isabella; but when he returned to his city in Hispaniola., he found everything in disorder. You remember that on his last voyage he had to man his ships with the refuse of the jails. This refuse no sooner found itself in freedom in a lovely climate in a country abounding in food and inhabited by a helpless people, than it broke loose from all restraint, and fell to robbing, murdering, and outraging the natives. A rebellion against Columbus was headed by a horrible wretch, named Roldan, who, strange to say, had been appointed chief-justice.

In the mean time, in Spain, the archdeacon had never ceased to intrigue against Columbus, to tell false stories about him, and to try to undermine him in the opinion of the king and queen. He could the more easily do this as Queen Isabella's faith in him was beginning to be somewhat shaken. She had distinctly forbidden the enslavement of the Indians; in spite of which five ship-loads of them—men and women, boys and girls—had arrived in Spain for sale. The queen set them free, and sharply rebuked the captains of the ships which had brought them. She thought Columbus should have prevented this. So when the archdeacon murmured that it was high time some one took Columbus's place in the New World she at first demurred, then hesitated, and at last consented; a hectoring, bullying soldier named Bobadilla was despatched to Hispaniola.

THE FRONT OF A SPANISH CHURCH.

This man no sooner landed than he trumped up charges against Columbus, and, before any trial, seized him, and though he was ill in health and broken in spirit, clapped him in irons and thrust him into a dungeon. Chains were riveted round his ankles and his wrists, and he was compelled to sleep on the cold stones of the prison, where his teeth could be heard chattering half the night. His two brothers were also seized and jailed by his side. Then, after a pretended inquiry into the facts, Bobadilla ordered Columbus on board ship, ironed as he was, and sent him off to Spain. When he landed, the king and queen promptly set him at liberty, gave him money, and soothed him with kind words. It is said that when Isabella saw him, with his bent back, his snow-white head, and his tottering step, she burst into tears.

She recalled Bobadilla. He, taking ship for Spain in company with Chief-justice Holdall, was wrecked and drowned on the way, and so there was an end of him. But the queen did not forgive the slavery business. The governorship of Hispaniola did not go back to the old admiral, but went to a friend of the archdeacon's—Ovando by name. It was not till May, 1502, after two years' idleness, that Columbus got leave to revisit the world he had found.

When he reached Hispaniola he found that he was nobody. Ovando was supreme, and his officers paid scant respect to the old admiral. He was given a couple of ships, and allowed to go on exploring as before. He reached the coast of Central America, and kept wandering up and down in search of a strait or passage to Asia. I need not tell you he found none. He found natives of various races, some of whom were at first friendly, but who rose in wrath and fury when the Spaniards misbehaved. The season was stormy, and Columbus more than once narrowly escaped shipwreck. Once or twice, when he found a place where he could land, he and his men went ashore, and nearly perished from hunger. Ovando let a whole year pass without sending them any provisions.

Returning to Hispaniola, Columbus demanded his share of the products of his discovery, according to the terms of his contract with the king and queen. Ovando would not let him have a ducat. Thus, in his old age, after all his toil and its splendid results, he found himself penniless and houseless. He begged to be sent home. Ovando gave him a ship which was leaky, which lost her masts and nearly went to the bottom in a storm. He shifted to another, which kept afloat, but was so slow that he was fifty-eight days reaching the mouth of the Guadalquivir. He was unable to walk when he arrived;

his men carried him ashore, and in a litter the battered and bruised old veteran was conveyed to Seville to die.

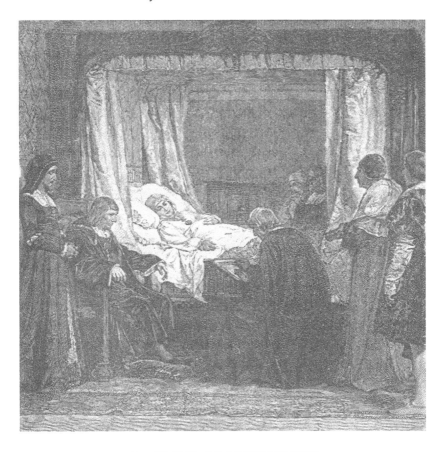

DEATH-BED OF QUEEN ISABEL.

Misfortune had laid a heavy hand on him. Less than three weeks after his arrival his good and stanch friend Isabella died. Her husband, Ferdinand, looked upon the New World as a place to get money out of, and neither cared how he got it., nor felt any gratitude to him who had enabled him to get it. At the time Columbus returned from his fourth and last voyage, Spain was receiving about half a million dollars (of our money) from the West Indies each year. One-eighth or one-tenth of this belonged to Columbus, under the bargain he had made with Ferdinand and Isabella. They had not paid him a dollar, and now when he wrote to Ferdinand to say that he had not money enough to pay his bill at the inn at Seville, the king not only sent him nothing, but would not even answer his letter. Columbus persisted, even had himself carried into the king's presence, followed him from Granada to Segovia, and from Segovia to Valladolid, but Ferdinand was cold and immovable.

"It appears," said the dying old admiral, "that his majesty does not see fit to fulfil that which he and the queen (who is now in glory) promised me by word and seal. For me to contend with him would be to contend against the wind."

He had a flicker of hope when the Archduke Charles, who married the Princess Juana., sent him word that he took the greatest interest in his discoveries. But Charles had other things to think of, and the old sailor gradually gave up the struggle.

His infirmities were pressing on him cruelly, and his pains were severe. He had found a resting-place in a small bare room, without carpet or curtains, in a mean inn at Valladolid, where hardly any one knew who or what he had been. His sons and one or two of their friends were with him, and a good Franciscan monk clothed him in a robe of the brotherhood. There he watched the approach of death. When he felt it come, on May 20th, 1506, he cried, "Lord, into thy hands I commend my soul!" and died.

When it was announced that Columbus was dead, King Ferdinand knew that he would worry him no more, and he ordered a splendid funeral. Seven years afterwards the admiral's body was removed to Seville: twenty-three years after that it was again removed to the cathedral at San Domingo, in Hispaniola. Nearly a hundred years ago, the Spaniards took from the cathedral at San Domingo a casket, which, as they believed, contained the remains of Columbus, and reburied it in the cathedral at Havana. But it seems doubtful whether they removed the right casket. It is now said that the one which was carried to Havana contained the body of some priest.

Wherever his mortal remains lie, his fame fills the world, and his family received honors which were denied to its founder. His son succeeded to his title of admiral and viceroy, and married the sister of the great Duke of Alva, of whom you will presently hear. His brother was given a high command in the New World. The family became one of the most considerable in Spain; one branch married into the reigning family of Portugal; the head of another branch married the Infanta Eulalia, and lately visited this country on the occasion of the World's Fair at Chicago.

You will, of course, agree with the Spanish grandee who said that if Columbus had not discovered America somebody else would. But you will perceive that so much may be said of all discoveries. The glory of a discoverer is none the less because some one else might have won it if he had been in time. When Columbus started out on his westward voyage the wisest men of his day said that the enterprise was foolhardy, and that its chief was a maniac. As you have read, it took eight years to convince the Spanish court that the experiment was worth trying. A man who perseveres against such obstacles, and whose efforts are crowned with success, you will always consider one of the heroes of whom the world must be proud.

When Columbus had made his landing on this hemisphere, on October 12th, 1492, other discoverers followed. John Cabot landed in Labrador on June 24th, 1497, Sebastian Cabot coasted along the shore of the Atlantic States in 1498—the year in which the Portuguese, Vasco de Gama, rounded the Cape of Good Hope. Amerigo Vespucci, after whom this continent is named, discovered the coast of Brazil between 1501 and 1503. There would have been more explorers, especially under the English flag, had it not been for the decree of the pope awarding all America to Spain. To explore in the face of that decree meant to make war on Spain, and England was not ready yet. So it came about that for the better part of a century after Columbus no explorers came to this continent except under the Spanish flag.

THE END OF FERDINAND AND ISABELLA

A.D. 1475-1516

IN order to give you a connected account of the conquest of Granada and of the discoveries of Columbus, I have passed over events in the reign of Ferdinand and Isabella of which it is necessary that you should know something, and have made little or no mention of some persons of whose lives you would like to hear.

One of these was Cardinal Mendoza, Archbishop of Toledo, and prime-minister of Spain for twenty years. He was a friend of Columbus when the great sailor sorely needed a friend. He was a man of lofty mind, a lover of learning, and a thorough gentleman of the world, adored by ladies as he was respected by men. His income was the largest in Spain, and he spent it royally, keeping an army of his own, and a palace full of young pages belonging to the first families, whom he took care to educate. The people loved him; as he paced the streets on his snow-white mule, whose hide could scarcely be seen for caparisons of cloth of gold and velvet, they fell on their knees and besought his blessing, begging to be allowed to touch his foot or his stirrup with their lips. He was a faithful and loyal servant to Queen Isabella; she rarely acted without consulting him. When he was on his death-bed she asked whom she would recommend as his successor. He designated a friar named Ximenes, and the queen appointed him accordingly.

He was a very different person from Mendoza. He was wise, politic, and vigorous; but also a bigot, a religious enthusiast, an ascetic, and a fanatic. As a young man he was always mortifying his flesh. He wore a shirt of coarse hair next his skin, and scourged himself at regular intervals. He lived in a log cabin he had built with his own hands in a chestnut wood, ate herbs, and drank from a stream. A person who led such a life as this in our day would simply be regarded as a crank, and his neighbors would watch him lest he went mad. But four hundred years ago in Spain these oddities were regarded as proofs of sanctity, and Ximenes was looked upon as a very superior order of saint indeed. People from far and wide went to his hut to confess their sins to so holy a priest. His reputation rose so high that in the very year when Granada fell and Columbus discovered the West Indies he was appointed confessor to the queen.

He was a lean, pale monk, who looked as if he had been starved—as indeed he probably had been—but he feared nobody, and was determined to do his duty as the understood it. When he was directed to inspect the various monasteries of his order, he travelled on foot and begged his food by the way-side, which caused much laughter among the gorgeous priests who lived like princes in their lordly palaces. I do not see myself that anything is gained for the cause of true religion by an affectation of poverty, nor do I understand why a priest who had plenty of money should have needed to beg his bread. But I observe that by so doing Ximenes made himself much thought of among the ignorant, and I suspect that was his object.

When he was appointed Archbishop of Toledo he was very much surprised, and said: "There is some mistake; the appointment is not for me." He said he wanted to live and die a simple priest in his cloister. But I do not observe that after he was well settled in his office he was squeamish in exercising his powers, though he allowed it to be understood that he still ate only the plainest food and wore a hair shirt under his silken robe.

After the fall of Granada he took the Moors in hand. Many of these, as you remember, became baptized to avoid trouble; others remained faithful to their old creed. One of the latter, named Negri, was seized by the archbishop, and given in charge of a special officer who was bidden to "clear the film from his eyes." The officer soon reported that a few days of jail and fetters and fasting had cleared his prisoner's eyesight, and, sure enough, Negri made no further objection to baptism. The darkness of the dungeon, observed the archdeacon, shrewdly, poured light on the soul of the infidel.

It was Ximenes who burned the Arabic Library at Granada, and it was his persecution of the Moors which led to the revolt which nearly wrested the city out of Christian hands. He never rested till for a time he drove both Moslems and Jews out of Spain.

But he was something more than a fanatic. He was capable of planning a policy for a nation, or a campaign for an army. In concert with the great soldier Gonsalvo de Cordova, of whom I shall presently tell you, he planned the campaigns in Italy where the Spanish troops won such renown. And having made up his mind to capture the city of Oran, in Africa, which was a great Moorish place of trade, and finding King Ferdinand cold on the subject because of the expense, he agreed to defray the whole cost of the expedition, and to pay the wages of the garrison out of his own income. Ferdinand was always ready to undertake any enterprise which other people were to pay for. He gave his consent to Ximenes's plan.

An army was landed in Africa, and marched against Oran. Ximenes mounted his white mule, and rode along the ranks in his cardinal's robes with a sword by his side. A friar carried a silver cross before him, and monks fol¬lowed him all in their priestly gowns, and armed with cimeters. He preached a stirring sermon to the troops, and offered to lead the assault; but that was not necessary. The Spaniards were roused by the stories of the booty which was to be found in Oran; they rushed into the place pell-mell, and put the people to the sword. The cardinal returned to his home at Alcala, followed by a train of camels laden with gold and silver plate.

After this he became more powerful than ever, and when King Ferdinand died he was recognized as regent of Spain, in the absence of King Charles, the grandson of Ferdinand and Isabella, and the heir to the throne. But the regency did not last long. Ferdinand died in January, 1516; in September Charles left Flanders and landed in Spain. The cardinal was ill abed, and did not go to meet him. Some weeks after the landing of Charles, Ximenes received a letter from the king stating that his services would be no longer required. It killed the old man.

He gave his last days to religion—he was eighty-one years old—and groaning aloud, "In thee, O Lord, have I trusted," he expired. His corpse was dressed in his priestly robes, and set erect in a chair of state, where thousands came to kiss the dead hands and feet. While he lived he had many enemies; after his death his memory was revered as that of a saint.

You will perhaps compare him with another great priest, Richelieu, who, a hundred years later, ruled France as Ximenes had ruled Spain. In some points they were alike. But in Richelieu the statesman rose above the churchman, while Ximenes never forgot that he was a priest. If Ximenes was a hypocrite in early life, he was rigidly honest towards the close. He believed that he was doing that which was agreeable in the eyes of God when, during his term of power, he burned alive twenty-five hundred people on the ground of their religion. He would have died rather than take the side of the Protestants against the Catholics as Richelieu did. He built up no family as Richelieu did; his vast wealth he spent in his lifetime on Spain and on the poor, and, at his death, he left it to a college he had founded. If he had only lived in an age of toleration, he would have been a man whose public life, after he became all-powerful, you could altogether admire.

During a great portion of the reign of Ferdinand and Isabella, Spain carried on war against France in Italy. Neither France nor Spain had any business in Italy. But—as you will learn when you read the *Child's History of Italy*—that country was plunged into the greatest disorder through the quarrels of the small powers which had divided it between them. France went to Italy in the hope of conquering territory. Spain followed to prevent France from doing anything of the kind. The war, which was long, bloody, and cruel, is not worth describing to you; but it brought to public notice a hero whose career was famous and glorious.

This was Gonsalvo de Cordova, whose family name was Aguilar. He first won fame at the siege of Granada, and he became the fast friend of the queen, when he waded waist-deep in the water, all equipped as be was in brocade and crimson velvet, to carry her ashore from a boat. Soon afterwards, a Spanish army having been ordered to Italy, Gonsalvo de Cordova was appointed to command it, and proved himself so skilful a soldier that he got the name of the Great Captain, by which he was more generally known than by his own proper name.

The Italian war proved a source of misery to the poor people of Italy, who were harried by the troops first on one side, then on the other. But among the officers of the armies the campaigns afforded rare opportunities for displays of knightly chivalry. An encounter between the Chevalier Bayard—of whom you read in the *Child's History of France*—and a Spanish nobleman named Alonzo de

Sotomayer, will give von some idea of these exhibitions of soldierly high-breeding.

Sotomayer had been the prisoner of Bayard, and said that while he was in that condition the Frenchman had not treated hint with the courtesy which knightly usage required.

Bayard answered that the Spaniard lied in his throat, and offered to make good his words by single combat, on foot or on horseback.

Sotomayer declared that he would fight on foot.

Both knights wore complete suits of armor, with their visors up; each carried sword and dagger. On reaching the field, where the two armies formed a ring around the fighters, each knelt down and offered a prayer to his favorite saint.. When they rose from their knees they flew at each other. Bayard moved as lightly as if he had been leading a fair lady down to dance, though the had only just risen from a fever. The Spaniard, who was tall and stout, tried to break the Frenchman down by heavy blows; but a dexterous sword-thrust of Bayard's went through the neck-piece of the Spaniard's armor. Maddened by the pain, Sotomayer seized the Frenchman in his arms, threw him, and rolled on top of him. It looked then as though the brave Frenchman had fought his last fight, for the Spaniard was a man of prodigious strength; but Bayard, expecting a wrestle of this kind, had kept his poniard in his left hand. He now drove it with all his might into the Spaniard's eye, and thence into his brain.

Instantly the music began to sound, and the minstrels to chant praises to the conqueror, who was held in as high esteem by the Spaniards as by the French.

Ferdinand had a mean mind, and Gonsalvo's victories made him jealous. The king had tried his own hand at fighting in Italy, and had been glad when the Great Captain rescued him from a trap into which he had fallen. Thus, on a small pretext, a new army which was raised to invade Italy was taken from Gonsalvo. The troops were so angry that they would gladly have risen in revolt had the Great Captain given the word; but he bade them obey without murmur, and retired in silence to his castle. There he spent his last days in farming, and died peacefully at the age of sixty-two.

You will not find many characters in Spanish history as faultless as Gonsalvo. In a cruel age, he was never cruel to a foe; in a greedy age, he never soiled his hands with plunder; in a loose age, he was a true and faithful husband to his wife, Maria. He was loyal to his king when he must have despised him. He was a skilful general, a valiant soldier, and a wise ruler of the Italian states he conquered. When he died all Spain went into mourning, and he was buried with much pomp at Granada.

Ferdinand soon followed him. His wife Isabella, who had been his good genius through life, died in 1504, broken-hearted at the sad fate of her daughter, who went mad. A year and a half after her death, Ferdinand married a beautiful young woman of eighteen, Germaine de Foix, he being fifty-four at the time. They were not happy together. She was gay, volatile, fond of amusement; he was morose, and in bad health. She gave birth to a child which only lived a few hours; after that a coolness rose between her and her husband.

In the winter of 1515 his heart began to trouble him, and his breathing became so difficult that he could not live in cities, but spent his time hunting in the woods. On one of these hunts he was taken ill, and was carried into a villager's house. The courtiers had been expecting something of the kind, and an envoy from his grandson and heir hastened to call.

"He has come to see me die," said Ferdinand; "throw him out!"

It mattered little; Ferdinand's hour had come. The envoy wrote to Charles that he was King of Spain.

So Spain lost a monarch under whom it had become the greatest power in Europe. Not through any merit on his part, for Ferdinand was rather a dull man, tricky, perfidious, and narrow; but mainly because of the great men who appeared in Spain under his reign, and of the genius and uprightness of his wife, Isabella the Catholic.

CHARLES THE FIRST

A. D. 1517-1558

THE successor of Ferdinand and Isabella was their grandson Charles, son of their poor crazy daughter Juana and her husband, Philip of Burgundy. He was born on February 24th, 1500. By a strange concurrence of fortunes he was heir to a number of thrones. From his father, who died when he was a child, he inherited the dukedom of Burgundy, which included Flanders, the Low Countries, Holland, Burgundy, Dauphiny, and parts of Languedoc, Provence, and Savoy. At the death of one grandfather, he became Grand-Duke of Austria; at the death of another, King of Spain. To cap the climax, when the Emperor of Germany died, he was elected to succeed him. Thus, with the exception of England, France, Portugal, and Northern Italy, he ruled over all Western Europe.

He was seventeen when he came to Spain to take possession of his throne. He was a dull boy, expert at manly exercises, but slow at his books. He had been brought up by a priest named Chievres, who was a cold, calculating ecclesiastic. Charles was cold, too, and sparing of his words. He spoke little while he was in Spain, as the knew the language imperfectly. It was observed of him that his only speeches were to ask for money—Spain being rich, and his own Flanders, where he lived, poor.

He remained three years in his kingdom. They were not altogether pleasant years. The sturdy Spaniards of Aragon and Valencia did not take kindly to a king who, though born in Spain, was a foreigner in speech and thought; it gave him some trouble to persuade them to acknowledge him as their monarch, and, above all, to give him money to spend in Flanders. But in the end they sullenly submitted, and he sailed for the Low Countries in May, 1520, leaving a Flemish priest, Cardinal Adrian, as regent in his place, with two viceroys to assist him. Castile protested violently against the king going out of his kingdom; but Charles sailed, none the less, on the day appointed.

He had been chosen, as I told you, Emperor of Germany, and had serious work before him. Martin Luther was thundering at the Church of Rome, and all Germany was applauding him for his war upon corrupt and vicious priests. The great work of the Reformation had begun. In Germany and Switzerland the Papal Church was tottering; a few more sledge-hammer blows by Luther and it would fall.

CHARLES THE FIFTH AND HIS FRIENDS IN MARBLE.

The Emperor Charles—in Germany he was fifth emperor of the name, while he was first of the name among the kings of Spain— summoned Luther to Worms to explain himself. The intrepid monk obeyed the summons, though he was warned that the priests would make away with him if they got him in their power. They did indeed propose to burn him as a heretic, but Charles, though he hated

Protestants to the full as much as they did, was afraid of the vengeance of the people if anything happened to their favorite preacher, and let him return home safely.

At the very time when Luther was founding the Protestant Church, another Catholic monk, equally vigorous and just as sincere, was founding a Catholic brotherhood which was destined to be the most powerful sect in the Papal Church. This was Ignatius Loyola, who had been a soldier in his youth. Wounded at a siege, he spent his time while his wound was healing in studying religion, and when he got well he established the order of the Jesuits—priests who were to lead pure lives, to devote themselves to the spread of religion, and to have no care or thought for anything but the good of the Church. You will perceive that Luther and Loyola worked for the same object, though by different means. You will see by-and-by the mistakes which Loyola made, and the evil consequences which followed.

In the meantime all Spain was in an uproar. The cities of the north, with Toledo at their head, declared that "the Fleming" should have no more of their money; that they wanted no Flemings to reign over them; that the King of Spain must live in Spain, and respect the rights of the fueros. A mob arose in Segovia, and hanged a king's officer with his head downward. Burgos flew to arms. The people of Valladolid, which was then the capital, rose in the same manner, and burned the house of the general of the king's troops. Charles's mother, poor crazy Juana, was found by the mob at Tortesillas, and was proclaimed queen. In a moment of sanity she promised to rule the kingdom justly; but in a few hours her mind deserted her again, and she would not speak or recognize any one.

The end of it was that the king's troops, who had been joined by the principal nobles, came up with the insurgents at Villalar, and being better led, better armed, and better disciplined than the levies of the cities, won a complete victory. The rebellion came to a sudden end, Charles, returning from Germany, refused to punish the rebels, and even granted some of their demands, which reconciled them to his authority.

There is a story which I like to believe of a courtier who went to the king to tell him where a certain leading rebel was bid.

154

"I am not afraid of him," said Charles, "but he has some reason to be afraid of me; you would be in better business if you told him I am here, than in telling me where he is."

Charles restored peace to Spain; but I am sorry to say that in the pacification the chartered cities lost their liberties, and did not regain them for many a long year.

In the wars which at that time were incessantly raging in Italy, there was a battle at Pavia between the French under their king, Francis the First, and the Germans under skilful generals serving the Emperor Charles. The latter won, and Francis the First was taken prisoner, having lost, as he said, all but honor. He was shut up in a castle at Madrid, and was there so harshly treated by Charles's jailers that his health gave way, and he nearly died. Fearful lest he should die on his hands, Charles released him after a captivity of a year. He was escorted by horsemen to the river Andaye, which separates France from Spain. When the river was reached, eight Spanish gentlemen with the king entered a boat on the Spanish side, and eight French gentlemen came out in a boat on the French side; the boats met in the middle of the river, Francis jumped into the French boat, landed, and mounted a horse, shouting, "I am yet a king."

As he had just stated in writing that he intended to break the promises he had made in order to induce Charles to release him, I hardly think that his statement of his losses at Pavia was quite correct. The pope, however, said he was quite right, and absolved him from his bargain.

Charles the First reigned thirty years after the release of his prisoner Francis. But the story of these years is one endless succession of intrigues, wars, treaties made and treaties broken, in which I do not think you could take much interest, and I will leave you to find them in larger books than this. Charles reigned over so vast a realm that trouble was always breaking out somewhere or other, and the emperor-king had to go journeying to set matters to rights. He was never still for a month at a time. He lived on the high-roads and the seas. He married in 1526 a beautiful girl of the reigning house of Portugal; the wedding was celebrated with pomp and splendor in the lovely town of Seville. But the bride saw little of her husband.

In these thirty years he visited Spain many times, but never succeeded in making the Spaniards like him. He never saw Spain except when he wanted money, and the Spaniards raged when they saw their hard-earned wages taken from them to pay troops in Germany or Italy or Flanders. If the nobles had stood by the cities when the latter rebelled in 1518 they might have held their own against the king; but they had taken his side, and he requited them by forbidding them to send deputies to the Cortes of the fueros. By setting nobles against people he was enabled to tax both classes unmercifully.

His endless labors broke him down at last, and in 1556, when he was fifty-six years old, he gave up his throne to his son Philip, and retired to a monastery at Yuste, in Estramadura. It was a lovely spot, high up in the mountains; the air was pure, and the days and nights cool; groves of lemon and myrtle and walnuts surrounded the monastery; from seats under their shades the ex-king could look over a wide stretch of rich plain, dotted with gardens and gaudy flowers.

Though he was in retirement, the retirement was splendid. Handsome tapestries hung on the walls, and against these fine paintings were suspended. He was served on silver plate. He had sixteen different robes of silk and velvet, many of them trimmed with ermine. Fifty gentlemen, chiefly Flemings, waited upon him. His time he spent in wood-carving, and in making watches and clocks and ingenious toys.

He was a voracious eater, and he loved rich food. Before he got up he ate part of a potted capon, with a sauce of sugar, milk, and spice. At noon he had a regular dinner, and a supper at six, at which a variety of dishes were served. In the evening, before going to bed, he ate a plate of anchovies, or some other savory food. His orders to his cook were to vary his diet; the servant once complained that he did not know what new dish to serve, unless he prepared a fricassee of watches. In the morning he drank iced-beer. At his meals he preferred Rhine wine, of which he consumed a quart at a sitting. You will not be surprised to hear that he was troubled with gout and indigestion.

CHARLES THE FIRST

He was a careful observer of the forms of religion, and was indeed a fanatical bigot, who believed that all mankind should go to the same church under penalty of death. As his end approached, his intolerance increased with his superstition. He drew a will bidding his successors east out heresy. He said he was sorry he had spared Luther.

The Archbishop of Toledo, Carranza, better known as the Black Friar, came to hear him confess, and to give him absolution. At the last, the archbishop held a silver crucifix before the dying king, who cried "Now it is time," and closed his eyes forever with a long-drawn sigh.

HERNANDO CORTEZ

A.D. 1518-1519

IN the reign of Charles the First two of the most famous Spaniards who ever lived added to the Spanish dominion countries far larger and richer than Spain itself. Their names will be known when the name of Charles the First is forgotten. They were Cortez and Pizarro.

When you read the story of their lives you will be puzzled to decide whether you should admire them most for their courage, their high spirit, and their fortitude in disaster, or hate them most for their rapacity and their cruelty to races which were weaker than the Spaniards. You will find that they invaded foreign countries, seized them without reason or pretext, robbed their inhabitants of their property, and murdered them if they objected. I notice that the French and the English and the Germans are doing something of the same kind at the present time on the continent of Africa. But I cannot think you can approve such things. Robbery is robbery, and murder is murder, whether the person robbed and murdered be black or brown or white or copper-colored; and the robber and murderer is none the less criminal because he is civilized and white, while his victim is savage and colored.

The excuse which Cortez and Pizarro gave for robbing and killing the people of the countries they invaded was that the latter were heathens, while they ought to have been Christians. I suppose it was very wrong in them not to be Christians, though, as they had never heard of Christ, it would have been difficult for them to be his followers.

At the present day good Christians try to convince heathens that Christianity is a better religion than the one which they profess. But if they do not succeed in convincing the heathens, they let them alone, trusting that time will bring them to a better frame of mind. In the time of Cortez and Pizarro it was thought to be the duty of a Christian, if he could not convince a heathen by argument, to convert him with sword and pike and dagger and fire. The notion prevailed in Spain that the murder of an obstinate heathen who refused to be baptized was an act that was grateful to God. That is a notion which you cannot admit. But in judging Cortez and Pizarro, you must remember that it was the notion of the time in which they lived, and that they were no worse than other Spaniards, or, for that matter, than some of your own ancestors. I am afraid that in the reason which they gave to their consciences for their conduct in the Americas, the Spaniards got their duty to God mixed up with their covetousness of the Indian lands and the Indian gold. But they always said they were acting solely for the spread of true religion.

Hernando Cortez was born in Estremadura. He had been brought up as a lawyer, but he was born to be a soldier and ruler of men. In the year of Queen Isabella's death he sailed for Hispaniola, resolved to win fame as a discoverer. He was then nineteen years old, brave, untiring, shrewd, and, like all heroes, a lover of women and beloved by them. For fourteen years he lived in Hispaniola on a farm which the governor had given him, and which he cultivated with slave labor, the Indians having been enslaved by the Spaniards; thus he grew rich. In 1518 news reached Hispaniola that on the mainland of the new continent countries had been discovered which abounded in gold, and whose people were willing to trade. An expedition was fitted out to visit them, and Cortez was placed in command.

He was then thirty-three years old, tall, slim, pale, with dark eyes and powerful muscles; he was careless about his eating and drinking, but dressed richly and wore fine jewels. He was, as you will see presently, a man of indomitable will. When all was ready, Velasquez, the governor of the Spanish colonies, jealous of the fame he might Will, tried to stop him. But Cortez was not the man to be stopped. He sailed with five hundred and fifty-three soldiers, one hundred and ten sailors, two hundred Indians, and sixteen horses—all in eleven vessels, the largest of which was one hundred tons' burden. The fleet sailed for Yucatan on February 18th, 1519.

Coasting along the shore of Yucatan, he landed at the mouth of the river Tabasco, which is in the present Mexican State of Tabasco, fought the Indians there, and finally came to anchor opposite the present Mexican city and sea-port of Vera Cruz. Here a difficulty arose from his not understanding the Indian language, and their not understanding him. This difficulty was overcome in a curious way.

After the battle at Tabasco the Indians gave him twenty young Indian girls to be slaves. One of these, whom Cortez named Marina, was beautiful and bright. She spoke several of the Indian languages, and when Cortez fell in love with her she very quickly learned Spanish too, as any girl might do under the circumstances. Marina now began to serve as interpreter between the Spaniards and the natives. She had been sold as a slave by her mother, and had no love for her own race.

With Marina's help Cortez and his companions soon got on good terms with the Mexicans of the neighborhood. The latter brought fruit, vegetables, flowers, game, and cotton cloths, while the Spaniards presented their visitors with glass beads, objects in glass and bronze, velvets, and ornaments. The Indian chief called, bearing cloaks made of the feathers of gaudy birds, and a basketful of figures in gold; and Cortez returned the compliment by presenting hint with a fine arm-chair, collars, bracelets, a cap of cloth of gold, and a brass helmet. Then Cortez said he desired to visit the king of the country, whose name was Mochtheuzoma, or, as we call it, Montezuma; and a swift messenger started to run the two hundred miles between Vera Cruz and the City of Mexico with a message to that effect from Cortez.

In an incredibly short space of time the messenger returned with word that Montezuma would not see Cortez. A second messenger brought the same answer. Cortez was discouraged.

In his distress, a Mexican chief visited him, and complained that his people were shamefully used by Montezuma, and that they would rebel if they could get help from any source. Cortez saw his opportunity, and laid his plans. But before he could carry them out a mutiny among his own men nearly upset them. A party of soldiers and sailors resolved to sail away to Spain, and actually put food and water on a ship for the purpose. Cortez found out the plot and executed the ringleaders; then, fearing that it might be repeated, he sank all his ships but one, and that one he sent down the coast.

The men were furious when they found their retreat cut off. "The general," said they, "has led us like cattle to be murdered in the shambles."

Said Cortez, "There is one ship left. Let those who are not content to stand by me go on board of her and sail for Cuba. That will be a good place for them to stand on the shore and see us land by-and-by laden with the gold and spoils of Mexico."

Nobody wanted to go after that.

But Cortez knew that no time must be lost. On August 16th, 1519, he started from the coast westward with four hundred foot, fifteen horses, seven big guns, thirteen hundred Indian warriors, and a thousand Indian porters to draw the guns. The rest of his force he left in the fort at Vera Cruz. The soldiers marched in wild spirits.

"We are ready to obey you," they cried. "Our fortunes, for better for worse, are cast with you."

On September 2nd the little army reached the chief town of Tlascala, and the people forbade the Spaniards to pass. They proved a foe not to be despised. The Tlascalans fought like lions, and they were far more numerous than the Spaniards. But they did not like the cavalry; they had never seen horses before, and when the cannon opened fire, and mowed down whole ranks of warriors, the Ind¬ian army broke and scattered. Their loss was prodigious, while the Spaniards suffered little from the bows and arrows and spears and darts with which the Tlascalans fought.

Still, the Indians tried the fortune of war again and again, always with the same result. They sent a body of spies to spy out the Spanish camp, in order to find its weak points. Marina detected them, and denounced them to Cortez, who, instead of putting them to death, had their hands cut off, and sent them home in that plight. At last the Tlascalans admitted that the Spaniards were stronger than they, and sued for peace and friendship, which Cortez was only too glad to grant, on condition that a Tlascalan army should accompany him to Mexico. To this the Tlascalans agreed, and they proved as loyal in their friendship as they were warlike in their enmity.

All this time, at regular intervals, Montezuma kept sending messengers to Cortez—whom he called Malinche—with smooth words and presents. But it was not till he heard of the final defeat of the Tlascalans that he consented to receive the Spaniards in his own capital City of Mexico. Then he promised to welcome them, and advised them to come by the way of Cholula.

The Spaniards were rejoiced to spend a few days in rest at the city of Tlascala. It was a large, well-built city, with so many people in it that thirty thousand men and women gathered in the market-place on market-day. Everybody was kind to the strangers, and the chiefs gave six of their daughters—the most beautiful girls in the city—to be wives of as many Spanish officers. Cortez, however, could not afford to dally there. As soon as his men were rested he marched to Cholula.

This was the chief city of a fine country, every acre of which was under cultivation, partly with the aid of irrigating ditches. There were vast fields of corn, and plantations of cactus, aloe, and pepper trees. Fine woods grew near the city, and streams flowed under the branches. The woods were long ago cut down by the Spaniards, and the streams dried up. Cholula reminded Cortez of Granada and Seville. He could not afford to stay there, however; but just as he had resolved to march, he was stopped by a startling piece of news from Marina.

That bright woman had found out that the Cholulans intended to fall upon the Spaniards as they left the city, having barricaded the streets to impede their march, and that a body of Aztecs had been sent from Mexico to make an end of those who escaped. The peril was immediate and frightful. The Cholulans were more than ten to one of the Spaniards.

Cortez made up his mind instantly. He would not wait to be attacked. He sent an officer to the Cholulan chiefs, telling them that he would march on the following day, and would be happy to say good-bye to them and their chief officers at his quarters. When they came they were shown into a large court-yard surrounded by a high wall, with houses here and there. Inside the yard he had ranged his men with their backs against the wall. When the Cholulans were all assembled, Cortez accused them of the plot they had contrived; then the gates of the yard were closed, and, at a signal, every Spaniard opened fire on the natives, who were huddled together in a mass, and could not defend themselves. They were killed to the number of several thousand; and the Tlascalans, at the sound of the firing, came in at the double quick from their camp, and fell upon the Cholulans who were collecting outside.

No more attempts were made to check the march of the Spaniards. They passed between the two great volcanoes, Popocatepetl and Istaccihuatl, both higher than any mountains they had ever seen; climbed the range which shut in the level plain of the City of Mexico, descended to the lakes, and on November 8th, 1519, Cortez met Montezuma at the entrance of his city.

He appeared in a litter shining with burnished gold, borne on the shoulders of nobles, and shaded by a canopy of feather-work, sprinkled with jewels, and fringed with silver, which was carried by barefooted servants. He was forty years of age, pale, tall, and thin, with black hair and a scanty beard. His aspect was dignified. He wore a cloak of cotton, sprinkled with pearls and other precious stones; on his head, green plumes waved as he moved; his feet were in sandals soled with gold. He descended from his litter to welcome Cortez in a few graceful words of courtesy; then, saying that his brothers would show the Spaniards the quarters he had prepared for them, he returned to his palace.

The Spaniards were open-mouthed at what they saw. Not even in their own Spain had they beheld such splendor as was now before them As they gazed on the vast causeway across the lake and the palaces of the city, they could not help thinking that a monarch who could erect such works would be likely to be able to defend himself against an attack by seven thousand men, only four hundred of whom were Spaniards.

IN THE CITY OF MEXICO

A.D. 1519-1520

YOU will have noticed that from the first landing of Columbus in 1492 to the arrival of Cortez at the City of Mexico in 1519, the Spaniards found no race in the New World that was not savage. The natives of the islands and of the shores which they invaded could not read or write; they knew little of any art or science; many of them wore no clothes; they had no settled government or laws; they built no cities; they were in nothing above the level of the Indian tribes which still linger along the frontier settlements of the United States.

The Mexicans or Aztecs were a very different people. They came from some place in the country which is now the United States— what place I do not know—pouring down from the North upon the rich table-land of the South, just about the time the Moors were establishing their empire in Granada. In Mexico they found a race called Toltecs in possession of the country, having wrested it from its former owners some three hundred years before. Whether the Toltecs were exterminated by the Aztecs, whether they perished from disease, or whether they moved farther south into Central America, no one knows. Nothing is certain except that they disappeared, leaving the Aztecs in possession of the region which is now Central Mexico. On an island in a lake in the valley of Mexico the Aztecs founded a city which they called Tenochtitlan, but which we call Mexico.

Being a fighting people, they spread their sway over the whole country round the city, and gradually stretched their borders from the Pacific to the Atlantic oceans, and from the Tropic of Cancer to Central America, Being an ingenious and intelligent people, they built their chief city of red stone, erected stone causeways across the lake, and constructed temples not quite as lofty but almost as vast as the pyramids of Egypt.

In these temples, which were called Teocallis, prisoners of war were sacrificed to the Mexican gods, and their flesh eaten by the chiefs and priests. The victim was led to the top of the Teocalli, where he could be seen from afar, was laid on a convex slab of stone, and held there by five priests, while a sixth cut open his breast with a sharp knife of itxli, and tore out his quivering heart. There were hundreds of such Teocallis in the cities of Mexico, and thousands of such victims sacrificed in them every year.

Apart from this savage custom, the Aztecs were a civilized people; they were careful farmers, and knew how to irrigate their fields; they were skilled miners; expert artisans, who could weave fine cotton cloths and feather-work; shrewd merchants, who travelled far and wide to procure goods for exchange; ingenious jewelers, who could make beautiful ornaments of gold and silver; dyers, who could reproduce almost every color; sculptors, who made statues of their gods; they treated their women well, and were kind to their children; they worshipped their king; they had a system of picture-writing in which they could express their thoughts; they understood arithmetic and astronomy, and could do long sums in addition by means of cords which had knots in them. Their system of laws was complete. They were brave, and knew much of the science of warfare.

This was the people whom Cortez had resolved in his secret heart to despoil of their country with his four hundred Spaniards.

When, on the day after his arrival, he visited Montezuma in his palace, which was splendid with fountains and tapestries and flowers and sweet-smelling herbs, the Spaniard was startled by so much magnificence; but in reply to a question as to what be wanted, he mustered up nerve to say that his business was to convert the Mexicans to Christianity. Montezuma. had no reply to make to this, but he supplied every man in Cortez's army with a new uniform, and on Cortez himself and his officers he bestowed rich gold ornaments, bidding them rest in their quarters after their fatigues, and assuring them that they should want for nothing.

Cortez well knew that he could not stay there forever. He knew that he was an unwelcome visitor. If he tried to return to the coast, the Aztecs would fall upon him by the way, and make an end of his little army. He resolved upon a bold stroke. With a party of trusty men he went to the palace, and partly cajoled and partly bullied Montezuma into moving into the quarters of the Spaniards, where, of course, he became a prisoner. You will wonder why Montezuma was so foolish as to place himself in his enemies hands. I cannot explain his conduct except on the theory that he had lost his head.

PYRAMID OF CHOLULA

He had not been long in custody when Cortez appeared before him one day, and, brusquely accusing him of having plotted against the Spaniards, ordered a soldier to put irons on his legs, and stood by while the fetters were riveted. The poor king moaned and quivered, but said not a word, though at the time one of his trusted officers, who had really conspired against the Spaniards, was actually burned alive before the window of the room in which he sat. His spirit was broken. He felt that he was no longer a king.

Cortez read his mind, and removed the fetters. He even let Montezuma go to worship at one of the temples, and go hunting in one of his game preserves—always under the strict eye of a powerful Spanish escort. But the king had no courage left. He did not try to escape, and when his nephew and other Mexican chiefs formed plans to rescue him, he showed Cortez how to seize the ringleaders, and did not object when Cortez put them in irons. He became a mere puppet in the Spaniards' hands.

TREE OF MONTEZUMA.

Then Cortez demanded that Montezuma and his principal chiefs should acknowledge that they held the country for the King of Spain, that Charles was the true sovereign, and that they were his vassals. To this also the poor broken-spirited king agreed, and compelled his chiefs to sign with him a paper admitting that Mexico was a province of Spain. With this paper, Cortez suggested that it would be only proper to send the King of Spain a present. Montezuma agreed again, collected a large sum in gold, jewels, and fine stuffs, added to it all his own and his father's treasure, and placed the whole at the service of Cortez. The gold alone amounted to over six million dollars of our money.

When the Spaniards saw this vast treasure gathered in one spot, they could not contain their greed. They insisted on dividing the booty, and very little of it ever reached the King of Spain.

Then Cortez demanded that the Mexicans should change their religion and become Christians. Here Montezuma made a stand. He said that his people would not endure anything of the kind, and he warned Cortez not to try their patience too far. The utmost he could concede was that the Spanish priests might celebrate mass on the top of a Teocalli by the side of the Mexican altars. This was done; but it irritated the Mexicans beyond bearing.

Shortly afterwards, during the absence of Cortez, who had gone to the coast to meet a detachment of Spaniards just landed from Spain, the people held one of their religious festivals. Alvarado, who commanded in Cortez's absence, had consented that they should do so provided they bore no arms. They came accordingly in their finest dresses, with all their gold and silver ornaments, but without their swords or shields; and they were no sooner engaged in singing their religious hymns and dancing their religious dances than the Spaniards fell upon them, butchered them all, and tore the ornaments from the dead and the dying.

Next morning every man in Mexico flew to arms, and attacked the Spanish barrack. They would have stormed it, and it would have gone hard with the garrison, for the long pent-up fury of the Mexicans was all ablaze, when Montezuma mounted the battlements, and ordered the attack to cease. You can form an idea of the docility of the Aztecs when you learn that the king's order was obeyed. The mob fell back, and resolved to besiege the Spaniards in their barrack. When Cortez returned from Vera Cruz with his reinforcements, he found himself caught in a trap.

The people of Mexico would sell the Spaniards no food. They would not let a man of them go out of the barrack in search of water, of which the barrack supply was exhausted. They shut them up with a wall which no one could pass. Cortez lost his temper for the first time, When Montezuma called to welcome him on his return, he growled:

"What have I to do with this dog of a king who lets us starve before his eyes?"

On studying the ground, he still felt sure that he could hold his own; but one morning a messenger he had sent out came back breathless and bleeding, crying:

"The whole city is in arms! The draw bridges have been raised, and our retreat is cut off!"

Soon a roar like an approaching thunder-storm filled the air. It grew louder and louder, and Cortez, from the top of the battlements, could see long black waves of warriors rolling up the streets towards the barrack, while the tops of the houses near by were covered with archers and javelin-men, who shook their fists and their weapons at the imprisoned Spaniards.

CORTEZ DRIVEN OUT OF MEXICO

A. D. 1520

UP the great street of the city, towards the barrack where the Spaniards were quartered, the Aztecs poured in a furious wave, swinging their banners and shrieking their yells. When they got within range, Cortez opened fire on them. But they were only staggered for a moment. They came on and on and on, and the shower of arrows and darts and stones never ceased till the going down of the sun. Lucky it was for the Spaniards that the enemy could not get into the barrack.

Next day Cortez made a sally, and whenever he met the Aztecs they went down before the charge of his heavy cavalry and his men in armor. But no matter how many he killed, their numbers seemed undiminished, and the rain of arrows was as constant as ever. Then Cortez asked Montezuma to call off his people.

The poor cowed king said he would take no part in the strife. He moaned:

"What have I to do with Malinche? I do not wish to see him. I only wish to die. My people will not stop at my request. It is of no use trying. You will never leave these walls alive."

But, hearing that the Spaniards would go away if they could, he put on his white-and-blue mantle and his diadem and his golden sandals, ascended a turret, and waved his hand to the mob. They were instantly hushed. He bade the people lay down their arms, and let the Spaniards go. He said that Malinche was his friend.

At this roars and shrieks arose from the crowd, and a noble shouted:

"Base Aztec, you are a woman—a woman, only fit to weave and to spin."

And a cloud of stones and arrows fell upon the turret; one of them struck the king on the forehead and knocked him senseless.

He was carried inside, and surgeons busied themselves with his wound. But he tore off the bandages and refused to be treated, or to eat or drink. Shaken as his constitution was, he began to sink very fast. A priest got at him, dinned religious argument into his aching head, and kept shaking the crucifix before his eyes, but he answered feebly:

AZTEC CALENDAR STONE

"I will not at this hour desert the faith of my fathers." To Cortez, who came to see him, he said:

"Care for my poor children. 'Tis the least you can do in return for what I have done for the Spaniards."

And so he died.

The street fight went on all the same. Cortez took the great Teocalli, and rolled the Aztec god down head-first into the street. But he could not hold the building. He asked the Aztec chiefs to meet him. They gathered opposite the turret on which Montezuma had stood, and Cortez, speaking by the musical voice of Marina, who stood by his side, threatened them.

"I will forgive everything," he said, "if you lay down your arms. But if you do not, I will make your city a heap of ruins, and will not leave a soul alive in it."

They scoffed at him, and cried:

"You are perishing from hunger and sickness; you have no food and no water; you must soon fall into our hands. The bridges are broken down, and you cannot escape. There will be too few of you to glut the vengeance of the gods."

Then Cortez knew that he must escape if he could. The City of Mexico was on an island in a lake; it was connected with the mainland by causeways, which were cut at intervals by canals over which were bridges. These were the bridges which the Aztecs had broken down. Cortez resolved to escape by the principal causeway, which was cut by three canals; to cross these he built a portable bridge.

In the early hours of the night of July 1st, 1520, after mass had been said, the Spaniards and their Tlascalan allies crept silently out of the barrack and slunk to the causeway. The night was rainy, and so dark that the men could hardly see each other; not a footstep of a sentry was heard; the streets were still as graves; sleep reigned over all. But when the advance of the Spanish army began to lay the timbers of the portable bridge, the noise awoke a guard, who shouted; in an instant the priests on the Teocallis took the alarm, sounded their shells, the big war-drum began to beat, and thousands of Aztecs poured headlong down the streets to the causeway.

Cortez crossed the first canal with little loss, but when the second was reached, and the bridge was called for, it was found that the weight of the men and horses who had passed over it had jammed and wedged its ends so tightly against the stone and earth that it could not be lifted. The Spaniards were caught. A few of the horsemen swam the second canal, and some of the infantry followed; but many of them had loaded themselves with Montezuma's gold, and its weight carried them to the bottom. After a time there were so many dead men and horses, and guns, and wagons of ammunition in the gap in the causeway that they formed a bridge, over which the Spaniards managed to scramble. The same thing occurred at the third and last canal. Each side of the causeway was lined with Aztecs in boats, who poured darts and arrows upon the Spaniards, leaped ashore and pierced them with spears or clubbed them, or when they fell helpless carried them off as prisoners for sacrifice. It was not till the gray of the morning that Cortez was able to draw off the remnant of his army into the country.

This night is called by the Mexicans "Noche triste"—the sad night. Sad night indeed it was. About two-thirds of the Spaniards and four-fifths of the Tlascalans fell in the fight, and those who had been killed outright were the least to be pitied. A wretched ending this for an expedition which had begun so well.

For six days the Spaniards retreated steadily, without seeing or hearing anything of the victorious Aztecs. But, when the sun rose on July 8th they beheld the plain of Otumba as far as the eye could reach swarming with waving banners, forests of spears, and masses of fighting men tossing to and fro like the waves of the ocean. Then Cortez had need of all his courage and all his spirit. His little army was weakened by wounds and privations. They had found little to eat but corn-stalks, wild-cherries, and the bodies of dead horses. They seemed only a mouthful for such a host as the Mexicans.

But Cortez drew up his men in line of battle with a firm face, and when the Aztecs approached, he met them with an intrepid charge. He must have been beaten and his force destroyed, but just as the tide of battle went decidedly against him, he saw the commander of the Aztec army surrounded by a gorgeous staff. Calling a few of his officers to his side, the charged furiously through the enemy's ranks till he reached the general, ran him through with his lance, and, seizing the Aztec battle-flag, waved it over his head. The sight caused a panic among the Aztecs. They turned face and ran away

174

headlong, while Spaniards and Tlascalans, forgetting their wounds and their hunger, pursued them until their legs gave way.

This unexpected victory saved the Spaniards from destruction; but the power and courage shown by the Aztecs taught Cortez that he must proceed with more caution hereafter. He first gave his troops a rest, during which they recovered their health and spirits. Then he sent to the coast and to Hispaniola for reinforcements, and succeeded in getting a few score men and horses, and a supply of ammunition. With this increase to his strength, the captured numbers of towns round Mexico, and compelled them to furnish him with recruits and provisions. In course of time he mustered an army which is said to have been a hundred thousand strong, though only a few hundred of these were Spaniards.

Cortez had satisfied himself that to retake Mexico he must get command of the lake which surrounded it. How he accomplished this is one of the most wonderful proofs of his enterprise. When he sunk his ships at Vera Cruz, he had been careful to take out of them their cordage and iron-work, and to store these safely on shore. He now sent a party of Indian porters for them. Then choosing a spot where tall trees were abundant, he bade a ship-carpenter, who was in his service, build him thirteen small vessels, and rig them as brigantines. When the vessels were built they were taken apart, carried in pieces over the mountains, a distance of sixty miles, and launched on the lake of Mexico. Arming them with small cannon, of which he had a few, and filling them with fighting men, he felt that he could now command the lake, and sweep the Aztec canoes from its surface.

This done, he set his army in motion in three divisions, and planted one at the end of each of the three chief causeways which led into the city.

So the siege of Mexico began in the last week of May, 1521.

THE CONQUEST OF MEXICO

A.D. 1521-1547

IT was now that the usefulness of the brigantines was shown. A few days after Cortez had begun his blockade the bosom of the lake was covered with Aztec canoes full of warriors. The tiny craft dashed hither and thither, hurling showers of arrows at the Spaniards, landing Indians at unprotected spots, and scurrying away when they were attacked. Cortez sailed his fleet right into their midst, ramming them as he went, and sinking and disabling so many canoes that the face of the lake was soon covered with drowning Aztecs. After this they rarely ventured to put to sea in their boats.

Then Cortez made a dash into the city, advanced as far as the old barrack which he had left on the sad night, and gazed at the great Teocalli on which the Spaniards had raised their altar, and from the top of which they had pitched the Aztec god. A new god had been set up in his place—a horrid, grinning god, daubed with blood; the Spaniards pulled him from his stand, and rolled him down the side of the Teocalli, with his priests on top of him. But Cortez did not find it easy to get out of the city. The Aztecs tried to cut off his retreat, and they were numerous and fought with the courage of despair. They failed, however, and Cortez renewed the attack next day, and the day after, and the clay after that. Once again he pushed to the old barrack and set it on fire. He burned also Montezuma's palace, and with it the royal aviary, a splendid building in which, it was said, there were specimens of all the birds in America. The beautiful songsters, and the gorgeous parrots, and the great fierce eagles were all burned.

When Montezuma died he was succeeded by his brother. When he died of smallpox the nobles chose a nephew of Montezuma's, Guatemozin, to reign over them. He was twenty-five years old, handsome, brave, and a fighter: the Spaniards he hated with a deadly hate. He swore on his Teocalli before his Aztec gods that he would wipe the white men off the face of the earth.

He did, in fact, defend his city bravely and intelligently. Hardly a day passed without a bloody fight. But the Aztec could not make

Cortez let go his hold. He was a Spanish bulldog. His lines gradually contracted round Mexico, and throttled it in their grasp. Cortez pulled down the houses as he advanced, and with their materials filled up the gaps in the causeways so that they could not be reopened. Meantime no food could enter the city. The inhabitants began to suffer terribly from famine. They ate the bark and leaves from trees, and drank brackish water. Such diet weakened them so that they had not strength to bury their dead.

Still they would not yield. In pity for their sufferings Guatemozin would have listened to Cortez's proposal for a capitulation, but the priests, who knew that Spanish conquest would finish their vocation, insisted on holding out, and the people obeyed them. Men who were crippled by wounds or helpless from disease, women who were starving, and saw their children starving before their eyes, still met the Spaniards with the cry of "No surrender!"

Then another twist was given to the chain which was grinding the great Aztec city; more buildings were burned and pulled down, and more soldiers of Guatemozin, who were almost too weak to hold their weapons, were done to death. The Spaniards did not have the heart to kill the poor defenceless creatures, but the Tlascalans, and the other native troops who were serving under Cortez, had no compunctions; they slew every creature that had life, even to the women and children. Day after day Cortez sent messengers to Guatemozin entreating an interview to arrange terms of peace; but though Cortez held seven-eighths of the city, and Guatemozin and his men were penned up in the other eighth with their wives and children, and the dead and the dying, without food, and in an air poisoned by disease, the Aztec emperor said he would not meet the Spaniard. He said he was ready to die where he was.

"Go, then," said Cortez to his messenger, "and prepare for death. The hour has come."

Then the attack began on August 21st, 1521, and the Indian allies renewed their massacres. Guatemozin, leaping into a canoe with his beautiful young wife, the daughter of Montezuma, endeavored to escape across the lake; but he was intercepted by a brigantine, made prisoner, and carried before Cortez. When he was taken all resistance ceased. To Cortez the captive king said proudly —

"I have done all that I could to defend myself and my people. Now deal with me, Malinche, as you will."

"Fear not," replied Cortez, "you shall be treated with all honor."

And he sent for Guatemozin's wife, whom he intrusted to the care of Marina—the gallant girl who had stood by her friend's side in all the dangers and hardships of the campaign, and who was richly entitled to a share of his triumph.

I wish I could say that Cortez kept his word. But I cannot. First, the Spanish soldiers, disappointed at the small amount of treasure they found in Mexico, accused Guatemozin of having hid it; at their request Cortez put the captive king to the torture to make him disclose where it was hidden. He confessed nothing, having probably nothing to confess. Then, on a charge that Guatemozin had concocted a plot against the Spaniards, Cortez had him arrested and hanged to a tree by the road-side.

His beautiful young wife survived him, became a Christian, and married in succession three Castilian nobles.

Cortez gave her a splendid estate. You may be glad, perhaps, to hear that Marina, who had been so loyal and useful. to Cortez, also became a Christian and married a Castilian knight, with whom she lived happily on an estate which Cortez bestowed on her. On her last journey in Cortez's company she passed through the place of her birth, and there met her mother, who had sold her when she was a child. The old woman was terrified, and fell on her knees, supposing that her daughter came to avenge herself. But Marina raised her, kissed her, made her many presents, and said she bore no grudge for an act which had been the means of enabling her to become a Christian.

After the conquest, Cortez rebuilt the City of Mexico, and restored it as it had been, all except the Teocallis. Then, an attempt having been made to overthrow him by the same Archdeacon Fonseca who had persecuted Columbus—he was now Bishop of Burgos—he returned to Spain. There the Emperor Charles received him in state, thanked him for the work he had done, made him a marquis, gave him an estate in Mexico on which there were twenty-four towns and villages, with twenty-three thousand natives whom he was free to enslave, and appointed him Captain-General of New Spain.

Thus rewarded and honored, he returned in 1530 to Mexico, and explored the Pacific Coast as far north as California. But his exploring expeditions cost much and brought him in nothing; at the end of ten years, in 1540, he found himself in debt. He returned to Spain, and begged King Charles to relieve him from his embarrassments. Charles was not in the habit of paying other men's debts. He received Cortez coldly, and would not answer his letters, which so preyed on the conqueror's mind that he fell ill at Seville and died.

In the will which he made before his death, there is one provision which will strike you as curious in one who was as unscrupulous as Cortez had often shown himself to be. He owned a number of Indian slaves. As to them he says:

"It has long been a question whether one can conscientiously hold property in Indian slaves. I enjoin upon my son Martin to spare no pains to come to an exact knowledge of the truth on this question, as a matter which concerns his conscience and mine."

After his death his body had almost as many adventures as it had met with in life. It was at first laid in the Medina-Sidonia vault, in the monastery of San Isidro, at Seville. Fifteen years afterwards his son removed it to the monastery of San Francisco, in Tezeuco, Mexico. From thence, after sixty years, it was moved, and was reburied with great pomp in the Church of St. Francis, in the City of Mexico. More than a century afterwards, it resumed its travels, and was reinterred, in a glass coffin bound with silver, in a church which Cortez had himself founded in Mexico. Finally, in 1823, a mob threatening the church, some descendants of Cortez secretly opened the coffin and took out the bones. Whether they were ever replaced I do not know.

PIZARRO

A.D. 1528-1532

IN the month of May, 1528, shortly after his return from Mexico, Cortez met in the little town of Palos, whence Columbus had sailed, a relation, whose name was Francisco Pizarro. He was a man of about fifty-seven years of age, tall, weather-beaten, but straight, and rather good-looking. He had been one of the first Spanish adventurers who had gone to seek wealth in Hispaniola, and had spent some seventeen or eighteen years in the New World without gaining fame or fortune. This veteran now told Cortez that there was in South America a country richer than Mexico, which could be conquered by a bold dash such as he had made on the kingdom of the Aztecs; that he, Pizarro, was resolved to make that dash; and that help, in the shape of money or advice, would be welcome. What Cortez replied, history does not tell us. Perhaps he had cares enough of his own not to concern himself about the schemes of others. Perhaps he did not believe Pizarro.

Yet the latter told the truth. On two separate occasions he had explored the west coast of South America from the Isthmus to the place where Truxillo now stands, and had landed, and had seen quantities of gold and silver, a rich country, and a cultured people. These voyages of discovery had been undertaken by him in partnership with a priest named Luque and an old soldier named Almagro. Luque furnished the money, Pizarro and Almagro undertook to do the discovering, the fighting, and the plundering, and all three were to divide the profit. A queer partnership for a priest to be a member of. Two voyages had been made; everything turned out as they hoped; but no conquest had been accomplished, and Father Luque had come to the bottom of his purse. Under these circumstances there was nothing to be done but to ask help from the King of Spain.

King Charles never gave money to any one. He kept it all for himself. But he granted Pizarro permission to conquer any countries he chose for the crown of Spain, and agreed that when he had conquered them, he should govern then with full authority. lie conferred high rank upon Pizarro, and agreed to pay him a large salary—out of the revenues of the conquered countries. Pizarro had promised to obtain from the king the same honors and powers for his partner Almagro as he got for himself; this part of his business he forgot. But be told such glowing stories of Peru, and boasted so loudly of his new rank as captain-general and governor that people advanced him money for his new expedition, and it is believed that Cortez helped him. At any rate, he managed to fit out three small vessels with a crew of one hundred and sixty men, and with these he departed. Four of his brothers, who, like himself, were hungry adventurers, joined his force.

In January, 1531, he set sail southward from Panama with one hundred and eighty men and twenty-seven horses. The men heard mass and took the sacrament before embarking; the priests blessed the expedition with especial fervor as a crusade against the infidel.

The first place they came to was a town in the province of Coaque, which was not far from the present city of Quito. The people, who were generous and hospitable, received the Spaniards without suspicion; whereupon, as one of Pizarro's captains said, "we fell on them sword in hand." The Spaniards stole all their gold and silver and jewels and fine stuffs; in fact, requited their kindness by making a clean sweep of all the natives had. The spoil they sent to Panama to show how bravely the expedition was coming on.

Panama was at the time full of vagabond adventurers and dare-devils, who had drifted thither from Hispaniola and Mexico. Their greed was roused by sight of the gold which Pizarro sent, and many of them fitted out small vessels to join him. In this way the Spanish force in South America was strengthened by recruits, among whom was the famous De Soto, who afterwards discovered the Mississippi; and Pizarro was able to move south to the Piura River, where he founded the town of San Miguel, which is inhabited to this day.

From that town, on September 24th, 1532, Pizarro marched at the head of one hundred and seventy-seven men, sixty-seven of whom were mounted. He knew that the King of Peru, who was called the Inca, and whose name was Atahnalpa, was at a place known as Caxamalka, on the other side of a spur of the Andes, with a large force of troops. The Spaniards crossed the mountains to meet him.

I must tell you here that the Peruvians, like the Aztecs, were a civilized people, though, unlike the Aztecs, they had no Teocallis, and very rarely offered up prisoners as sacrifices. They worshipped several gods, but the chief god was the sun, who had temples in which priests and virgins, who were not allowed to marry, held religious services. The Inca was all-powerful, but there was a system of laws which even he had to obey. Under him were a number of nobles who served him in the wars, who paid no taxes, and many of whom lived in the Inca's palaces and ate at the Inca's table.

The land of Peru was so divided that every head of a family (and every man was obliged to marry) held a portion of it, which he farmed. One-third of the crop went to the Inca; one-third to the sick, to the soldiers, and to others whose calling kept them in cities; the remaining third belonged to the holder of the land, and if it was not sufficient, he could get corn from the public storehouses without paying for it. Thus, there were no poor in Peru, and hardly any rich, except relations of the Inca. The people were warlike, and had subdued the nations round them.

Their farming was thorough. Their lands were irrigated, and manured with guano. They grew corn, potatoes, bananas, tobacco, and a number of vegetables. On the hills flocks of vicuna sheep bore a wool which was even finer than the merino wool of Spain. The country was full of gold mines; the walls of the sun god's temple were hidden by plates of gold. Strange to say, the Peruvians had no iron, and the steel weapons of the Spaniards filled them with surprise.

The chief city of Peru was Cuzco, in a valley of the Andes. It was surrounded by a wall of immense thickness; at one point a huge fortress built of great stones towered above the palaces of the Incas and the nobility. It was said that it took twenty thousand men twenty years to erect this fortress. Several thousand Peruvians lived in Cuzco in houses built of mud and reeds.

Like the king of the Aztecs, the Inca lived in lofty state. He wore a dress made of the finest wool of the vicuna, dyed in the brightest colors, and girdled with a belt shining with gold and precious stones. In his turban stood two feathers of a rare bird; no one but he was allowed to wear those feathers. Every year he travelled through his empire in a litter blazing with gold and emeralds, and carried on men's shoulders. At night, the litter reached an inn, which had been built for the purpose, and where the Inca was regaled. Before he started out in the morning the people swept the road over which he was to travel, and strewed it with flowers. When lie died, his vitals were taken out of his body and deposited in a temple with his plate and jewels; a thousand of his women were put to death on his tomb. The body itself was embalmed, clothed in the dress the Inca wore in life, and set upright in a gold chair by the side of a long row of his ancestors.

This was the people whom Pizarro had resolved to conquer and despoil.

THE CONQUEST OF PERU

A.D. 1532-1538

WHEN the Spaniards marched down the winding path which led from the dark forest of the mountain to the plain below, they saw on the slope opposite them a green meadow flecked with white dots as thick as snow-flakes. These were the tents of the Peruvian army, and Pizarro knew that he was face to face with the foe. He marched bravely on, nevertheless, and entered the town of Caxamalca, which was empty of people. This was on November 15th, 1532.

Hernando Pizarro, at the bead of a few horsemen, rode to the Inca's camp, and said that his brother had come to teach the Peruvians the true faith.

For some time Atahualpa answered not a word. But at length he observed:

"Tell your captain I will see him to-morrow."

At daylight on that morrow, Pizarro filled the buildings on each side of the great square of Caxamalca with his cavalry and his infantry, to whom he gave secret orders. Mass was said, and the troops led by the priests sang the hymn, "Rise, O Lord, and judge thine own cause." Atahualpa did not leave his camp till the afternoon, and then advanced with a strong body of well-armed troops, intending to encamp outside of the city for the night; but Pizarro pressing him, and saying that everything had been prepared for his entertainment, he changed his mind, and entered the town with unarmed attendants only.

In the great square he found no one but a priest, who began explaining to him the doctrines of the Christian religion, and advised him to be baptized, and to acknowledge that he held his kingdom as a vassal of Charles, King of Spain. With that he handed him a Catholic breviary. The Inca's eyes flashed as he replied:

"I will be no man's vassal. I am greater than any prince on earth. As for the pope of whom you speak, he must be crazy to talk of giving away countries which do not belong to him. I will not change my faith. My God lives in the heavens, and looks down upon his children." And he threw the breviary to the ground.

At this Pizarro waved a white scarf, the signal gun boomed, the cavalry charged out of their hiding-place; the infantry dashed forward, the cannon opened fire, and in a few moments the unarmed Peruvians were overwhelmed by the furious onset of the Spaniards. Atahualpa would have fallen had not Pizarro rescued him. He was secured and carried off a prisoner ender guard; but in the half-hour which the fight lasted many thousand, some say ten thousand, of his followers were slain, and the rest, seized by a panic, fled in every direction.

Pizarro had followed the example of Cortez. He had made himself master of the person of the king he intended to overthrow. What to do with him was now the question.

After an imprisonment of a day or two, Atahualpa learned that what the Spaniards wanted was gold. He told Pizarro that if he would set him free he would cover the floor of the room in which they stood with gold, and would pile up the gold as high as a man could reach. The room was twenty feet long by seventeen feet wide, and by standing on tiptoe, Atahualpa could reach up nine feet. Pizarro agreed. Messengers were despatched to every town in Peru requiring them to send their gold and silver to Caxamalca, and in a few days it began to arrive in considerable amounts. At the end of a few weeks, though the room was not filled nine feet high, enough gold was collected in it to be worth fifteen and a half million dollars in our money.

The soldiers began to clamor for a division. They feasted their greedy eyes on more gold than any one of them had ever seen before in all his life. They said that such a vast treasure would tempt the Peruvians to attack them for its recovery, and they were only a few hundred against countless thousands. Pizarro agreed, and the treasure was divided. By a solemn paper—which he signed with a cross, for he could neither read nor write—he admitted that Atahualpa had paid his ransom, and was entitled to his freedom. But he said that for reasons of state he would keep him prisoner a little longer.

Then arose stories of risings among the Peruvians to rescue their Inca, and to punish his captors. These rumors frightened the Spaniards, who wanted to get out of the country with their booty, and disquieted Pizarro. He gave ear to persons who told him that the captive Inca was at the bottom of the plots. And he brooded over the idea until one day he seized the Inca, and put him in irons.

A regular trial was held. Atahualpa was accused of having murdered his brother—which he had not done; of having wasted the substance of the kingdom—which meant that he had let the Spaniards seize the gold; that he worshipped idols, and had several wives—which were customs of his country. A few witnesses were heard; and without delay or debate the Inca was sentenced to be burned to death that night in the square of Caxamalca.

Two hours after sunset, on August 29th, 1533, the troops assembled by torchlight. Atahualpa was led out chained hand and foot, was bound to the stake, and fagots were heaped up round him. A friar named Valverde, who had signed a paper approving the sentence condemning him to death, tried to convert him at the last, and when every other argument had failed, offered to commute his sentence to death by the garote, if he would be baptized. Atahualpa consented; the iron ring was fastened round his throat, and he was strangled— his last words to Pizarro being, "What have I done to meet such a fate from you who have had nothing but kindness at my hands?"

The gallant De Soto was absent when the execution took place. When he returned he did not mince his words. To Pizarro he said:

"You have done basely. The Inca was slandered. He was not plotting against us. For the crime you have committed God will call you to answer."

At the death of the Inca the kingdom of Peru went to pieces, and Pizarro marched to the capital, Cuzco, without resistance, and it and all the other cities of Peru yielded to the Spaniards. The conquest of Peru was complete, and the future capital, Lima, was founded.

But the conquerors who had been so cruel and rapacious in their treatment of the Peruvians, now quarrelled among themselves. Pizarro's old partner, Almagro, who had never quite forgotten Pizarro's neglect of his claims in his bargain with King Charles, was in Peru at the head of a force of his own, and when Pizarro settled down at Lima he made his headquarters at Cuzco, and claimed to rule from thence. Two of the Pizarro brothers falling into his hands, he thrust them into prison.

Francisco Pizarro got them out by making a new treaty of friendship with Almagro—they were always making treaties with each other and breaking them—and then, when he had organized an army, he marched it against Almagro, under Hernando Pizarro. There was a battle fought under the walls of Cuzco on April 26th, 1538, and Almagro was beaten. His conqueror locked him up, and one morning dark-faced men crept stealthily into his cell, fastened the iron collar round his neck, and garoted him. He had been tried and sentenced, and did not know it. So passed away the second of the three partners—the priest, Luque, having died in his bed some time before.

Hernando Pizarro, who put Amalgro to death, returned to Spain, laden with gold; was seized by order of Bishop Fonseca, and was locked up for twenty years in a dungeon. He was forgotten, in fact. When he got out he was a bent, lame, white-haired old man without money or friends. Yet I read that he lived to the age of a hundred.

His brother, the conqueror, who was now known as the Marquis, was sitting in the dining-room of his house at Lima with friends round him, when a party of Alrnagro's old followers entered the house with drawn swords. He had not time to fasten his cuirass, but, wrapping his cloak round his left arm, laid about him with his right, like a warrior at bay:

"What! ho! traitors! have you come to murder me in my own house?"

And he ran the nearest of his foes through the body. But, in the next moment, a sword thrust pierced his neck, he staggered, and a dozen weapons were plunged into him as he fell. So that was an end of the last of the three partners.

Another brother, Gonzalo, was beheaded. For many years Peru was a scene of endless conflict between the conquerors; and it must be said that they were as cruel to each other as they had been to the Peruvians. Of this sickening strife you would not care to hear anything in this *Child's History of Spain*. But I must say a word before we leave the subject of an old soldier whose name was Carbajal.

He was one of the greatest fighters of the day, a skilled soldier, and one who boasted that he never spared a fallen foe. At the end of a long career of warfare he was taken prisoner and sentenced to die. He was then eighty-four years old. He was carried to the place of execution in a basket drawn by two mules, and, as the old soldier was stout, it was necessary to use force to squeeze his body into the basket, "The old baby," said he, "does not fit in the cradle." On his way to his death he sang and whistled. The words of his song were from an old Spanish ballad:

> The wind blows the hairs off my head,
> Mother,
> Two by two it blows them away,
> Mother!

PHILIP THE SECOND

A.D. 1556-1568

THE successor of Charles the First was his son Philip, who was born at Valladolid on May 21st, 1527, and was consequently twenty-nine years old when he came to the throne. His mother had died when he was twelve, and he had been brought up by tutors under his father's instructions. In his youth he was pale and slim, with blue eyes and rather a pleasing expression; in middle and old age his features grew pinched, and his cast of face morose. At all stages of life his temper was sour, he was cold-blooded, deceitful, tricky, and suspicious. He was a man who lived without pleasures. He spent his life in reading dispatches, with his thin nose bent over the paper, and his quill pen scribbling comments on the margin.

When he was sixteen he was married to Mary, infanta of Portugal, a young lady who was fifteen, and quite pretty. She travelled from Portugal to Spain to be married, and as he had never seen her, he disguised himself with a slouch hat and a gauze mask, and mixed with the crowd which assembled to greet her, so as to take a good look at her face. She rode a mule; her saddle was silver; her dress was of silver cloth embroidered with flowers of gold, and over the dress was a Castilian mantle of violet-colored velvet. Her hat was velvet with plumes of white and blue.

The young couple lived happily together for two years. A boy baby was then born to them, and the mother died: what became of the baby I will presently tell you.

Some years afterwards Philip betrothed himself to Mary, Queen of England, who had at one time been courted by his father. She is the queen who has been called Bloody Queen Mary, because of the numbers of Protestants who lost their lives in her reign by reason of their religion. She was indeed a bitter and bigoted Catholic, and, like most people in that day, she believed that it was right and proper to put people to death because they did not believe what she did.

The wedding took place at Winchester, and shortly after it the queen and her husband made their public entry into London. Generally speaking, the English did not like the marriage. They were prejudiced against the Spaniards, and those of them who were Protestants, and these, I think, were the majority, would much rather the queen had married a Protestant prince. They were afraid that in some way the marriage would make England subject to Spain, which was at that time the most powerful state in Europe.

PHILIP THE SECOND

But Philip had brought with him quantities of silver from his possessions in Mexico and Peru, and the sight of the carts laden with the bright metal rolling through the streets of London cooled the enmity of the mob. He did his best to soothe the jealous temper of the great English lords with his wheedling tongue, and had almost won their hearts, when he was called to Flanders to hear from his father's lips the news of his intended abdication. He left his wife in September, 1555, and did not see her again till March, 1557.

In the meantime he had come into his kingdom, and had waged two successful wars—one against the pope, the other against the French, and had shown his people in Spain that lie knew how to make himself obeyed. The war in Flanders and Picardy was fierce and bloody; on one side fought the French; on the other side the Spaniards, with Englishmen, Flemings, and Germans to help them. There was a battle at St. Quentin, which the Spaniards won; and there was a battle at Gravelines, which the Spaniards also won, mainly through the valor and skill of a Fleming, Count Egmont; but the French took Calais, which was English, and just as a final decisive battle was going to take place the King of France and the King of Spain discovered that they had no money to carry on the war, and made peace.

Meanwhile, Queen Mary, who had been in bad health for years, died on November 17th, 1558, and Philip was a widower again. It appears that he believed it was not good for man to be alone, for he had scarcely put on mourning for his wife when he proposed to her sister, Queen Elizabeth. Elizabeth was too wise a woman either to accept or to reject him. She was herself a Protestant, and she knew that the English people would not forgive her if she married a Catholic; but, at the same time, she did not want to offend so powerful a monarch as Philip. So she coquetted with him, and neither said yes nor no; till he, weary of answers which might mean anything, married Elizabeth—or Isabella, as the Spaniards called her—of France, who was fourteen at the time. Elizabeth of England took the marriage in dudgeon.

Your master," said she to the Spanish ambassador, "must have been much in love with me not to be able to wait four months."

Philip married his wife Isabella by proxy in June, 1559, and did not see her face till January, 1560, when she joined him in Spain. She was tall, with dark eyes and dark hair; full of wit and merriment, after the manner of her country, and in this a contrast to her gloomy husband, who spent his time pouring over papers with a scowl on his yellow face. The wedding festival was joyous. In the public squares tables were set with good things which all were free to eat; the fountains ran with wine. I am afraid that after the holiday was over poor little Isabella did not find her life as pleasant as it had been in her own sunny Franco.

WORK-ROOM OF PHILIP THE SECOND.

She dined alone, with thirty of her ladies standing round the room. One of these carved the meat for her; another poured out the wine. The others talked with gentlemen who flirted, and kept their hats on; etiquette forbade that any of them should address the queen. After dinner she retired to her room, where her jester tried to amuse her with stupid jokes, and ladies sang and played the lute, often out of tune. I fear that the life was dull for one so young and gay.

In order to divert her mind, her husband sometimes took her to a bull-fight, which disgusted her, and sometimes to an *auto-da-fé*, where she saw Protestants and Jews burned at the stake. This was the chief entertainment at Valladolid, where the court lived. It was a strange performance to take a young lady to see.

CRUCIFIX TO WHICH PHILIP THE SECOND PRAYED.

At six in the morning the church-bells tolled, and a procession of troops, priests, inquisitors, and magistrates accompanied the prisoners of the Inquisition from its dismal fortress to the great square. Some of the prisoners were dressed in black; these were heretics who had abjured their heresy, and whose lives were spared on condition of their giving up their property to the Church and serving a term in jail. The others were dressed in loose sacks of yellow cloth, painted with figures of dancing devils who represented the inmates of hell. These were the culprits who were to be burned alive. Many of both classes had to be supported as they walked, their limbs had been so twisted and crippled by the tortures they had suffered in the dungeons of the Inquisition.

When they were all in place, some high churchman preached a sermon on the sweet mercies of the Church; then the sentences of those who were to be fined and jailed were read; the others, in the yellow sacks, were handed to the executioner to be dealt with, as the grand inquisitor said, "in all kindness and mercy." The kindness and mercy consisted in chaining them to iron stakes, piling fagots round them, and burning them to death in sight of the people and the court.

A victim led past the king cried to him:

"Is it thus you allow your innocent subjects to be persecuted?"

To which Philip replied:

"Wert thou my own son, I would fetch the wood to burn such a wretch as thou art."

I can hardly think that pretty Isabella enjoyed such spectacles.

After a time the Inquisition rather overdid their business I think. They accused the Archbishop of Toledo of heresy, and kept him in prison for seventeen years, torturing him from time to time to remind him in whose hands he was. This shocked the pope, and he removed the head inquisitor, whose name was Valdes. But the holy office succeeded in stamping out Protestantism in Spain, so that it has never reared its head from that day to this; and it demoralized the Spanish people so that their sense of right and wrong became confused, and they have never recovered from the obliquity.

It was while the Inquisition was busy with its bloody work that Philip lost his son and his wife, both at the age of twenty-three. The son, Carlos, whose mother was Mary of Portugal, grew up to be a headstrong, passionate, eccentric youth; he felt that no one loved him, and that he was friendless; there were but two people whom he loved, his uncle, Don John of Austria, and his step-mother, Isabella of France; everybody else he hated, and showed his hate so plainly that he was said by his father to be mad. At last the story got wind that be intended to kill his father, and Philip made him a prisoner in his room. He was not long a prisoner. In August, 1568, he died.

Less than two months afterwards Queen Isabella died, a few hours after her baby was born. She died of a disease which the doctors could not understand; she was chiefly treated with relics.

After both had been laid in their graves a dark and dreadful story began to be whispered that the queen and her stepson had been in love with each other, and that Philip, having found it out., had put them both to death.

I think he was capable of doing so; but it is not yet proven that he did.

The suspicion was first started by the warmth of the affection which Carlos showed for his stepmother, and by her kindness to him. They had been betrothed before Philip ever thought of marrying Isabella; it was natural that the son should feel bitterly at losing the girl he intended to make his wife.

The case was so suspicious that the pope demanded a full explanation from Philip, and I think that if it had been satisfactory, it would have been made public. Popes in those days were arbitrary; but they were not always intrepid. No blame came to Philip from Rome.

I think you must conclude that the case was a dark mystery which can never be unraveled. I am afraid that Carlos who had been betrothed to Isabel did really love her more warmly than befitted a son-in-law; but there is no reason to suppose that her affection for him was deeper than became a mother-in-law.

THE DUKE OF ALVA

A.D. 1559-1570

GRAVER matters even than the death of wife and son were making the gloomy soul of Philip gloomier than ever. Rebellion against Spain had broken out in the Low Countries—by which name, in consequence of their lying on a level with the sea, Holland, Belgium, and Flanders are known.

Under the Emperor Charles these countries, which had for some time been provinces of Spain, had grown prosperous and rich. Antwerp was the greatest place of trade in the world, full of busy factories, great warehouses, and wealthy banks. Traders and manufacturers from every country in Europe went there to start in business. Big-pooped vessels were seen loading and unloading at its wharves, and long strings of loaded wagons—taking the place which railroads do now—rolled along its streets. All classes of people were well-to-do.

The merchants lived like princes; mechanics had neat dwellings, which were kept spotlessly clean, and were handsomely furnished; the working-class was well clothed and well fed; it was hard to find a peasant who could not read and write. Now these people, being readers and thinkers, and listeners to those who had travelled, were disposed to become Protestants. Charles had tried to stop the heresy, as he called it, by burning and beheading those who left the old church; but though he put many thousands to death, he said on his death-bed that his effort to destroy Protestantism had been a failure.

Philip, frowning in his dark chamber, now resolved to accomplish that which his father had been unable to do—to root out heresy. And as it was absolutely necessary for him to remain in Spain, he appointed to carry out his purposes, and to be regent in the Low Countries in his stead, his half-sister, Margaret of Parma. This was a remarkable woman; the courtiers called her a man in petticoats. She had the will, and the hard, cold temper of a man. Her only pleasure was hunting; on her upper lip and chin there grew a down like a beard. She was devout; in Holy Week she always washed the feet of twelve poor girls.

To advise this man-woman Philip chose as her chief counsellor Cardinal Granvelle, who was as fond of persecution as he was himself. The great nobles of Flanders and the Low Countries generally hated Granvelle, whose mean, narrow soul they had long ago measured. Egmont and the Prince of Orange could not bear him, nor could the people. But they submitted. Not always, however.

At Valenciennes two Calvinist preachers were arrested for heresy, tried, and chained to the stake to be burned. But the people rushed to the place of execution, scattered the fagots, loosed the chains, and carried off the preachers in triumph. Margaret was equal to the occasion. Her brother had taught her that "rigorous and severe measures are the only ones to be employed in matters of religion." Granvelle advised her how to act; she sent an army to Valenciennes, caught the leaders of the mob and hanged them. Granvelle exulted.

Then the nobles, the Prince of Orange, Egmont, and the citizens generally, demanded that Granvelle should be dismissed. Margaret refused. Egmont wrote to the king to demand the recall of the hated cardinal. Philip, smiling a bitter, cruel smile, refused. But the cardinal, who had read that unpopular ministers sometimes lost their heads, remembered that he had not seen his old mother for fourteen years, and that he must, as a good son, pay her a visit. So he disappeared for a time. I don't think Philip and his sister won the first game in the match with the Low Countries.

You must understand that it was not the Protestants alone who were opposed to religious persecution in the Low Countries. Most of the nobles were Catholics; Egmont, who was one of the fiercest opponents of the Inquisition and Philip's cruelties, was a stanch Catholic. He went to Spain on behalf of his country to say that people of all faiths, including most of the Catholic priests, believed that nothing would satisfy the people of the Low Countries but freedom of conscience and freedom of worship.

Philip replied, grimly stroking his thin beard, that if that was the case they should have both. But Egmont had no sooner turned his back than the treacherous king broke his promises, and wrote to Margaret that the laws against the Protestants must be enforced with the utmost rigor; that no heretic must be allowed to live, that the

Inquisition must be restored with full power, and that the whole force of the government must be employed to sustain it.

The letter in which he wrote these things fell like a thunder-clap on the Low Countries. Margaret declared she would resign her regency. Philip would not accept her resignation. She begged him to come to Brussels himself. He promised he would, and of course did not. Egmont ground his teeth with rage at having been hood-winked. The Prince of Orange, more self-contained, said: "I fear me we shall see the beginning of a fine tragedy. These despatches will drive men into rebellion, and I do not see myself how I can endure them."

Thousands of industrious Flemings, foreseeing the future, crossed the water to England, carrying their trades with them. Others sharpened their knives and their axes, resolved that if the Inquisitors came near their houses there would be two sides to the argument.

At length the pent-up fury of the Protestants burst out. They sacked convents, monasteries, and churches; breaking the statues, cutting the pictures to pieces, smashing the altars with their furniture, and tearing down pulpits and chapels. This went on until Margaret promised she would not obey her brother's orders, and would not interfere with the meeting-houses of the Protestants; then peace was restored. She wrote to Philip that he need not be bound by her bargain unless he chose to. She was a worthy sister of such a brother. As for him, when he got the news he set his bloodless lips firmly, plucked his beard till some hairs were torn out, and muttered:

"It shall cost them dear. By the soul of my father, it shall cost them dear."

And he ordered the Duke of Alva to take command in the Low Countries.

The Duke of Alva was a soldier of repute, and a high grandee of Castile. He looked upon the world as a camp in which it was mutiny, punishable with death, to dispute the orders of the general commanding He was sixty years of age, and as hard as a flint His first act was to entrap Egmont and Hoorne, who were the best-loved leaders of the people, and to send them prisoners to Ghent. Then he organized a court to try such prisoners as might be brought before it.

You can fancy what the judges were from the name the people gave to the court—the Council of Blood.

Before the Council of Blood in the first months of 1568 several hundred of the best people of the Low Countries were brought and sentenced to death. They were executed day after day, some by hanging, some by beheading, some by burning. Most of them were Protestants, but some were Catholics who w ere in favor of religious freedom. On Ash-Wednesday five hundred burghers were torn out of their beds and carried before the Bloody Council. One of the members of the council was so worn out by signing death-warrants that he fell asleep, and had to be awakened to vote on the guilt or innocence of the prisoner on trial. lie would rub his eyes and croak, "To the gallows! To the gallows!"

But iron-hearted Alva was not satisfied with the execution of common people. He hauled Egmont and Hoorne out of their prison at Ghent to be tried before the Council of Blood.

Egmont was honored and loved by every one in the country. He had won for Spain the battles of St. Quentin and Gravelines. He was a firm Catholic, and had never wavered in his faith. He had always been loyal to his king. But Philip was so suspicious that he was afraid of what he might do, and there is no doubt but that Alva acted by his orders. Egmont had a wife and eleven small children. The former had begged on her knees to be allowed to see her husband during the nine months he had been in prison: Alva had sternly refused. All Egmont's property had been seized, and his children would have starved but for a small sum of money which, out of the proceeds, Alva allowed to be sent to their mother.

On the morning of June 5th, 1568, the prisoner heard mass, and made his confession. He wrote a letter to Philip, which he dated "On the point of death," saying:

"Whatever I hate done, I have done from a sincere regard for the service of God and your majesty. Wherefore I pray your majesty, for the sake of my past services, to take pity on my poor wife, my children, and my servants."

At ten o'clock he dressed in a crimson damask robe, over which was a Spanish mantle figured with gold. He wore black silk breeches, and a black silk hat. As he was led by soldiers through the streets the shops closed, business ceased, and the church-bells tolled. Grief was on every face. He walked firmly up the scaffold steps, and after a brief prayer turned to the executioner, who, with a single blow of his sword, struck off his head.

This shocking murder of one of the purest men the Low Countries ever produced roused the people to fury, and rebellion broke out in every direction. The rebels chose William of Orange to be their leader; he carried on a fitful warfare against the Duke of Alva for five years. There were no striking successes on either side. But though, on the whole, Alva won more advantages in the field than William, being an abler soldier, yet he could not help seeing that mainly through his cruelties and his arrogant disposition, the Low Countries were forever lost to Spain. He said to himself when he left the country in 1573 that he had caused eighteen thousand Netherlanders to be exe¬cuted in six years; he might have added that he had cost Spain every friend she had in that part of the world, and every foot of land she had ever owned.

To him and Pizarro, and men of their stamp, the horrible reputation which the Spaniards bore in the sixteenth century was due. Your ancestors, who lived in those days, believed that every Spaniard was a monster of cruelty and wickedness—a devil in human form. Vessels which were fitted out to roam the seas from England, France, Holland, Italy, and Portugal, attacked Spanish ships wherever they found them, and gave the crews no quarter, whether war was raging or not. Spaniards were counted a race apart from the rest of mankind; not really human, but diabolical, to be hunted down and exterminated like vicious wild beasts. If you read the books which were written at that period you will be astonished at the pitiless hate which the very name of a Spaniard aroused all over the world.

If you travel in Spain to-day you will find a courteous, humane, kindly, generous, hospitable people, whom it is delightful to know. But men like Philip the Second and Pizarro and Alva stamped their imprint on the race to which they belonged, and for a time it suffered for their crimes.

DON JOHN OF AUSTRIA

A.D. 1547-1578

IN the year that Cortez died there was born in Germany a son to a beautiful young girl named Barbara Blomberg. The child was taken from his mother when quite young and was sent to Spain, where he was brought up in the family of a hidalgo named Quixada. He grew up a tall, fine, handsome lad, fond of outdoor sports, and not very fond of his books; but so good-tempered and generous that every one loved him.

When he was thirteen years old, he was told by Quixada that King Philip wished to see hint, and sure enough, next day, as he was riding through the woods, he met the king, who alighted from his horse, gazed long and earnestly at the boy, and asked him:

"Do you know who your father was?"

Now that very question the boy had often put to himself and to Quixada without getting any answer. He flushed scarlet, and his breath came quick and fast; but he could not utter a word. The king spoke kindly:

"Don't be afraid, my boy; the Emperor Charles the Fifth, who is now in glory, was your father as well as mine." And turning to the courtiers he added, "Gentlemen, let me introduce my brother."

Up to this time the lad had been called Geronimo. Philip now ordered that his name should be John of Austria, though he had no more to do with Austria than you or I have.

He was given a household, and was sent to college, where he studied assiduously, and was particularly fond of histories of wars and books about soldiering. At eighteen he ran away from college in order to join the Knights of Malta in their fight against the Turks, but was stopped on the way by the king, who said he was too young for such work. Everybody in Spain heard of the affair, and men and women were never tired of talking of his gallantry.

When he was twenty-one his brother gave him the command of a small fleet which sailed to chastise the Corsairs. He was eight months away. During that time he gave the pirates such a lesson—sinking their vessels, thrashing them in fair fight, rescuing their Christian prisoners—that they were crippled for a long time, and Don John returned to Madrid triumphant.

The heart of the Spanish people went out to him. He was genial and sunny in manner; his smile was good-humored; his curling blond hair rippled as he swung it off his forehead; he was straight as a pine; he dressed in gold and white, with a crimson scarf loosely knotted over his chest; his cap was blue velvet, with nodding plumes. No one could ride or fence or dance or play at tennis as well as he. I can quite understand how the girls of Madrid thought there was no one in all the world as charming as he, and how they sat at their lattices watching for him to pass.

War breaking out again between Spain and the Moriscoes—I shall have something to tell you of it in the chapter after the next—and the Spanish commanders meeting with defeat after defeat, Don John was sent to lead the army. He was hampered by counsellors whom his brother sent to advise him; but at last he got his chance, and he put down the rebels in quick time.

The chief of the Moriscoes rode to the tent of the Spanish general and alighted. Don John stood by the door of the tent, surrounded by his officers. Said the Morisco:

"We implore your highness in the name of his majesty to show us mercy and to pardon our transgressions, which, we admit, have been great."

And he knelt before Don John, and handed him his cimeter, while the Moorish flag was thrown at his feet.

Stooping forward, Don John raised the Moorish general, returned him his sword, bidding him henceforth employ it in the service of Spain, and gave him a royal welcome to his tent.

After this there was nothing to keep Don John in Granada, and there was a general cry for him at Madrid. The King of Spain, the Republic of Venice, and the pope were fitting out a fleet to contend with the Turks for the mastery of the Mediterranean. The Sultan of Turkey had said he would make the Mediterranean a Turkish lake, and that no vessel should sail its waters unless it paid tribute to him. France did pay tribute; but Spain, Venice, and the pope refused.

They felt that sooner or later the mastery would have to be settled in fair fight, and though Turkey was admitted to be stronger than any one of them singly, they argued that the three together could more than hold their own against the Turks. So they gathered a great fleet and a powerful army, and when the question arose who should command it, every voice agreed, Don John.

The combined fleet contained three hundred royal galleys, besides smaller fighting ships, and on board them were twenty-nine thousand soldiers, and a great force of artillery. To meet them, the sultan mustered a fleet of two hundred and fifty royal galleys, besides smaller vessels; on board of them were one hundred and twenty thousand fighting men, besides galley-slaves who rowed at the oars. To these, who were Christians, the Turkish commander said, when the battle was expected:

If your countrymen win the day, Allah give you the benefit of it! If I win it, you shall surely have your freedom. If you feel that I do well by you, do then the like by me."

Don John sailed by way of Naples, and there had hard work to tear himself away from the beautiful Neapolitan girls, who would far rather have let the Turks have their own way with the Mediterranean than that such a darling as he should run the risk of being killed or his splendid face disfigured by wounds. But Don John was on too serious business bent to let them beguile him. He speedily joined the allied fleet at Messina.

Thence, on October 7th, 1571, he weighed anchor, and sailing eastward over the blue Ionian sea, he descried at the mouth of the Gulf of Lepanto the great Turkish fleet spread in a half-circle, with the crescent flag floating aloft, evidently waiting for their prey. A council was held, and most of the admirals and generals were for waiting and engaging the Turk in the open sea, where his vast force of soldiers would not help him. But Don John, having heard them all, bade his officers hoist the signal for battle, and battle in close order.

SPANISH GALLEYS IN A SEA-FIGHT.

He leaped into a boat and gave a short order to each division commander to be read to his men. It ran as follows:

"You have come to fight the battle of the cross—to conquer or to die. But whether you are to conquer or to die, do your duty this day, and you will insure a glorious immortality."

At noon the fleet engaged on a front three miles long; the battle lasted till four in the afternoon. At that hour one hundred and thirty Turkish vessels had been taken, eighty had been burned or sunk, and the rest had escaped. The Turkish admiral had been killed, and the slaves to whom he had promised their freedom got it from Don John. The Christians lost fifteen galleys and about eight thousand men; the Turks are said to have lost in killed and prisoners thirty thousand.

Ali Paella, the Turkish admiral, had been thrown clown by a boarding party, who made for him to kill him. He told them where he kept his money and his jewels, and all but one left him to secure them. That one, thinking that Ali's head was the most valuable jewel he could capture, cut it off, and carried it to Don John.

"Wretch!" said the young commander, "what do you bring me that for?"

And the ordered the man out of his sight. Ali had two sons, young boys, who were on board his ship. Don John sent for them, took them into his own cabin, treated them as if they were his friends, and at the first opportunity sent them home to Constantinople. For this their sister sent him a jewel of great price, but he returned it, saying that a Spanish gentleman could not accept such presents, and that he had only done his duty.

His prize-money resulting from the victory was so large as to be a fortune; he distributed every dollar of it among the wounded sailors and soldiers of the fleet, and the orphans of those who had fallen.

There were not honors enough, nor smiles enough, nor flowers enough at Messina to heap on the conqueror when he returned. Men roared themselves dumb in cheering him, and the fairest ladies of the beautiful Sicilian city scrambled and fought with each other to kiss his hand.

When the news reached the pope he fell on his knees, and cried in the language of the Bible:

"There was a man sent from God, and his name was John!"

The victory did indeed save Christendom on the Mediterranean. If it had been lost, that sea might in reality have become a Turkish lake.

But I suspect that there was one man who was not overwhelmed with joy at the victory. That was John's brother Philip. For I notice that the king began to show signs of envy and jealousy which boded no good to his half-brother.

John was appointed to command in the Low Countries, where, after Alva, no Spaniard could hope to win the goodwill of the people, or prevent the province from slipping out of the grasp of Spain. And Philip took care that Don John should not have men enough or money enough to accomplish anything.

He did the best he could with the means at his command. Once he nearly lost his life in an ambuscade set for him by the angry Netherlanders; he was rescued just in time by his nephew, Alexandre Farnese, the son of the man-woman Margaret. Another time he was penned up so long in a swamp that he caught a fever, and never recovered from it.

The books differ about the cause of his death. Some say he died of the fever. Others pretend that he was poisoned, which I think is likely. At any rate, when he died, King Philip said it would be too expensive to bring his body home in a cavalcade, he had it cut into three pieces, and brought home in bags tied to the saddlebows of horsemen. When it reached Madrid, the pieces were sewed together with silver wire, and the body was shown to the people.

THE KNIGHTS OF MALTA

A.D. 1565

IN order to give you a connected story of Don John, I described the battle of Lepanto without referring to the siege of Malta, which took place six years before, and in which Christian and Moslem came to close quarters.

The Turks, who were a warlike nation from Asia, captured Constantinople over one hundred years before Philip the Second came to the throne, and during all of those hundred years they had striven mightily to uproot Christianity in the Mediterranean countries, and to plant the religion of Mahomet. They founded or seized a number of cities in northern Africa, and planted colonies which were subject to their sultan. They overran the European coast of the Mediterranean as far as Italy, and laid hands on many of the islands of the Levant. One of the islands which they took was Rhodes.

This island was the home of an order known as the Knights of St. John, who were monks, and likewise soldiers and sailors. They fought for the cross against the infidel, but they did not disdain to plunder the infidel when they had beaten him in fair fight. From their island home of Rhodes they put to sea in fighting ships, which gave battle to the Turkish frigates, corsairs, and merchant ships, and quite often captured them and carried off their cargoes. In this way the order had grown rich and powerful. It was thought honorable for princes and noblemen to belong to it.

When the knights were driven out of Rhodes they cast about for a new home, and the Emperor Charles offering them the island of Malta, they gladly accepted it, and prepared to continue their career as sea-rovers from that base.

Malta lies in the middle of the Mediterranean sea, about sixty miles from Sicily, and two hundred from Tripoli, in Africa. It is fifteen miles long and nine miles wide. It is really a mere rock in the sea, with no soil on it except what has been brought in bags and boxes from Sicily. It is swept by the terrible south wind from Africa, and it is only by sheltering plants against this wind and against the fierce rays of the sun that anything can be grown there. But it stands in the path of vessels sailing up the Mediterranean, and it has an excellent harbor, in which the largest ships can anchor; it has, consequently, been coveted by maritime nations, and is now much thought of by the English, who hold it. It looked barren and desolate to the Knights of St. John after the smiling plains and the flowery valleys of Rhodes. But the fine large harbor was for the knights a good place from which to launch their cruisers against the Turks and against the cities of Africa; and the knights, with all the men they could hire, bestirred themselves to build a town there, and to build strong forts at its mouth, calling them St. Elmo and Il Borgo.

Pretty soon the knights began their old work, and Maltese galleys swarmed in the Mediterranean. The Sultan of Turkey, whose name was Solyman the Second, was enraged to hear of the capture of his vessels by the craft fitted out in this little island, and to find that he had to do his work over again. He resolved to make an end of the knights, once and for all. He fitted out a fleet of a hundred and thirty galleys, with a hundred smaller vessels; armed them with the heaviest artillery known in those days, filled them with thirty thousand of his best troops, and despatched them against Malta.

The grand-master of the knights knew of his coming, and begged help from the Christian powers. Volunteers enough came to raise his force to nine thousand men, including seven hundred knights. King Philip of Spain bade him have no fear; that he would send him a fleet and an army that would demolish all the Turks in Turkey. "Was he not," he said, "the eldest son of the Church, and the champion of Christendom against the infidel?"

The grand-master of the knights was not quite satisfied, as he probably knew Philip, and what his promises were worth. But he held his peace. He was a tall, gaunt old warrior, with a silvery beard, and at this time sixty-eight years of age, His name was Parisol de la Valette; he was a French Provencal, and had been a member of the order for over forty years. His will was like iron; the knights obeyed him as children obey their father. He now bestirred himself to put his forts in a position of defence, and to prepare for the coining conflict, in which he knew that the life of the knights and the existence of the order were at stake.

Early in the dawn of May 18th, 1565, over the dancing waves of the blue Mediterranean, the great Turkish fleet was sighted from the height of St. Elmo. It was coining on with a fair wind under full sail, and with Turkish pennons floating in the air. Every Christian was at his post. Valette had sent the old and infirm to Sicily; he wanted to send away the women, too, but they would not go.

The Turkish galleys swept past the front of the island, and landed their soldiers at the southeastern corner. A swift boat was promptly despatched to the viceroy of King Philip in Sicily, praying him not to delay; he wrote back that he could not possibly come before the 15th of June.

There were now four or five Turks to every Christian on the island, and the former had artillery compared to which the Christians' pieces were pop-guns. But the grand-master, as calm and serene as ever, walked round among his men, bidding them be of good cheer. On May 26th the Turks got their guns in position, and opened fire on St. Elmo. It was in no position to stand a heavy fire; in a week its walls were shattered by the tremendous rain of iron and stone cannon-balls. By a sudden dash the Turkish soldiers captured the outworks. But they could get no farther, though the knights were unable to dislodge them.

The grand-master was as intrepid as ever, and kept up the men's courage with brave words. It was then the 3rd or 4th of June, and the Spanish troops had been promised for the 15th.

The knights, however, began to feel the strain. Neither night nor day did the rain of shot cease, and the garrison were worn out by watching and fighting. Some of them went to Grand-Master Valette for permission to surrender. The stern old warrior heard them with a frown on his brow, and a flush on his weather-beaten cheeks.

"I will not surrender," he said. "The duty of a Knight of St. John is to die for the cross, and to die in the way that his commanding officer directs. I direct the knights to hold the post at all hazards. As for you, gentlemen, you may retire to the convent, where you will be safe; I will replace you with others whom I can trust."

The knights went back to the fort abashed, and ready to die. Still the 15th of June came and went, and no sign of the Spanish fleet. On the 16th the Turks made a hot assault on the fort, their ships of war taking part by firing from their big guns; the fight lasted all day, and so many were killed that the ditch was filled with corpses. But the Christians still held out, and the flag of St. John still floated from the flag-staff. A message from Sicily said the Spaniards might be expected on the 22nd.

The 22nd came, and still no sign of the Spanish fleet. Then the Turks, having tightened the lines round the place, charged up the hill-side once more, and dashed at every opening in the walls. Once more they were beaten back. But when night came the knights saw that the struggle was over. The grand-master did not yield a hair's-breadth, but the ammunition was exhausted, the soldiers' weapons broken, their walls were in ruins, and almost every man so badly wounded that he could hardly crawl along the ramparts. They spent the night in confession and prayer; they took the sacrament, repeated aloud the vows of their order, and waited for the end.

It came on the following morning. No sign of the Spanish fleet showing from the highlands, the Turks, like a great wave of the ocean, swept into and over the fort; every living creature was put to death, save only nine soldiers who surrendered to the corsairs, and were saved to be sold as slaves. The cross of St. John was hauled down, and the Moslem crescent waved in its place.

The knights still held the fort of Il Borgo, and a smaller work at La Sangle, and the grand-master ordered that these should be defended so long as a single man was left to handle a pike. The old man worked himself at strengthening the defences, though he had been wounded in the leg. Upon these works the Turks now pointed their guns, and battered at them till their walls, like the walls of St. Elmo, were crumbling to pieces. On July 15th the Turkish general judged that they were sufficiently breached, and he flung his troops upon them. Again the little garrison drove them back, but the loss was heavy. Grand-Master Valette sent once more to the viceroy of Spain in Sicily, to say that he could not hold out much longer. The viceroy answered that he would surely come with an army by the end of August.

Il Borgo, which was the chief point of attack, was in a horrible state. The men were worn out, and many of them wounded. Many women had taken the places of their husbands; some of them lay dead in the streets by the side of the men. A soldier managed to escape to Sicily, and told the people there what was happening at Malta. It would have done the cowardly and treacherous soul of Philip good to have seen the frenzy of rage which broke out among the warm-hearted people of Sicily. It behooved his viceroy to bestir himself. If he had dallied further, the people would have seized his ships, and crossed to Malta on their own account. As it was, his fleet sailed at break of day with twelve thousand soldiers on board.

When the ships, flying the Spanish flag at the peak, were seen from the Christian forts, the garrison burst out in shouts of joy, and strong men sat down on the ground and cried.

That night the Turks silently boarded their ships, and with the first glimmer of dawn set sail homeward.

And so Malta, thanks to the skill and gallantry of old Valette, after whom the present capital of the island was named, and to the courage and fortitude of the Knights of Malta, was saved to Christendom for all time.

THE MORISCOES

A.D. 1566-1609

YOU remember that when the Moorish empire of Granada was overthrown by Ferdinand and Isabella the Moors were allowed to remain in Spain on condition that they would be baptized as Christians, and would cease to hold religious ceremonies in their mosques. They accepted these hard terms because they could not help themselves, but in secret they remained Moslems as before.

The Inquisition was not ignorant of their real sentiments, and constantly urged the king to adopt more stringent measures with the infidel. Charles did at one time draw up an edict for the purpose, but he refused to let it be carried out. When Cardinal Espinosa became minister of Philip the Second the clergy were more successful. A royal edict commanded the Moriscoes, as the Moors were now called, to stop using their own Arabic tongue, and to speak and write nothing but Spanish; to change their names for Spanish names; to give up their own dress, and dress like Spaniards; to cease bathing; to stop singing Moorish songs and dancing Moorish dances. More cruel than anything, the Morisco women were forbidden to cover their faces in public, though in all Moorish countries it was and is still considered immodest for a woman to appear in public with her face uncovered. The ordinance was published on November 17th, 1566.

You will not be surprised to hear that the whole Morisco people declared that they would rather die than submit. They armed themselves, and prepared for resistance. King Philip had to send an army into Granada, and the old war began again.

It lasted several years, and, like all wars for race and religion, was carried on savagely on both sides. When the Moriscoes swooped down on a Spanish village they spared no one; when the Spaniards captured a Moorish fort or town every Morisco, young or old, male or female, was put to the sword. In one town, which the Spaniards took after a siege, the gutters ran with blood as they run with water after a rain-storm.

But, as you may imagine, the parties to the contest were too unequal for it to last long. There were not Moriscoes enough to resist the power of Spain. They fought gallantly; and their leaders, Aben-Yumeya and Aben-Aboo, did wonders with their little force; but when John of Austria was sent to the seat of war with a considerable army the Moriscoes were crushed.

The king then scattered the surviving Moriscoes through Spain. Granada was emptied of them. Every day a caravan of men, women, and children was started for some distant place in Castile or Estremadura or Valencia or the North; and as it was nobody's business to see that they were not driven too fast or were fed on the way, numbers of them died on the journey from fatigue and hunger. After a time the rest were settled in new homes among strangers.

I confess I am not as sorry as perhaps I should be that the exile of the Moriscoes from Granada desolated that beautiful city. Nearly all the mechanics and gardeners had been Moriscoes; when they were gone, there were no carpenters or masons or painters or smiths or florists in the place. Neither houses nor tools could be mended, and the beautiful pleasure-grounds, which had been the pride of the city, became wildernesses of weeds.

Nor did the Inquisition find that the dispersion of the Moriscoes put an end to secret heresy, as it had reckoned it would. The little Morisco colonies scattered here and there clung all the more closely to each other, and to their faith and their customs; the country priests reported that they still washed the holy water off their children's faces after baptism, and still talked in Arabic to each other when they were alone. It was found that wherever they went their industry and their skill enabled them to excel the lazy fighting Spaniards in farming and handicraft. Whereupon the Spaniards began to chorus with the priests that the Moors must go.

Nothing came of the cry in the time of Philip the Second. But when his son, Philip the Third, came to the throne, the clergy renewed their efforts. Archbishop Ribera of Valencia never ceased to worry the king, saying that there would never be pure religion in Spain, and the native Spaniard would never be able to make a living, so long as the Moors remained. The Archbishop of Toledo agreed with him, and thought the best way to deal with the Moriscoes was to kill them all, especially the young children, in order to prevent their intermarrying with Spaniards. Ribera and the king rather objected to this, as being too much in the style of King Herod of Judea.

An appeal was taken to the pope, who expressed a view which rather surprised the archbishops. His holiness said that if Ribera and the other priests had done their duty, they would have converted the Moriscoes long ago, and that the idea of killing or exiling them was unchristian. The archbishops had to wait.

IRRIGATING NEAR ALICANTE.

But the dull Spanish farmers and workmen, who saw the Moriscoes making a living where they starved, kept harping on the necessity of driving them out, and, in an evil day, Philip the Third consented. On September 9th, 1609, an edict was published requiring all Moriscoes to be in readiness to be carried to Africa in three days.

The edict was carried out to the letter, in spite of opposition from the nobles of Valencia, who knew the value of Morisco labor, and parted reluctantly with the best field-hands and workmen they had. About one million people, the most useful inhabitants of Spain, were put on ship by force of arms, and transported to Africa. Some of the vessels were wrecked on the way, and the passengers perished. Other passengers were murdered by their guards, and their wives and daughters taken as slaves. The property of all was taken from them to defray the expense of their removal.

What a blow this inflicted on Spain I cannot describe. The great mass of the Spanish people understood war and nothing else. All works of drainage and high farming were conducted by the Moriscoes. They carried on the factories and sugar-mills. They managed the rice plantations. They cultivated the vineyards and the orchards. When they were gone, all the sources of wealth dried up.

A few children of both sexes were stolen at the last moment by priests, who proposed to educate them as Christians, and a few nobles in Valencia obtained permission from the king to keep six out of every hundred Moriscoes to teach the natives how to farm their estates. With these exceptions the whole race was driven out of Spain to lose itself among the savage races of northern Africa.

SPAIN UNDER PHILIP THE SECOND

A.D. 1560-1598

SPAIN was never richer or more powerful than in the early part of the reign of Philip the Second. The Moors and Moriscoes prosecuted their industries, and some of the Spaniards had learned lessons in farming from the infidels. Great quantities of silver and some gold came in every year from the New World; I am not very sure that they were a source of wealth. To get the silver and gold, Spain had to send a fleet of galleys across the ocean, and to keep numbers of Spaniards in Mexico, Peru, and the islands. The ship-builders and sailors and soldiers and adventurers had to be supported, and I am not certain that after their cost was deducted from the value of the silver and gold there was much profit left. You know that if it costs you a hundred and two cents of labor to get a dollar's worth of silver you are not growing rich at the business.

There was a great deal of wealth among the clergy and the nobles. The former owned about half the fertile land of Spain. The income of the Archbishop of Toledo, who was called the primate of Spain, had increased to about two hundred thousand ducats a year, which is equal to nearly a million dollars of our money. The Archbishop of Seville had about half as much, and all over Spain the archbishops, bishops, abbots, priors, and even the common priests, were wealthy. As they paid no taxes, could not sell their land, and impressed upon every dying man that it was his duty to give something to the Church, their riches grew like a snowball that rolls downhill.

Next to the clergy, the nobles were the richest people in the country. There were twenty-three dukes, each of whom enjoyed an income nearly equal to three or four hundred thousand dollars a year of our money, and counts and barons and knights past counting. These grandees spent most of their time on their estates, which were sometimes so vast as to include several towns, and tens of thousands of acres of good land. Their castles were full of retainers, major-domos, equerries, hidalgoes, cavaliers, pages, men-at-arms, and what not. They led lives of splendor and pomp; but they rarely did anything useful, and I am afraid that some of them could not read or write. In the winter they lived in town-houses in Madrid, where they gambled with each other, and the young people made love; but I do not find much mention of them either in the army or in the offices of state. They paid no taxes, however, and I dare say they were satisfied with their station in life.

A GARLIC SELLER.

It was the business of the people who were neither priests nor nobles to find money to support the court, and to carry on the wars which Philip was always conducting in every quarter of the globe. And towards the close of Philip's reign they were in no condition to bear the expense. The people at large had grown poor—very poor. Great tracts of land which had once been highly productive lay waste because, under the ignorant system of farming which the Spanish peasants followed, their crops barely sold for enough to pay the king's taxes. Religious persecution and race prejudice had thinned out the people and crippled business. Mechanics complained that they could not get work. Beggars swarmed on the highways. In cities which had been hives of industry, the common people did not know from day to day where they would get their bread on the morrow. With all his rigor, king could not screw out of the people enough money to pay the expenses of government. He was always borrowing, and he rarely paid his debts.

He did not always pay his soldiers, and they robbed their way through Spain when they were on the march. When a regiment passed through a village, the villagers often left their houses and ran to the mountains to avoid what might be worse than robbery.

All through the reign of Philip, representatives of the people met in a Cortes. The kings had at first agreed that no tax should be levied without the consent of the Cortes, and that they should make the laws. But Philip changed all this; he took away from the Cortes the right of making laws and levying taxes. When the Cortes remonstrated, he replied that he would see about it. Had they not the right to petition?

They did petition, and some of their petitions were queer. They asked that the common people should be made to dress and live plainly; that no woman should wear finery; that men should not have fringe on their coats, and should not wear starched shirts. This petition the king granted. They asked that no one should have more than four dishes of meat and four dishes of fruit at one meal. This he also granted. He also agreed that common people should not ride in coaches; that towns should keep an inn open for travellers; that women should not read novels; that boys should get their schooling at home and not abroad, and that no more dolls or pocket-knives should be imported from France; but when the Cortes petitioned the king to put a stop to the growth of the estates of the Church he hesitated; and when they said that in so poor a country as Spain had become the king ought to be able to get along without a household of fifteen hundred persons, besides three hundred guards, and twenty-six ladies in waiting and four doctors for his wife, he smiled, and said he would think about it.

COFFINS OF THE KINGS, IN THE ESCURIAL.

I suppose there never was a kingdom in which the people were so near starvation while the king was lavishing money on useless objects as was Spain under the last years of Philip the Second.

Several of the great cities of Spain—Cordova, Toledo, Seville, Granada, Valladolid—had in turn served as the capital city. Philip chose as his capital the city of Madrid, which is the chief city to this day. It is a cold, windy place on a bleak plain, where it rains nearly all winter.

Twenty-four miles from the city, in the mountains, he erected a queer assemblage of buildings which he called the Escurial. It contained a palace, a monastery, and a burial vault. The outer wall is half a mile long. Thirty-two years were spent in building, and the cost was about six million dollars. All said and done—the Spaniards thought it was one of the wonders of the world—it was and is a gloomy, cold, dreary, and desolate pile. In Philip's time it was filled with fine statues, beautiful paintings from Italy, gorgeous tapestries, which were the work of the floors, and relics without number; sixty fountains spurted jets of water into the air, and magnificent arches and doorways were met at every turn. It was long ago stripped of everything that made it glorious; it is now a mere tomb, in which the bones of Charles the First and Philip and a few members of their family rest. When you go to see it you will be oppressed by low spirits which you cannot shake off.

It was to this dark and sad home that Philip brought his fourth and last wife, Anne of Austria. She was young, beautiful, and gay; she loved music and dancing and frolic; she tried to surround herself with people of her own age and her own temper, who could laugh and be merry. The gloomy shades of the Escurial were far better suited to the bilious old king whose wife she had become than to her; I think the poor little queen must have been rejoiced when she could run away from the palace and spend an afternoon in the quiet parlor in the house of one of her friends.

This place suited him exactly. He loved to sit in the dark and brood over his cares. They were many and grave. He had fitted out a great armada to conquer England; it comprised the finest galleys in the navy, and contained the best troops in the service; but the English, with a far smaller fleet, had captured and sunk many of his ships, and the rest had been scattered by storms. Only a small part of the grand armada ever got back to Spain.

THE TOMB OF PHILIP THE SECOND AT THE ESCURIAL.

For twenty years Philip had been a victim to gout, and when he was sixty-nine other diseases attacked him. He became so weak that he had to be carried about in an arm-chair. His thirst was unquenchable, and the doctors forbade him to drink. After enduring these sufferings for many months at Madrid, he had himself carried to the Escurial in June, 1598. He was in such agony that it took him six days to travel the twenty-four miles. When he arrived, he was cheered up by a consignment of relics from Germany, and he had himself carried round in his chair, pointing out where they should be set.

CHOIR OF THE CHURCH IN THE ESCURIAL.

Tumors and boils broke out all over his body, and the least touch gave him more exquisite pain than he had ever inflicted on heretics. For fifty-three days he could not be moved nor have his shirt changed. But his mind remained active. He gave his son advice how to conduct the government, and talked freely on religion to the priests. He had his father's coffin opened, and the crucifix which had been held before him when he died fastened to the foot of his bed; he also had his own coffin placed beside the bed.

When he was told that his hour had come, he was quite calm, confessed, and received communion. So, with his family and a number of churchmen round him, he passed away on September 13th, 1598.

TWO MORE PHILIPS

A.D. 1698-1665

PHILIP THE SECOND was succeeded by his son Philip the Third, who was twenty-one when he came to the throne. He was a weak, submissive creature, who never had a mind of his own. His father decided that for reasons of state he should marry a daughter of the Archduke Charles. As there were several of them, the king showed his son the portraits of all, and bade him choose which he would take for his wife.

"Whichever you please, papa," was the dutiful reply; and he did accordingly marry Margaret. The marriage took place at Valencia, and cost a million ducats, besides presents to foreign ambassadors, though Spain was in the direst poverty.

Philip was too feeble and too lazy to carry on his government. That business he left to his favorite, an equerry named Denia, whom he created a duke, and whom the pope made a cardinal, though he had never been a priest. This cardinal-duke knew so little about governing that when money ran short in the royal treasury he coined copper pieces, and forced people to take them at the value of silver coins of the same size. He laid taxes on everything, but they yielded nothing, because business was dead. The Spaniards ceased to make linen or woollen cloths for wearing apparel, or paper to write on, or spades to dig with; all these things came from abroad.

One thing alone prospered—that was the Church. There were more priests than ever, and more churches. The cardinal founded five new monasteries and two new churches; in the cathedral at Seville one hundred priests officiated, though six could have done the work. Almost every family had one son or daughter in the Church; the other sons and daughters became servants in rich men's houses, or beggars or thieves. The king himself was so well aware how good a thing it was to belong to the Church that he got the pope to make his ten-year-old son a cardinal, and then created him Archbishop of Toledo. He, at all events, was sure not to come to want.

THE VILLAGE CURATE

The only event of public importance which took place in the reign of Philip the Third was the acknowledgment by Spain of the independence of the Low Countries in the year 1609. This enraged the Spaniards, and made the cardinal-duke unpopular. He had lately picked up the son of a common soldier, named Calderon, and raised him to such power that he was called the favorite's favorite. At last the people's patience was worn out, and they rose in rebellion, drove the cardinal-duke into retirement, and locked up Calderon in jail. One day, when they were particularly hungry, they took him out of jail and murdered him.

After this Philip grew tired of playing king. He was in poor health, and the general poverty which he saw round him threw him into low spirits. His royal income was far less than that of his father. He did not see how matters could be mended. So, when a serious disease attacked him, he hardly struggled against it; beyond ordering a statue of the Holy Virgin of Antioch to be carried through the streets of Madrid in a solemn procession, he made no effort to cure himself. He took leave of his family with many words of affection, and bemoaned the mistakes of his kingly career, saying that he would act differently now if he were spared. But he did not have the chance. He died peacefully on March 31st, 1621.

His successor was his son, who is known as Philip the Fourth. He was sixteen when he came to the throne, and lived forty-four years afterwards. But in all that time he never did anything by which he is remembered, except that he led an idle, dissolute life with vile women and viler men. The business of governing Spain he left to a count-duke named Olivarez, who had a hankering for war and glory, and a habit of getting the worst of every quarrel in which he engaged. To wage successful war money is as necessary as men, and Olivarez had none, though he undertook wars in the Low Countries, in Germany, in Italy, as well as at home.

One of the consequences of his folly was an uprising in Catalonia, in which the royal governor was killed, the royal troops expelled, and Spain set at defiance for thirteen years.

To put down the Catalans, Olivarez ordered Portugal to furnish him with an army. Portugal had been annexed to Spain by Philip the Second, and had not taken kindly to Spanish dominion. It raised the army, but when it was armed and equipped, the Portuguese nobles, under the lead of a gallant woman, the Duchess of Braganza—she was of the Medina-Sidonia family of Spain—asked each other why it should not be used against Spain? Portugal was governed at the time by a woman, Margaret, grand-daughter of Philip the Second, who was called Vice-Queen. When the insurgents began business by killing her secretary, she met them with intrepid words, declaring that she would overlook a trifle of that kind, but that the people must lay down their arms, or she would not beg their pardon from the king.

The leader of the insurgents said they wanted no pardon. And leading Margaret into a room, he forced her to sign orders for the surrender of all the fortresses which the Spaniards held; which done, he quietly took possession of all of them, and that night Lisbon was as quiet as if nothing had happened; the Duke of Braganza was proclaimed King of Portugal, the shops were all open, and the Spaniards were carrying their knapsacks over the border into Spain.

DOING PENANCE.

Under the long reign of Philip the Fourth the decay of the nation and the growth of the Church kept pace with each other. More than once the Cortes renewed their protest against the increase of Church property, and the king promised to check it. But he made no effort to do anything of the kind. Meanwhile he increased the taxes on meat, wine, oil, and vinegar. People were driven out of Spain by these taxes. Toledo lost one-third of its people, Segovia, Burgos, and La Mancha nine-tenths, Granada nearly one-half, Seville one-half, including nearly all its rich manufacturers.

The prevailing discontent induced Philip to dismiss Olivarez, but as he put his nephew in his place there was not much gained by the change. The wretched king, whose soul was wrapped up in his dissolute pleasures, felt each new piece of bad news as a shock; when he was told of the coronation of King John of Portugal, he cried, "It is the will of God," and fainted away. He died shortly afterwards, in 1665, which was the best thing be could do.

You may perhaps be surprised to hear that these dark years of misery and decay for the Spanish nation were the Golden Age of Spanish letters and art. Never till our own time did Spain produce so many writers and painters as it did during the reign of the three Philips.

It was during this period that Cervantes wrote his *Don Quixote*, which has been the delight of the reading world for two centuries, and which you can enjoy to-day with the same pleasure it inspired when it was first written. It is told of the third Philip that, seeing a student walking the street and laughing to split his sides as he read a book, he observed: "That fellow is either mad or is reading Don Quixote."

As famous as Cervantes was Lope de Vega, who wrote eighteen hundred plays, and many other works of prose and poetry. His plays were a mine from which French, English and Italian authors stole some of their best pieces.

Among the poets of that day, whose writings you will enjoy if you learn Spanish, are Gareilasso de la Vega, who wrote pastoral poetry; Calderon de la Barea, who entered the Church probably to make sure of bread; and Luis de Leon, who wrote beautiful religious poetry while he was a prisoner in the dungeons of the Inquisition. Among historians you would like Hurtado de Mendoza, Bernal Diaz, Las Casas, Ovido, and Gomara, from whose writings we learn all that we know about the Spanish conquests in America. Until the reign of Charles the First there was hardly any literature in Spain.

At the very time these gifted men wrote, Murillo, Velasquez, and Ribera painted such works of art that the Spanish school took rank with the schools of Italy. Their paintings are still the admiration of lovers of art. It cannot be easily explained why these men of genius suddenly appeared in a cluster just at the time when the fortunes of Spain had begun to decline, and why, after a course like that of a meteor they vanished, leaving no successors.

CHARLES THE SECOND

A.D. 1665-1700

THE next king in order was Charles the Second, who was three years old when he came to the throne. During his minority his mother was regent; and she took as her adviser the grand-inquisitor, a German Jesuit named Nitard, whom the people hated. They thought the right man to be at the head of affairs during the king's childhood was his half-brother Don Juan, whose mother was an actress. Of this Don Juan his father, Philip the Fourth, had thought a good deal, had made him prior of an abbey and general of an army; but the queen-regent disliked him, and between him and the Jesuit Nitard it was war to the knife.

After much effort Don Juan succeeded in rousing the sleepy Spanish nobles, and getting them to follow him to the queen-regent to demand the expulsion of Nitard. Said the queen:

"Very well, let him go."

And she got the pope to make him a cardinal, and put in his place a pretty boy from Granada, whose name was Valenzuelo, and whose calling was that of a page. As you may imagine, neither Don Juan nor the Spanish nobles thought that a page was much of an improvement on a Jesuit as a royal favorite; they laid plots against Valenzuelo as they had against Nitard, and when King Charles came of age, at fourteen, they persuaded him to appoint his brother, Don Juan, prime-minister. The pretty boy had just time to make his escape to the monastery of the Escurial.

Don Juan was hot after him with a party of troopers. They tracked him to the monastery. He had crawled behind the wainscot of an empty room, but after lying hid there for several hours, while he could hear the troopers tramping round with their big boots and clattering with their swords and spurs, the closeness of the air overcame him, he lost consciousness, and when Don Juan came up he found the man he was hunting in a dead faint. They sent for the barber, and had him bled, which brought him to. After which they packed him off to the Philippine Isles, bidding him never more show his face in Spain.

Then Charles became king in name, his brother, Don Juan, king in reality, and the queen-regent nobody. This did not last very long. A whisper crept round that the king wasn't quite right in his mind. To set him right, everybody said that the thing to do was to get him a wife; so they married him to pretty Marie Louise of France. I do not know why Don Juan should have objected to the marriage, but he did, and when it was celebrated in spite of him, he went home and died, and the old queen-mother returned to court. Meanwhile the king was certainly very queer, so queer that his loving wife Marie Louise couldn't make him out, and worried herself into a consumption of which she died.

People then said that his queerness arose from his having married the wrong woman, and they married him again—this time to an Austrian princess. But the Austrian could not understand her husband any better than the Frenchwoman had; she had no children, and she brooded and fretted and cried a good deal.

THE MONASTERY AT THE ESCURIAL

The trouble with the king was that he believed he was bewitched, or possessed of a devil. In those old days, you know, people generally believed in witchcraft and devils; I think I have heard of the banging of some witches in Massachusetts. King Charles was satisfied that there was a devil inside him which gave him excruciating pain, and put all sorts of wrong thoughts into his head. If he had been a common man, I think the Inquisition would have treated his case with a little torture and a warm fire at a stake. As he was a king, the priests tried to exorcise him with holy water, relics, and powerful preaching.

The poor sick man was set on a stool, and a loud-voiced monk hectored and bullied him, crying:

"Come out, Beelzebub! avaunt, Sathanas. Aha! "Tis thou, Nebul! Come out, thou villain Abaddon! Ha! Belial, thou knave! Thou canst hear the sound of my voice, eh? I exorcise thee! Get thee behind me!"

While he thus roared, the monk would splash the king's face with holy water, and shake him violently as though there was really some creature inside his body who had to be shaken out of his mouth. You will be less surprised than the monks were that these remedies did not do the king the least good, but, on the contrary, made him more nervous and depressed in spirit than ever. Finally, it was determined to adopt still stronger measures.

In the vault of the Escurial lay the bodies of Charles's ancestors, as far back as the first of his name. He went down into the dark and damp chamber of death, where the great black crucifix stood, where spiders built their webs, and bats flew whirring from air-hole to air-hole, and he ordered the covers of the coffins to be unscrewed. Then he gazed long and earnestly at the faces of the dead, some of which were falling into dust, while others were still fresh as if they had died but yesterday. When he came to the coffin of his first wife, Marie Louise, whom he had really loved, he noticed that her face was mild and tranquil. Overcome by the sight, he shrieked:

"Marie Louise, I will soon be with thee."

And he rushed out of the vault into the open air, quite mad. A few days afterwards the died.

COURT OF THE EVANGELISTS, IN THE ESCURIAL

In his reign Spain had sunk into a shocking condition. Every business had been ruined except religion. When Philip the Second came to the throne there were sixty thousand looms running at

Seville. In the time of Charles the Second there were but three hundred. Under Philip the Second, Toledo had fifty woollen factories; under Charles the Second, there were but thirteen, the Moriscoes having transferred the business to Tunis, in Africa; under Philip the Second, everybody all through Europe wore Spanish gloves; under Charles the Second, no gloves were made in Spain. At Burgos and Segovia the streets were deserted, and most of the houses empty.

At Madrid and in the neighborhood people starved. At the convent doors the monks furnished a bowl of broth and a piece of bread to all applicants; even soldiers crowded in with the beggars to get their share. At times in Madrid, bread riots cost many a life; one day five women were stifled to death in scuffling for bread at the door of a bake-house; the police, who could not get their pay, joined the vagabonds and lived by robbery.

I suppose there never was before or since an example of a nation so thoroughly ruined by bad government as Spain presented in the year 1700.

PHILIP THE FIFTH

A.D. 1700-1746

AT the death of Charles the Second, three princes—two grandsons of Philip the Fourth, and one grandson of Philip the Third—claimed the throne of Spain. Charles decided that one of the grandsons of Philip the Fourth—Philip of France—should succeed him, and as in this he was backed by King Louis the Fourteenth of France, the young man was duly crowned; whereupon the two other candidates made war upon him. This contention is known in history as the War of the Spanish Succession; almost every power in Europe took part in it.

It lasted thirteen years, and at the end of it Philip was acknowledged King of Spain. But he lost Sicily, which went to the Duke of Savoy; his Italian possessions, which went to the Emperor of Germany; and Gibraltar, which went to the English. Thus Spain was reduced from being the foremost power in Europe almost to the second rank. But I am not sure that the loss was not a real gain, for the long war, during which the soil of Spain was overrun by a multitude of foreigners, had the effect of waking the Spanish spirit, and rousing Spaniards to something of their old manhood.

It did not rouse the king. He was a poor, weak creature, who always wanted a woman to lead him. When he was crowned king, at the age of seventeen, he married Marie Louise of Savoy, who was fourteen; and to take care of the two children, Louis the Fourteenth of France gave them a governess in the person of Madame Orsini, who was a wily intriguer. The young king spent most of his time in bed, and would not let his wife out of his sight; while the two young people were chattering and playing games, Madame Orsini, with the assistance of a man named Orri, and financiers whom Louis the Fourteenth had sent to advise her, governed the kingdom.

The Frenchmen made improvements in the government, and put the finances in better order. Notwithstanding the war, there was not so much poverty as there had been under Charles the Second, and business showed a tendency to pick up. Madame Orsini was a good Catholic, but she was not so much in love with the Church as to let the priests take everything that was in sight; she put a stop to the operations of the Inquisition. When the fortunes of war went against him, Philip would have abandoned the struggle, and gone to Mexico or Peru; but his little wife, strongly backed up by Madame Orsini, restored his courage by her brave words, and put life into him.

AT MID-DAY IN THE SUN.

One day, unluckily for him, she died. Then he fell into a deep depression, went to bed, and would not get up, and would see no one. Madame Orsini was in despair. In her tribulation she sent for an Italian priest of her acquaintance, and sought his counsel. His name was Alberoni; he was a man of cunning and vigor. Said he to Madame Orsini:

"The thing to do with the king is to get him another wife."

Madame agreed, and they two ran over on their fingers all the princesses in Europe, one after another. At last, Alberoni said, in an indifferent tone, that there was a fat little girl at Parma, who had been brought up on Parmesan butter and Parmesan cheese, and who had not a thought beyond her embroidery; she would work under Madame Orsini's thumb, if she were made Queen of Spain. Madame thought that would be just the right kind of girl for Philip to marry. So she sent Alberoni over to Parma to marry her by proxy, and bring her back to Spain. Her name was Elizabeth, or Isabella, Farnese.

The new queen lost no time in crossing to Spain, where King Philip was waiting for her, and journeyed to Madrid. At the last station on the way, Madame Orsini met her, and welcomed her in the name of the king. The young lady turned upon the old one, and in a voice of fury asked how she dared present herself before her in such a dress. Madame Orsini tried to explain and apologize, but Elizabeth would listen to nothing. Calling an officer, she bade him arrest the old lady, and carry her out of Spain that very night. It was bitter weather, the ground was covered with snow, and Madame Orsini had no cloak, and was in evening dress: but the officer's orders were clear. He drove her to the frontier without a stop, except to change horses, and landed her in France. She was never heard of again in Spain—she who had ruled the country with a rod of iron.

Next day Elizabeth met Philip and married him.

And now, my dear," said she, "I think we shall have peace."

She appointed Alberoni prime-minister, and Spain soon saw that she had made a wise choice. The pope hastened, at Elizabeth's request, to create him a cardinal. He really did much for Spain. He put the finances in order, so that there was a little money in the treasury; he restored some industries; he put the army and navy on a better footing; he regulated the trade with the Spanish colonies. But Queen Elizabeth, who was a restless, ambitious woman, insisted on recovering the territory Spain had lost by the War of the Succession; under her orders, Spain declared war against nation after nation. They at last combined against her, and at every point the Spanish armies were beaten. Finally, she sued for peace, but for a long time she did not seem able to come to an agreement as to the terms.

ON THE ROAD TO THE BULL-FIGHT.

She had in her service a Parmesan servant whose name was Laura; she put on the queen's shoes and stockings, and was the only person who saw her alone. This Laura, who was in the pay of Italy and France, whispered to her while she was tying her shoe one morning that peace could be made, and good offices found for the members of the queen's family, if Alberoni were dismissed. That night—it was December 4th, 1719—she spent several hours discussing affairs quite pleasantly with the cardinal and the king. Next morning a secretary entered the cardinal's chamber before he was up, and handed him a letter, dismissing him from office, and ordering him to leave Madrid within a week.

Then peace was arranged. But the king fell back into his old fits of melancholy, and could not be got out of bed. He moped and mourned, until one day he rose, dressed himself, and startled everybody by following the example of his ancestor Charles the

First, abdicating the throne, and retiring, not to a convent, but to the palace of San Ildefonso. His son Philip, who was sixteen, was crowned king in his stead. This did not last long. The boy king took smallpox and died of it; whereupon his father, saying that there was no rest for him anywhere, again took his seat on the throne.

He reigned for twenty-one years more. They were years of intrigue and fitful wars, which resulted in nothing but a waste of lives and money. One personage loomed up in them whom it may be worth your while to remember.

This man's name was Ripperda; he was born in the Low Countries, but was of Spanish descent. In early life he settled in Holland and became a Protestant, because most of the Dutch were Protestants. After the overthrow of Alberoni he got himself appointed Dutch minister to Spain; and he then became a Catholic again. He now persuaded Queen Elizabeth to employ him in trying to revive the industries of Spain. He succeeded in planting a woollen factory, and perhaps some others. But he was ambitious, and took no rest till he became ambassador, and, finally, prime-minister. It was his misfortune that he talked too much; he betrayed the secrets of the Spanish court, was detected, and imprisoned in the fortress of Segovia. Here he would have probably ended his days, but for a servant-girl who had fallen in love with him. She managed to get him out of jail, and became with him a wanderer on the face of the earth. He fled in turn to Portugal, England, the Low Countries, Russia, and Morocco—where he became a Moslem. But everywhere the implacable vengeance of Elizabeth followed him, and he was driven out of country after country. At last he hid himself in a small seaport on the Adriatic, where he changed his religion once more, and died in the Roman Catholic faith.

Philip the Fifth was conversing with his wife on July 9th, 1746, when he was struck by a sudden fit of apoplexy, and died before a priest or doctor could be got. He was not so bad a monarch as some of his predecessors; under him knowledge made some progress in Spain, and poverty was not as wide-spread as it had been. He was at heart a Frenchman, and at this time the French were more intelligent than the Spaniards.

After his death his angry wife retired to an obscure home in Spain, and was never heard of more.

FERDINAND THE SIXTH

A.D. 1746-1749

FERDINAND THE SIXTH, the second son of Philip the Fifth, was the next king. He was thirty-eight when he was crowned, and was the husband of a Portuguese princess named Barbara, who was so plain that, when he first saw her, be was for sending her back to her father, but so bright and good that after he knew her he came to adore her. Like his father, Ferdinand was subject to fits of low spirits and melancholy, and these were the means of procuring him the service of a most useful minister. For on one occasion, when the king had been many days in bed crying, and refused to get up, or to wash himself, the queen secretly introduced into the next room the famous singer Farinelli, who sang so melodiously that Ferdinand started up, ordered the sweet singer to be brought before him, and asked him what reward he wanted for giving him such exquisite delight.

Farinelli, who knew why he had been sent for, answered: "Nothing, except that your majesty will get up, wash yourself and dress, and go out for a walk."

Ferdinand could not part with him, and the singer became one of his chief advisers till he died. He was an honest, worthy fellow, gave good advice, and never took a bribe, which was considered extraordinary at Madrid.

Other good advisers whom the king drew round him were an old Spanish grandee named Carvajal, who was such a miracle of honesty that he considered a compliment a crime; and a peasant who is known by the name of Ensenada, and who, I suspect, bright as he was, was not so stiff-necked on the subject of bribes. His real name I do not know. When he was called into the king's counsels he was made Marquis of Ensenada, which in Spanish means "In himself, nothing."

This was very humble, no doubt; but I do not find that after he was well seated in power he was remarkable for humility.

These three men now undertook to cure the evils under which Spain had been suffering ever since the middle of the reign of Philip the

Second. And I confess it fills me with astonishment to see how much they accomplished, considering the ignorance of the people, the helplessness of the king, and the power of the Church.

They reduced the taxes on food and other things so that the people could pay them without starving. They put a stop to the stealing of public money by those who undertook to collect the taxes. They built roads and improved the harbors; they encouraged the establishment of factories; they stimulated ship-building; they repealed the laws which had driven foreign trade from Spanish ports; they saw to it that the king paid his debts; they regulated the expenses of government in proportion to its income, so that there was something over every year, and when Ferdinand died there was a large sum in the treasury. They punished corrupt judges with severity, and rewarded pupils at the colleges who showed proficiency in learning; finally, they destroyed the power of the pope in Spain. Under Philip the Second he appointed twelve thousand priests to serve in Spain; at the close of Ferdinand's reign he had only the right of appointing fifty-two. There were still one hundred and eighty thousand priests in Spain, and they still owned half the kingdom. But a reckoning was at hand.

In 1754 Carvajal died, worn out with faithful work. Two years afterwards Ensenada was detected in assuming power which did not belong to him, and was dismissed. France and England were at war. It was in 1756 that the English General Braddock, under whom Washington was serving, was defeated by the French at Fort Duquesne. Each nation tried to get Spain into the war on its side, and if it had not been for the firmness of Queen Barbara, one of them would probably have succeeded. She said Spain had had enough of war; what money the people earned they wanted for themselves.

The heart of this noble woman was broken by the terrible disaster which befell her native city of Lisbon, in Portugal, on November 1st, 1755. On that dreadful day the people had hardly got out of their beds when they heard a rushing sound, as of underground thunder; then, in an instant, the earth began to shake from side to side, and the strongest houses to totter and fall; then the waters of the river flowed out to sea, leaving the bottom bare, and sweeping out into the ocean every craft that floated; then, after the lapse of perhaps a minute or two, the waters returned in a wave fifty feet high, and drowned every living creature in its path. It is said that in the space of six minutes, fifty thousand people lost their lives, including many friends and relations of the Queen of Spain.

She roused herself from the shock to furnish food and clothing to those who had lost everything by the earthquake. But, this done, her despair returned. Her health gradually declined, and on August 27th, 1758, she died.

Her husband, who was passionately attached to her, could not get over his grief. At times his paroxysms frightened his friends; he seemed to be going mad, like Charles the Second. He would not eat; he could not sleep; he would not speak when spoken to. Just a year after his wife's death he breathed his last.

He left a country which, in comparison with what it had been, was prosperous and happy; which shows you that the condition of a kingdom does not always depend on the quality of its king.

CHARLES THE THIRD

A.D. 1759-1789

NOW we come to a king who surrounded himself with wise counsellors, and who honestly tried to carry out the work which Alberoni and Carvajal and Ensenada had begun. This was Charles the Third, who had been King of Naples, and had had twenty-five years apprenticeship to the business of governing. He knew, when he came to the throne of Spain, that his reign was to be a fight to the death between him and the Church, and though he was a devout Catholic, he went into the fight with a firm purpose to win if he could. There could not be two masters in Spain. He must either put down the Church, or it would put him down.

This fight was going on in Portugal, France, and Italy, as well as in Spain. The strength of the Church grew out of the general ignorance and superstition of the people, who obeyed the priests through their terror of hell in another world. How dense the ignorance was you would not believe if it were not actually proved. There was but one public library in Spain, and that had recently been started at Madrid. No one bought books, except books of devotion. A student at the great University of Salamanca was five years there before he ever heard of mathematics. The priests, who were the only teachers of youth, refused to admit the discoveries of Sir Isaac Newton, and denied the circulation of the blood. The doctors refused to let the streets of Madrid be cleaned, because that would be flying in the face of Providence. There was no one in Spain who could teach botany or astronomy or physics or public law. There was no one who could make a map of Spain, or build a ship, or rig it after it was built. The peasants did not even know how to build their own houses, or to mend their tools.

A people so ignorant were easily led into superstition, and controlled by priests who claimed to be able to doom then to eternal perdition, or to secure their admission to heaven. Spaniards came to obey their priests as if they had been real agents of God, as they said they were; and when the king went counter to the priests, the people went counter to the king just as far as the priests chose to lead them.

Foremost among these priests were the brotherhood of Jesuits, which, as you remember, had been founded by Ignatius Loyola for the loftiest and purest purposes. Its members had long ago abandoned their original aims, and now openly sought little else besides making themselves all-powerful. Most people in Spain and Portugal, indeed, thought they were stronger than the king.

In the year in which Charles came to the throne, a young lady was found in a street in Lisbon dead, with many wounds on her body, which was wrapped in a sheet; and the same night the king was shot at and severely wounded. The Prime-Minister of Portugal, whose name was Pombal, claimed to have traced the crime to a plot set on foot by the Jesuits. He found passages in their books which justified crime, if the criminal fancied that good would result from it, and, by a single stroke of his pen, he exiled all the Jesuits from Portugal and the colonies, including Brazil. This was in September, 1759.

A SPANISH MONK.

France followed; the prime-minister, Choiseul, ordered all Jesuits to leave France on a given day.

In Spain, Charles hesitated to break with so powerful a body as the Jesuits. But events forced his hand. His minister ordered the streets of Madrid to be lighted, and forbade the Spaniards from wearing the large cloak and slouch hat with a flapping brim, which often served robbers and murderers as a disguise. At this turmoil arose. It is said—I know not how true or false it may be—that the Jesuits put the notion of rebelling into the minds of the mob. They were apt to object to measures which they had not inspired. However this may be, the mob rose in arms, took possession of Madrid, and drove Charles out of the city. He had to yield to their demands to dismiss his minister, and to let the cloaks and slouched hats remain.

But he bided his time. He found a stalwart Spaniard, the Count Aranda, who had been abroad, and was a man of intelligence and intrepidity; him he made prime-minister. Aranda had the king write letters with his own hand to the governors of every province in Spain and Spanish America—the letters to be opened in private on a certain day and at a certain hour, and not before.

After sufficient time had elapsed, at midnight, on March 31st, 1769, every Jesuit college in Spain was surrounded by soldiers, the doors broken open, and the Jesuits bidden to rise and dress. When they were gathered in the refectory a royal decree was read to them, expelling them from the Spanish dominions. Every member was allowed to take with him his money, his linen, and his breviary; un¬der the escort of dragoons they were all conveyed in carriages to the sea-coast, where they were shipped in vessels and transported to Italy. I dare say that on that cruel journey some of them remembered how their order had insisted on the expulsion of the Moriscoes, less than sixty years before.

They were ferried across to Civita Vecchia, in the dominions of the pope, but his holiness refused to allow them to land, saying that he could not support all the priests who were driven out of other countries. For three months they were tempest-tossed on the Mediterranean, vainly trying to get permission to land somewhere, and being refused everywhere. At last they were allowed to set foot in Corsica, where they slept in warehouses and barns and stables, and were fed by charity. Many of them who were old died of exposure and privation. The end of it was that the King of Spain agreed to pay the pope so much a head for each of them, and on this condition they were let into Italy.

The King of Naples and the Duke of Parma followed. the example of Spain, and expelled the Jesuits. But the simple people of Spain stood by them in their afflictions, and when the king, as the custom was, asked the people what boon he should grant them on his birthday, the mob replied with one voice:

"Give us back the Jesuits!"

The police discovered that they had been tutored to say this by the Archbishop of Toledo, and Aranda very quickly sent hint out of the kingdom to join his friends.

At last the pope himself became disgusted with the evidence of the Jesuit intrigues, and by a formal bull he suppressed the order. So for a time there was peace, as far as they were concerned.

Having got rid of the chief obstacle to reform, Aranda Set to work to improve the condition of Spain. He abolished the pope's court. Up to his time every church was a sanctuary where a criminal could defy arrest. He provided that there should not be more than two sanctuaries in capital cities, and one in smaller cities. In our time, the police would consider that more than ample In the Morena Mountains, which was a haunt of robbers, he founded a manufacturing city, which, he called La Carolina; and, as there were no Spaniards who could be trusted to handle looms or machinery, he imported six thousand Germans and Swiss to carry on the business.

The misfortune was that most of these new-comers were Protestants, and when Aranda retired from office the Inquisition swooped down upon them and scattered them. Olavide, Aranda's friend, tried to protect them; but the Inquisition laid hands on him, confiscated his property, shut him up in a monastic prison for eight years, and pronounced him incapable of ever holding any office of power or profit.

Aranda's successor was another gallant Spaniard, named Florida Blanca. It was his sad fate to engage in more wars than Spain could

246

rightfully afford. He joined the French in war against England at the time of the American war of Independence, and accomplished no results. He tried more than once to take Gibraltar from the English; but always without success. He put down a rising of the native Peruvians in South America, and I am sorry to say that the Peruvian chief, Tupac-Amara, was inhumanly butchered with all his family. He took Minorca from the English.

But his chief work was at home. He did his best to encourage manufactures; and though he pursued his object in the wrong way, namely, by levying high protective duties on foreign goods, he did get some branches of industry on their feet. He was able to reduce the taxes without impoverishing the treasury. He brought in foreigners to work the mines. He improved the roads and canals, and reorganized the police. He compelled the wealthy clergy to make provision for the poor.

With the Inquisition he was always at war. That body accused Charles, who was a man of devout piety, of being an infidel tainted with French heresies; and, among the people, many were ignorant enough to believe it. Florida Blanca retaliated by requiring the Inquisition to submit their sentences to the king before they could be executed. Thus he held a rod over their head which curbed their blood-thirstiness. In the reign of Philip the Fifth, the Inquisition burned or sent to the galleys or imprisoned for life the enormous number of three thousand persons; in Ferdinand the Sixth's reign, only eighty persons were so punished; in Charles the Third's reign, only sixty. Sixty seems a terrible number of victims to have been sacrificed to bigotry in twenty-nine years; but the grand inquisitor was disgusted, and thought the business of the Inquisition was going to the dogs.

In the year 1789, Charles's son, Gabriel, whom he loved with a passionate love, caught smallpox from his wife, and died. The broken-hearted father went back to his palace, and never concerned himself about anything afterwards. In less than a month he was seized with inflammation of the lungs, and died.

He was one of the best kings Spain ever had, but he could not raise his people to the level of his own intelligence. He had but one passion, which was hunting. Shortly before he died, he wrote to his brother that he had killed with his own hand, in the course of his life, five hundred and fifty-nine wolves, and fifty-three hundred and twenty-three foxes.

THE PRINCE OF THE PEACE

A.D. 1788-1851

THE eldest son of Charles the Third was an idiot, and had been declared incapable of inheriting the throne. His brother Charles, who had been known as the Prince of the Asturias, succeeded his father in 1788. He was a man of forty, ignorant, devout, and narrow-minded. He had married a dreadful woman, Maria Louisa, who combined all the faults which a queen could possess; she was tyrannical, meddlesome, short-sighted, superstitious, and dissolute.

When Charles came to the throne, Florida Blanca consented to help him with his advice. But the priests did not like the old statesman; they poisoned the king's mind against him, and with the help of the queen they overthrew him. He was dismissed from office, and locked up in a castle where he was left without food, and would have starved had not his brother sent him supplies in secret. King Charles appointed Aranda in his place; but the priests did not like him either, nor did the queen; so he was presently dismissed. Then said Maria Louisa:

"We must make Manuel Godoy prime-minister."

And the dull, stupid king consented. This Godoy was a young man who had served in the life-guards, and was said to be the handsomest man in Spain. The queen had seen him at a review, and had taken a fancy to his face and figure. She had forced her weak husband to create him a duke, and now, before he was twenty-five, she made him prime-minister. Soon afterwards he got another title — Prince of the Peace — because he had made a peace with France, and by that title he was generally known.

He was a young man of good family, and had been well educated, but he had no principle and no control of his passions or his appetites. He married early in life a pretty Spanish girl named Pepita Tudo. When he rose to high favor with the queen, he sent his wife to live in a distant country town, and that was the end of her. He was so handsome, and so dashing, and dressed so beautifully, and rode such prancing horses, that all the girls in Spain were in love with him. Among these was one whose father was an uncle of the king, and likewise a cardinal and an archbishop. Queen Maria Louisa ordered the prince to marry her, which he did without wincing. And this nice party, the pig-headed king and his shameless wife, the wild scape-grace and the cardinal's daughter, all held high revel, and feasted and dressed and rode and hunted as though life were nothing but a frolic, and there were no grave burghers in Madrid to knit their brows at such goings-on.

Just at this time, partly in consequence of the like doings in France, the French Revolution—of which you have read in *A Child's History of France*—broke out; the French king, Louis the Sixteenth, lost his head, and the French clergy, from bishop to altar-boy, were driven into the highways and byways to earn their bread. The priests of Spain took their part. They had plucked up heart since Charles the Third died, and Aranda and Florida Blanca had been got rid of. Under those statesmen the Inquisition kept quiet; now it began to clamor about its being the duty of good Spaniards to make war upon French atheists and infidels. Priests preached sermons to this effect, and the poor simple Spaniards, never stopping to think that affairs in France concerned Frenchmen and not Spaniards, cried aloud to be led against the French heretics. At Madrid, the fury against the French rose to such a pitch that the blind and the lame, who lived by begging, sent their earnings to government to help pay the expenses of the war.

Godoy was willing to make war on France, or any other nation, or to do anything else which the people wanted, so long as he was let to ride his fine horses, and to eat his gay suppers with the queen and the cardinal's daughter, and the other gay and jovial members of the court. He declared war, set France at defiance, and pretty soon had the pleasure of seeing the Spanish troops soundly thrashed by the French Republicans. The French blood was up, and French soldiers came streaming over the Pyrenees by the thousand, and overran all northern Spain.

This was not what the priests wanted, or the people either, and they began to bawl for peace as lustily as they had bawled for war, and Godoy said:

"Oh, very well! If you want peace, you shall have it."

A PROFESSIONAL BEGGAR.

And he signed a treaty with France, and went on feasting and frolicking and riding and dancing with the queen and the cardinal's daughter, and the prettiest women in Spain, while King Charles sat gloomily in a corner, reading his breviary and mumbling Aves.

Then disputes arose with England, and Godoy declared war upon that country. The Spanish fleet joined the French fleet, and attacked the British fleets. There was a battle off Cape St. Vincent, and the Spaniards were beaten; there was another battle off Trafalgar, at which the British admiral was Lord Nelson, of whom you have heard, one of the bravest and most skilful sailors who ever sailed the seas; he entirely demolished the allies, and put Spain once more out of conceit with war.

By this time the Spanish people began to hate Godoy. They had never liked the loose and wild life which he led. They were quite aware of the behavior of the court, and of the lavish folly with which a parcel of idle and profligate women squandered money while the treasury was empty and the poor were starving. Pretty soon they had still graver reasons to dislike the prince. It seemed impossible for him and the queen to remain quiet. As if they had not tried one bout with France and been obliged to eat humble pie, they must now try another while Napoleon was away in Germany fighting with Prussia. Godoy summoned all able-bodied Spaniards into the field to fight France. A week afterwards, in October, 1806, Napoleon won the battle of Jena, and for the time made an end of Prussia. Then he read the proclamation of the Prince of the Peace with a grim smile.

"Write me a letter," said he, to one of his generals, "to this Spanish popinjay, and say that I want sixteen thousand of the best troops in Spain to garrison some Prussian forts which I have taken."

Godoy neither ate nor slept till sixteen thousand men were despatched.

"Now," said Napoleon, "write me another letter to this Spanish upstart to say that if Spain dares to trade with my enemy, England, to buy any English goods, or to send any wine or fruit to England, I will grind the Spanish monarchy to powder, and will hang the Prince of the Peace on a gibbet so high that every one shall see him."

Godoy replied that he would rather be dead than trade with the English, that he abominated all Englishmen, especially since the battle of Trafalgar, and that he thought the French were the salt of the earth, and the Emperor Napoleon an angel, who had been sent into the world as a blessing.

At all of which Napoleon smiled more grimly than ever.

King Charles the Fourth and his merry queen nearly died of fright when Napoleon began to threaten. When Godoy came to them and said be had made it all right with the emperor, and that Napoleon and he loved each other a little better than brothers, the imbecile king could not sufficiently reward his wife's friend. He made him generalissimo of the army, lord high admiral of the fleet, protector of commerce, and serene highness. Loaded with all these new dignities, and surrounded by a splendid retinue, all on prancing horses, with trumpets blowing and girls strewing flowers, the prince made his entry into Madrid, as if he had saved his country.

But he had reached the turning-point in his destiny. A French army carne creeping, creeping over the Pyrenees, and wormed its way through the mountains of Galicia and the Asturias into Portugal. The Spaniards knew what this meant. All at once, without any warning, they rose in the night and attacked the favorite's house, set it on fire, set fire to his brother's house, pillaged both of them, and burned them to the ground. Strong men cried with rage when they found that Godoy had escaped them. They wanted to tear him limb from limb with their nails. Think how long they had hated him and swallowed down their hate!

Hardly a day had passed before they caught him. Ah! his story would not take long to tell if, on that day, some brave Spaniards had not interposed between him and the mob, and locked him up in a prison for safe-keeping. So fierce was the fury of the people that the miserable creature cowered and shivered behind the strong stone walls of his prison when he heard the howls and the roar outside. He did not stay long in jail. Napoleon needed a tool to help him plunder Spain. He sent an army to escort the prince to Bayonne, and employed him to assist in the degradation of his country.

After the war in Spain was ended, Godoy lived in Paris, and when Napoleon fell, he found himself pretty lonely. Spaniards would have nothing to say to him, and he was afraid of going out at night for fear of being stabbed in the back. His money ran short. He would have starved if the French government had not granted him a pension of a thousand dollars a year. In 1842, when he was an old man, Spain restored to him some of his estates, and he lived in a sort of splendor till 1851, when he died, far from all those who had loved him.

THE OLD KING AND TILE NEW ONE

A.D. 1807-1808

KING CHARLES THE FOURTH had a son who was born in 1784, and whose name was Ferdinand. As he grew to manhood he hated Godoy, at which you will not be surprised; but what may surprise you is that he hated his father and mother quite as bitterly. This Ferdinand wrote to Napoleon in 1807 that Spain was being ruined by Godoy, and would he be so kind as to interfere a little? Nothing could have suited the ambitious emperor better. But he was too wary to answer Ferdinand's letter, and when the Prince of the Asturias — as Ferdinand was called — wrote again to say that lie was old enough to be married, and would the emperor bestow on him the hand of some girl of his family, Napoleon nodded, smilingly, but said never a word.

Ferdinand was so loose a talker that Godoy soon learned all about his letters to France, and King Charles was told by his minister that his son had plotted his death. The old king put himself at the head of his guards, marched to Ferdinand's quarters, arrested him, and locked him up in prison. Charles wrote to Napoleon that he had been saved from a terrible danger, planned against him by his own dear son and heir, and that He was afraid that it was his duty to punish the boy so as to make an example of him.

Two days afterwards Ferdinand begged his father's pardon, and said he was sorry for what he had done. Whereupon the old king wrote that "where a guilty party solicits pardon, the heart of a father cannot refuse it to a son." And Charles and the Prince of the Asturias showed themselves to the people arm in arm, and embraced in public.

By this time Napoleon had made up his mind what to do. He had an army in Portugal; he used it to drive out the royal family, and he bade his General Junot take command of the kingdom. This done, he turned round on Spain, and moved another army into Catalonia. He was going to interfere a little, as the Prince of the Asturias had invited him to do. But all the time he remained King Charles's best friend. On the very day when the French moved on Barcelona,

Napoleon sent the Spanish king a present of twelve beautiful horses, with a letter saying that he would call on him soon.

When Charles knew for certain that the French occupied Catalonia, he resolved to follow the example of the royal family of Portugal, and run away to the American colonies. His carriages drove to the palace door, and a strong body of cavalry and artillery was mustered to escort them to Seville, where he intended to take ship. But a mob gathered, surrounded the carriages, filled the air with cries and threats, cut the traces of the horses, and drove the old king back into the palace. In the crowd stood the Prince of the Asturias, cool and sneering.

PEASANTS IN THE MARKET-PLACE.

"Were you going to run away, too?" asked a by-stander.

"Not at all," said he; "I stay with my people." Whereupon the mob declared that Ferdinand was a true Spaniard, and the very man to be king.

That night Charles abdicated, and Ferdinand was proclaimed king. Charles wrote a letter in which he said that his health required rest and a milder climate, that his abdication was made of his own free will, and that his beloved son would govern wisely and well. Two days afterwards he wrote to Napoleon that he had not in the least acted of his own free will, but had been forced to abdicate, and would the emperor please set him back on the throne?

On March 20th, 1808, he told the foreign ambassadors that his abdication was his own choice, and had given him much pleasure. On the following day he wrote to the foreign courts that he had abdicated in order to avoid bloodshed, and that the act was therefore null.

The knavish son of this knavish father was going to be pretty roughly awakened from his fool's d ream. On the day after he became king he called on General Murat, who represented Napoleon at Madrid. Ferdinand went in great state, with a gorgeous staff and a grand escort. Murat stood erect and stern in the centre of the room. The king said he was glad to meet him as the emperor's envoy, and added other pleasant speeches. Murat never opened his mouth. The king made a few more remarks, with a rather forced smile on his lips. Murat did not answer a syllable, but stood like a man of stone, and looked straight before him gravely and frowningly. Ferdinand, after fidgeting with his sword and gloves, had no choice but to go.

It was made known to Ferdinand that the emperor was coming to Madrid, and he was told that it would be but polite to go and meet him. He started forth accordingly, taking care to send word in advance to Napoleon that Spain would give hive every assistance in destroying the independence of Portugal, and making it a French province. Napoleon never answered a word.

When Ferdinand reached Vittoria in old Navarre, near the French border, he was warned that he had better go no farther. Wise old Spaniards bade him beware of putting himself in the power of the emperor. But General Savary, who spoke for Napoleon, said he would let Ferdinand cut off his head if any trouble calve, that Napoleon loved Ferdinand like a brother, and better than most brothers; and the King of Spain crossed the Bidassoa.

Napoleon did receive him like a brother. He threw his arms round Ferdinand's neck, kissed him, and said everything that was sweet and kind and flattering. That day the emperor sent his own carriage to bring Ferdinand to dine with him, received him at the foot of the staircase, and all through the meal paid him the most delicate attentions. Ferdinand went home in high spirits, feeling that the emperor was a true friend. He had scarcely taken his seat in his own parlor when General Savary was announced. The general entered with a severe face, and made a very short speech.

"My master, the emperor," said he, "has made up his mind. You must immediately resign the throne of Spain. He proposes to put one of his own family on that throne."

And afterwards he explained that if Ferdinand gave no trouble, a small throne might perhaps be found for him elsewhere.

Ferdinand was dazed at first; when he collected himself, he said that he had not the least intention of giving up his throne. Then, said Napoleon, we must send for your father.

You will better understand the bitter struggle which was now beginning if I give you some notes of the state of Spain from a book written at this time by the Spanish historian — Vargas Ponce.

He said that Spain had generals enough to command the armies of the world, but no soldiers. There were at Madrid more churches than houses, more priests than burghers, more altars than kitchens. Wax figures of saints lay side by side with robbers and bad women. Religious processions blocked the streets. The courts of law were busy night and day, but justice was not to be had. A judge would sentence a man to death after a trial of twenty minutes, but would take ten years to decide the title to a mule. Every trade was a monopoly; the seller of oil could not sell wine, the seller of meat could not sell salt, the seller of wine could not sell oil or meat or fruit; none of them could sell oats or any article for which he did not hold a license. Nobody cared to have regular work. A true Spaniard slept so many Hours in the daytime, no matter if he had nothing to eat when he waked. He would go hungry to a bull-fight, and when he had not a coin in his pocket he would stand in the street and beg of passers-by.

The proud nobility of Spain which had figured so grandly, as you remember, in the history of the old days, had passed out of notice at this time. Very few of them served in the army, and still fewer in high employments of state. It was thought to be the correct thing for grandees and dukes to wait on the king, to hand him his shirt when be dressed, and to hold his stirrup when he mounted his horse; their wives combed the queen's hair, and handed her her tooth-brush. These duties were all they cared to fulfil. Yet the property owned by the nobles was enormous. They had got much of the land which was taken from the Jesuits, and they did not know how to cultivate it. Most of it lay fallow. They were lazy, ignorant, superstitious, and perfectly contented. No matter what the king or the prime-minister did, they had no objection to make.

It was this condition of Spain and the Spanish people which made Napoleon think he could easily conquer the country and annex it to France. He said to himself that an imbecile king, an ignorant and slothful people, a besotted nobility, and a rapacious Church could not defend the country against his veterans if they were directed by a mind as broad as his. Unluckily for him, and happily for Spain, there was a chord in the Spanish heart which, if touched, could still rouse the people to energy—that chord was impatience of foreign dominion. The Spaniard would starve or beg or go about in rags, but he would not be the slave of the foreigner, and especially of the Frenchman. He was ready to endure the rule of an idiot, so long as he was born a Spaniard; but he would rather die than submit to a Frenchman, however able or virtuous he might be. Napoleon was now going to find this out.

KING JOSEPH

A.D. 1808

GENERAL MURAT lost no time in obeying the emperor's orders to send King Charles and his wife to Bayonne. Napoleon met Charles at the foot of the stairs, and supported him as he climbed them, on which the old doting king cried to his wife:

"See, Louisa, he is carrying me."

Next day they settled down to business, and Napoleon easily persuaded the weak old man to assign to the emperor his rights to the throne of Spain, in consideration of a palace and a fat income. But Ferdinand was still obstinate. The emperor threatened him, his father bullied him, but he stuck to his determination not to give away his throne. Napoleon had resolved to have it. But he wanted to get it under cover of a regular transfer from Ferdinand. He was much embarrassed, and was revolving plans in his mind, when news came that there had been a brush between the French troops and the mob at Madrid in which some lives had been lost. This gave the emperor his cue.

He bade the king and his wife pour willies of red-hot abuse at their obstinate son. But he stayed obstinate in spite of the names they called him. Napoleon roared at him, shaking his fist in his face, and screaming that the French blood which had been shed at Madrid put a new face on the matter. He stamped on the ground, and in round words bade Ferdinand choose between cession and death.

Of course, after this, there was nothing to be done except to yield. On May 10th, 1808, Ferdinand signed away his throne in exchange for a castle in France and six hundred thousand francs a year. As soon as he had signed, he, his father and his mother, were carried as prisoners to a castle in the heart of France, and kept there till the end of the war.

Then Napoleon appointed his brother Joseph, who had been King of Naples, King of Spain, without so much as asking the Spaniards what they thought about it. Joseph was a mild, kindly gentleman, who cared much more about books and pictures than kingdoms; he begged his brother to let him alone and choose some one else. But Napoleon was one who insisted on being obeyed. Joseph had to yield, and he prepared to take possession of his kingdom.

Meanwhile, Murat, who was in command at Madrid, managed to bring about a conflict between his army and the mob, and slaughtered the latter in the most cruel way. The poor Spaniards had no arms and no discipline; the French mowed them down with grape-shot, and raked then with musketry fire when they escaped into the side streets. Murat said he did this to give the Spaniards a lesson, so that they should trouble the French no more. The lesson had precisely the opposite effect.

In every province of Spain, from the Pyrenees to the Mediterranean, the people rose against the invader. They formed in each province what they called a Junta, which was a standing convention of the leading people of the province; these conventions mustered in the fighting men, and armed them as they could. England, which was at war with France, sent them arms, ammunition, and clothing; with these, small armies were equipped and prepared to act together.

Meantime, King Joseph, with a strong force at his back, crossed the Pyrenees and entered Madrid. Orders had been given that the people should decorate the city as usual on the entry of a king; that tapestries should be hung from the windows, peals of welcome rung on the church-bells, and cheers given by the crowd. Joseph was disappointed. There were few people in the streets, and they did not cheer; nothing but dirty old rags hung from the windows, and the church-bells tolled mournfully.

Upon the very day when the new king met this chilling reception at the capital, an old Spanish soldier named Castanos fell upon a French army under General Dupont, at a place called Baylen, at the foot of the Sierra Morena, and utterly defeated it. Dupont surrendered with twenty thousand men. Castanos had agreed that the prisoners might return to their own country. But many of them were Swiss and Poles and Germans; they enlisted in the Spanish armies. The others, I am afraid, were attacked by the furious Spanish peasantry on their way home, and never reached France. In this Spanish war—where one people were fighting for conquest and the other for liberty—there was very little mercy shown on either side.

As soon as King Joseph got the news of the battle at Baylen he packed his trunk and left for home. Madrid was no place for him. It was beginning to thunder all round.

On June 15th, 1808, the French General Lefebvre, at the head of a fine army, marched up to the famous old town of Saragossa, which had stood so many sieges, and sum¬moned it to surrender. As it had only an old wall for all defence, he did not expect to have to fight. But the old blood which had flowed in the veins of the Saragossans a thousand years before still ran red and hot; they bade him come and take the town if he wanted it. He made a dash at the wall and was beaten back; then he sent for reinforcements and invested the place.

For nearly two months he bombarded Saragossa, until nearly every house was battered down, and the people had to sleep in their cellars. But they defended every house and every wall, even when the French had got into the place, and at last, raging at losing so many men and making such little headway, Lefebvre resolved to raise the siege. On the morning of August 14th, when the Saragossans got up to renew the dreary fighting, they saw the enemy in a distant dust-cloud marching away up the river.

It was at this siege that Augustina, the Maid of Saragossa, made herself famous. She was a canteen girl, who carried wine and lemonade round to the soldiers during the bombardment. Noticing that one gun was silent, the gunner having been killed, she leaped to his place, and served the gun to the end of the day, aiming and firing it herself. For this the Government of Spain made her a lieutenant, and gave her a pension.

> "Ye who shall marvel when you hear her tale,
> Olt! had you known her in her softer hour,
> Marked her black eye that mocks her coal-black veil,
> Heard her light, lively tones in lady's bower,
> Seen her long locks that foil the painter's power,
> Her fairy form with more than female grace,
> Scarce would you dream that Saragossa's tower
> Beheld her smile in danger's Gorgon face,
> Thin the closed ranks, and lead in glory's fearful chase.

"Her lover sinks—she sheds no ill-timed tear,
Her chief is slain—she tills his fatal post,
Her fellows flee—she cheeks their base career,
The foe retires—she heads the sallying host,
Who can appease like her a lover's ghost?
Who can avenge so well a leader's fall?
What maid retrieve when man's flush'd hope is lost?
Who hang so fiercely on the flying Gaul,
Foil'd by a woman's hand, before a batter'd wall?"

This was a bad beginning for the French conquest of Spain. But the man who had planned that conquest was not one to abandon his projects because of checks at the start. The Emperor Napoleon concentrated two hundred thousand French veterans under some of his best generals, and flung them into Spain. On November 8th he followed them himself, and from that time, for several years, the Spaniards won no more victories. Soult and Victor destroyed the Spanish armies in the northwest. The army of Aragon and Catalonia was scattered. Saragossa was besieged again, and though it was heroically defended by General Palafox, a pestilence broke out in the garrison, and it had to surrender. The English, who had landed armies in Portugal and Spain to oppose the French, were forced to re-embark them; the only competent general they had, Sir Arthur Wellesley, who afterwards became Duke of Wellington, having been recalled, and Sir John Moore, who had commanded them, having fallen in the battle of Corunna.

On December 2nd, 1808, Napoleon appeared before Madrid, and summoned it to surrender. It could not help itself. It opened its gates. Napoleon was very angry. He scolded the Spaniards sharply.

"What!" said he, "I give you a king of your own, an excellent king, my brother Joseph, and you are not satisfied. If you give me any more trouble, I will give you no king at all, and will govern you as a French province."

You see, nothing could convince this man that he did not own the earth.

The Spaniards submitted, and for five years Spain was ruled by Joseph, who was nothing but a clerk of Napoleon's.

THE FRENCH SPAIN

A.D. 1808-1813

JOSEPH was King of Spain in name, if not in fact, from the winter of 1808–9 to the June of 1813. During this time there never was an hour when he could have trusted himself in the smaller towns of Spain without an escort of armed men. There never was a day when Spanish hatred of the invaders cooled, or when the Spanish peasant did not go to bed with a loaded gun by his side to shoot any passing Frenchman.

From first to last, Napoleon poured into Spain some four hundred thousand men, under the ablest generals of his army. Of these, over three hundred thousand left their bones south of the Pyrenees. They fought bravely, they were well led; but, as they well knew, they were engaged in a wrongful and mean attempt to subvert the liberty of a neighboring race, and their enterprise was stamped with failure from its birth.

The Spaniards had no army, though there were on the national pay-roll five captain-generals, eighty-five lieutenant-generals, one hundred and twenty-seven field-marshals, two hundred and fifty-two brigadiers, and two thousand colonels. All over the country there were small bodies of armed men, burning to fight the French, but led by generals who could not agree with each other, and would not act together against the common enemy. These generals were under the orders of Juntas, which met in the several provinces, and the Juntas could not agree any better than the generals. You will be surprised to hear that no great man arose—as generally happens on such occasions—to take command of the Spanish nation. No Spanish Washington or Bolivar or Cromwell grasped the hour in an iron hand.

But if there was no great Spanish army under a great general, the country swarmed with free-shooters, who murdered Frenchmen, and fought bravely enough when driven to bay. The towns were full of cruel mobs, which sometimes fell upon French prisoners furiously and savagely, and who, when the French got the upper-hand, were themselves furiously and savagely punished. At Valencia, a horrible wretch named Calvo induced a party of poor French prisoners to try to escape, by telling them that a plot had been formed to assassinate them. As soon as they got clear of the prison wall, and were creeping stealthily towards the trees they could just see in the still, dark night, Calvo and his band fell upon them and made an end of them. Calvo was afterwards caught by the authorities, and was sent a prisoner to Minorca. I believe he was forgotten there. At least, nobody seemed to know what had become of him, and I am not surprised at it.

In those days, when King Joseph was sitting on an imaginary throne at Madrid, and French generals were exercising very real authority at Barcelona and Burgos and Cordova and Toledo and Granada and Salamanca and Valladolid, the air was always full of whispers of treason. It was death to be suspected of siding with the French, and many a poor Spaniard lost his head because some enemy accused him of corresponding with the invaders.

That was the charge which was brought against a burgher of Catalonia. The mob insisted on seeing his mail-bag opened, in order to get hold of the letters which they said they knew he was getting from France. His daughter, a straight, black-haired, black-eyed girl, said she would open the bag in their presence. She did so, and when she came to one letter, she hastily tore it up and swallowed the pieces. Some one cried, "The little devil has fooled us."

She pressed her hand to her side, and a scarlet blush spread over her face as she answered:

"Did you think I would let you see a letter from my lover?"

And so her father was saved—for that time.

On April 22d, 1809, Wellington arrived in Portugal with a small army of English soldiers. The English had made up their minds that the fight to a finish between the emperor and themselves might just as well be fought in Spain as elsewhere. They sent their best general there, and bade him try to make an army out of the Spanish and Portuguese peasants who were fighting as guerillas in the mountains. These were not the best possible material; they were not accustomed to obey. It was contrary to their custom to spare a fallen foe. But they were brave as steel, and could march great distances almost without food.

Wellington succeeded in getting them in shape; mixing them with his English troops, he built up a very tolerable army—so good in fact, that, though the French always had more men in Spain than he had, he never fought a battle till he was ready, and never fought a battle which he lost. When he wasn't sure of winning he wouldn't fight, and the French couldn't make him.

It would fatigue you if I described these battles. It will be enough to tell you of the last, the battle of Vittoria, which was the decisive battle of the war.

In May, 1813, King Joseph made up his mind that the time had come for him to run away once more. He levied a tremendous tax on all the towns and villages he could reach, and packed the silver and gold in wagons and country carts. He stripped the churches of their pictures and their gold and silver plate. He took ornaments and jewels and works of art wherever he found them. With this plunder, and his guns and ammunition, and with a large party of gay ladies of his court, he started north at the head of the remnant of his army—about seventy thousand men—and got as far as Vittoria on June 20th.

He had not been gone from Madrid for many hours before Wellington was on the march with about a hundred thousand men to intercept him. He knew exactly where Joseph was going, and what route he would take. On the morning of June 20th the Spanish scouts reported that the French had crossed the mountain, and were spreading over the basin of Vittoria, which is a pretty level plain about ten miles long by eight miles wide, enclosed on three sides by spurs of the Pyrenees and low ranges of hills.

Wellington made his plans that night, and before the French knew that he was near, in the gray dawn of the misty morning of June 21, the English soldiers in their scarlet coats, the Dutch and Spaniards in blue and dark-brown, came climbing up the mountain, scampered down on the other side, and burst their way through copses of chestnut, oak, and cork trees, in which birds were singing merrily, and the little river Zadorra was leaping and bounding from jag to crag on its way to the Ebro. In front of then, through the morning haze, belated wagons of King Joseph's army were seen raising dust-clouds on the road to Vittoria. In the distance were the French tents scattered on both sides of the roads to Bayonne in France, and to Pampeluna in old Navarre, while near the horizon the silver Ebro rolled peacefully to the ocean.

Wellington had circled round the French, and though they fought bravely, as they always do, they were so hampered by the multitude of wagons and useless camp furniture that they could hardly form in line of battle, and the morning was still young when they knew they were beaten. The defeat soon became a retreat, and the retreat a rout. King Joseph gave the word to take the Pampelana road, and it was soon so blocked that the French had to cover their rear with fifty cannon to protect the flying army.

As it was, they lost almost everything. King Joseph lost his carriage, in which there was a picture he had stolen, his clean clothes, and his purse; when he got to Pampeluna he had but one coin in his pocket. Wellington captured a hundred and fifty-one brass cannon, and small-arms and ammunition-chests past counting. In the army-chest were five million and a half dollars in gold and silver. Joseph did not save a dollar. His officers and soldiers seem to have lost their money too, for after the battle the ground was covered with coins, for which the English and Spanish troops soon found use.

I have told you that when Joseph left Madrid a number of fine ladies—and some ladies who were not so fine—went in his company, reckoning on a pleasant jaunt to France. Some of these were left behind when the army fled. They were placed under escort, and in a day or two a few were sent home in their own carriages. Others followed the troops, riding on artillery wagons or behind troopers on their horses. These threw away everything that could impede their flight. Thus, the victors found the battle-field strewn with velvet and silk brocade dresses, gold and silver plate, pictures, jewels, laces, cases of fine wine, poodles, parrots, monkeys, French boots, books of devotion, and novels.

The common soldiers reaped such a harvest of plunder that some eight thousand men were absent from duty for several days after the battle, and were found carousing in the village with the proceeds of the spoil.

This was the end of the attempt of Napoleon to conquer Spain, and it was, I think, the chief cause of his downfall.

FERDINAND THE SEVENTH

A.D. 1814-1833

BEFORE the French were driven out of Spain, the people had elected a Cortes to frame a new constitution based on popular liberty. The work had been done, and well done. It abolished the Inquisition, and took away the privileges of the nobles. It provided for a king who should govern according to law; and the Spaniards had no objection to Ferdinand being that king.

Ever since he assigned his throne to Napoleon he had been a prisoner in a castle in central France. He was not in close confinement. He could ride and drive through the grounds about the castle, could entertain his friends, and amuse himself at any game he pleased, except playing king. Now that Napoleon appeared to be going downhill, he claimed the throne which he had abdicated five years before. Napoleon said he might have it and welcome.

On March 20th, 1814, he re-entered Spain, and read for the first time the constitution which the Cortes had framed in his absence. It was not to his liking, and he said so. The priests of Catalonia and Navarre said it was not to their liking either. They got crowds of ignorant peasants to shout:

"Down with the constitution! Let us have an absolute king! Long live King Ferdinand!"

On the strength of this expression of public opinion, King Ferdinand issued a proclamation declaring that all the acts of the Cortes, including the framing of the constitution, and the decree abolishing the Inquisition, were null and void, and that everything must be put back on the old footing. Gathering round him a band of soldiers, he marched to Madrid. Most of the members of the Cortes had fled to Cadiz; those who remained he locked up in jail, and afterwards sent to the galleys, or forced to serve as privates in the army. He restored the Inquisition, recalled the Jesuits and gave them control of the schools, and proclaimed that any one who spoke ill of him or of his government should be put to death. The Spaniards began to think they had not gained much by driving out the French.

GOING TO MARKET.

You will not be surprised to hear that Ferdinand's behavior led to revolts. Riots broke out at Valencia, Barcelona, and Cadiz; while New Castile, Estremadura, and Andalusia began to get ready for rebellion in the old way. The contagion spread and spread from one province to another, from one city to the next, until all Spain was ripe for explosion, and only needed a spark. Then the craven king crept into a corner and issued a proclamation convening the Cortes, and promising to do everything that was wanted by his people, "who have given me so many proofs of their loyalty." This was in March, 1820.

The Cortes met. Many of its members were taken out of the jails where the king had shut them up. Others were persons whom he had threatened with death. It restored the constitution of 1812, again abolished the Inquisition and expelled the Jesuits; then, as the chief obstacle to good government in Spain was want of money in the treasury, it suppressed all monasteries and convents but eight, and confiscated their property to the service of the State. King Ferdinand at first refused to sign the decree for this, but when a crowd surrounded his palace, and he was told that the troops were of the same mind as the people, he signed it, and ran away to the Escurial.

In the gloomy shades of that dismal abode he planned a *coup-d'etat*, and secretly appointed a general whom he could trust, named Carbajal, to the post of captain-general, with supreme command of the troops. The Cortes found out what he had done, and sent a committee to the Escurial to warn him. He fell into abject terror, removed Carbajal, and asked the committee if his life would be safe in Madrid. Thither he returned, trembling and quaking; his knees shook so that he could hardly walk up the stairs of his palace, and, with a haggard face, he locked himself in his room. A day or two afterwards, when he tried to drive out, the mob stoned his carriage, and be had to return home.

A time followed when there was really no government in Spain, and Madrid was in the shocking condition to which Napoleon had put an end in Paris. There was a king whom everybody despised. There was a Cortes which was as incapable of governing as the French Assembly had been. There were a number of clubs which undertook to dictate to the king and the Cortes. And above all, there was a mob of brutal, blood-thirsty miscreants whom the troops sometimes fired upon and sometimes sympathized with.

There was a poor half-crazy priest, who wrote a pamphlet against liberty; he was arrested for it, and condemned to ten years' imprisonment. But the mob were not satisfied. They thought he should have been more severely punished. They tore him out of jail, with shouts of "Blood! blood!"

The poor priest, holding a crucifix high above his head, begged his life in the name of the Redeemer.

The mob rushed upon him, and the leader beat his brains out with a hammer.

You may perhaps not be so much shocked at this, when you remember that all mobs are brutal and blood-thirsty. But the newspapers of Madrid applauded the murder of the priest, the Cortes called it a noble deed, and the city rabble formed a club to commemorate it under the name of the Order of the Hammer. Curses were coming home to roost indeed.

In the turmoil a gallant general named Murillo loomed up, and put down mobs with the bayonet wherever he found them. But he could not be everywhere. There was a dreadful monk, who was known as the Trappist, who mustered an army of peasants, and made war upon the army of the Cortes with terrible vigor and savage cruelty. Seville and Cadiz set up a government of their own, and declared war upon the government at Madrid. The Cortes at Madrid ordered its troopers to give no quarter to the rebels. The Junta at Cadiz commanded its troops to kill their prisoners after every battle. The gutters of the cities of Spain ran with blood, and there was no money anywhere to buy food. All this time the miserable king wandered from place to place, wringing his hands, and asking everyone what he should do.

He found out at last. He persuaded the King of France, who hated liberty as much as he did, to send an army into Spain under the Duke of Angoubime. You know how the Spaniards loved the French, and you can fancy how pleased the former were to hear that their old foes had come to keep then in order. The duke, at the head of one hundred and fifty thousand men, swept down through northern Spain, and took Madrid without resistance, king and Cortes having gone first to Seville, then to Cadiz. It did not take the French long to capture the latter place, and then, with every show of respect, they proceeded to restore Ferdinand to his throne. He assured the Cortes and its friends on leaving Cadiz that he bore no malice, and that they could trust to him. But when their backs were turned, he shook his fist and muttered, "They will see they will see!"

A STREET BARBER OPERATING ON A CUSTOMER.

And they did see. The most gallant and noble-hearted of the popular leaders was General Riego. He was arrested, and put on his trial. The lawyers were such cowards that not one of them dared to defend him. He was found guilty and sentenced to be hanged, which in

Spain is considered an ignominious form of death. He was stripped of his uniform, and draped in a white cloth, with a cap of liberty on his head. His hands were tied behind his back, and he was set on a hurdle, which was drawn to the place of execution by an ass, while a row of priests marched beside the ass chanting the service for the dead. The gibbet was so high. that Riego had to be hauled up to the scaffold. There the rope was passed round his neck, and as it was cut by the executioner a bystander smote him on the cheek with his fist.

The French troops remained five or six years in Spain, and while they were there there were no more riots. Ferdinand ruled according to his own sweet will. As he grew old, he began to be troubled about the succession to the throne. He had been married three times, but had no children. In 1829 he married once more, the bride this time being Christina of Naples. In October, 1830, she gave birth to a girl-baby, who was christened Isabella. It had at one time been the law that a woman could not reign in Spain; but both Charles the Fourth and Ferdinand had issued what they called pragmatic sanctions, declaring that females could succeed to the throne as well as males.

Against this decision Ferdinand's brother now protested, and bullied the king till he revoked his decree and declared that Carlos was the heir, and not the girl-baby. As soon as Carlos's back was turned Ferdinand changed his mind, as he often did, and said that Isabella was the rightful heir. When Carlos heard of it, he started for Madrid to make the king change his mind once more. Unluckily for the former, before he reached the capital city Ferdinand died, and Isabella was proclaimed. The disappointment of Don Carlos led to a long and bloody war, of which I will tell you something in a future chapter.

There may have been worse kings of Spain than the one whose reign came to a close on September 29th, 1833, but I cannot recall any one of them who did so much injury to his country as Ferdinand the Seventh.

THE SPANISH-AMERICAN COLONIES

A.D. 1810-1822

WHEN Ferdinand the Seventh came to the throne, Mexico, Central America, several of the West India islands, and all of South America, except Brazil, belonged to Spain. When he died, nothing was left to Spain but Cuba and Porto Rico.

The successful revolt of the British colonies against England set the people of the Spanish colonies to thinking; when convulsions spread through Europe after the French revolution, and during the reign of Napoleon, the thinking was of independence. When Ferdinand sold his birthright to Napoleon for a castle and a pension, the Spanish Americans said to each other that he should not sell them. They had, moreover, grievances of their own. They were heavily taxed for the benefit of Spain. They were not allowed to buy goods of any nation but Spain. And all the offices in Spanish America were filled by natives of Spain. There were Spanish garrisons in the strong places, and Spanish priests in the churches; the Inquisition was in full feather, and good Catholics in America, as well as in Europe, were beginning to think it was not as grand an institution as they had once supposed. As in Spain, the Church had got most of the property in Spanish America into its hands. It was, in fact, the ruler of the country. In all Spanish America the priests would not allow one Protestant church to be opened.

The first gun was fired in Mexico. In the year 1810, Miguel Hidalgo, a Spanish priest of Dolores, in the State of Guanaxuato, raised the standard of rebellion. He was a white-haired man of fifty-eight, tall and stout, with a strong face and powerful limbs; a man who had been a reader and a thinker, and who had satisfied himself that Mexico ought to cut loose from Spain. He called his people to arms, mustered quite a large army, beat the government troops in several battles, took city after city, and had nearly attained his purpose when fortune forsook him. He was not a soldier, and after a time he began to lose battles. Then his men deserted him. His officers were captured. The Spanish officials hunted him hotly, and in March, 1811, they caught him.

He was shackled hand and foot, and carried on a mule to Chihuahua. After his trial, which you may be sure did not puzzle the judges much, he was made to kneel, and his priestly garments were torn from his back. Then he was shackled again. Before daylight on the morning of July 31st he was taken, limping from his irons, into the back yard of the prison, and set in front of a platoon of soldiers. He laid his hand upon his heart. But they missed it, and three shots had to be fired into his body after he had fallen to make an end of the old hero.

When he died another priest named Jose Morelos arose to take his place, and for three or four years led the insurgents with success. At one time all southern Mexico, including the City of Mexico and Vera Cruz, was in his hands. He was a daring leader, who never counted odds. The common people adored him. On one occasion a young lady who had a sweetheart serving under him was caught sending letters and money to her lover, and for this was locked up in a convent, with a fine chance of losing her head. A party of Morelos's young men got together one night, dashed up to the convent, broke open the doors, tore the young lady out of her prison, and carried her off to the camp where her sweetheart was on duty.

But the Spanish authorities now mustered into their service a young soldier named Iturbide, who was quite as dashing as Morelos, and more skilful in the business of war. He took the priest's conquests from him one by one, separated his forces, and beat them in detail. Gradually he drove the rebels into the mountains, and there, in a range not far from the City of Mexico, he at last, in November, 1815, penned up Morelos in a glen without an outlet. As the Spanish cavalry galloped up, Morelos dismounted to take off his spurs so as to climb the mountain on foot.

"Surrender!" shouted the leader of the cavalry.

"Ha!" replied Morelos, taking his cigar from his lips, " Senor Carranco, we meet again."

He met the usual fate. His gown was stripped from his shoulders, and he was sentenced to die. The Inquisition jailer—think how times had changed!—offered to let him escape. But he declined, saying,

"God forbid that I should imperil your innocent family to prolong my own life."

On the execution-ground he prayed:

"Lord, thou knowest if I have done well; if I have done ill, I implore Thy mercy!"

As he knelt to meet his end, he was shot in the back.

The war lasted five years more, the advantage being always on the side of the royalists. The insurgents were driven from place to place, their chiefs executed, their friends thrown into prison. In 1820 the rebellion looked as if it was thoroughly ended. It was just at that very moment that it triumphed. The story is quite curious.

General Agostin Iturbide, of whom I have told you, had fallen out with the Spanish viceroy, had thrown up his command, had travelled abroad, and on his return had lived quietly on a ranch. He now formed a plan to play in Mexico the part which Napoleon played in France. He suddenly sought and got command of the troops, under pretence of stamping out the last embers of the revolution. Putting a long distance between him and the viceroy, he opened negotiations with the remaining rebel chiefs, and got them to join him with their forces. The news spread far and wide that the great general who had led the Spaniards was now on the side of the patriots, and Mexicans who had given up the struggle as hopeless sprang to arms once more.

Iturbide soon found himself at the head of a force which it would have been folly to resist. He marched to the City of Mexico without striking a blow, and General O'Donoju, who represented Spain, agreed to evacuate the country. Iturbide entered the city on September 27th, 1821, and proclaimed the independence of Mexico.

I may as well tell you here—though it is not part of the history of Spain—that eight months after he proclaimed the independence of the Mexican republic, Iturbide declared himself emperor. He was overthrown in less than a year, and ordered to leave the country, being warned that if he returned it would be at his peril. He did return, and the colonel in charge of the port where he landed had him shot without consulting his superior officers.

The only other story of the independence of the Spanish colonies which you would care to hear is that of Bolivar. Originally, the province of Peru included Chili, Paraguay, Buenos Ayres, Ecuador, New Granada, and Venezuela. These several states gradually separated, and had viceroys of their own. In 1810 and 1811, just at the time when Mexico began to strike for independence, Chili and Venezuela did the same; and New Granada and Ecuador followed the lead of their neighbor Venezuela. For several years the royalist troops were able to put clown the insurrections. But at last there arose in Venezuela a leader who belonged to the kind of men that win.

This was Simon Bolivar, a native of Caracas, and a colonel in the army; he was then thirty-two years old. He had no regular army and no money. But he had grit and genius; and after a war of nearly seven years, he met the royalists in a pitched battle at a place called Bocaya, on September 19th, 1819, and defeated them so thoroughly that they agreed to evacuate the country.

Then he crossed over into New Granada, and set that State and Ecuador free, too; and he gave the Spanish Americans of South America such heart that Chili won her independence likewise; and Buenos Ayres, which is now the Argentine Confederation, was not long in following suit. Even Peru, which was the slowest to move, joined the procession at last, and the Spanish flag disappeared from South America.

When Bolivar returned to his capital, after securing the independence of his country, he was called "The Liberator," and was unanimously elected president. He performed his duties well and faithfully, but at the close of his term he refused a re-election. The president who was chosen in his place did not please the Venezuelans, and they begged Bolivar to take office again. But he would not. They entreated him, saying that they would elect him whether he chose or not. Then he left the country, assuring the people that there were many men as capable of being president as he, and that he would not be accused of having been led by ambition in what he had done.

After a time, he returned to Venezuela, and found political strife hot between rival parties. He labored faithfully to reconcile them, and succeeded. But some small-souled creatures accused him of having been actuated by base motives in what he had done, and their gibes wounded him to the heart. He was fifty years old, had spent his life in active work and warfare, and was broken down. He withdrew to his farm, and there moaned and writhed under the injustice of his countrymen, until his constitution gave way, and he died.

I do not think that this Child's History has ever had to deal with a purer, honester, and braver man than Simon Bolivar.

There is one little story about him, which may give you a side-light upon the man, and the people who lived with him.

Somewhere in Venezuela there was a statue of the Virgin, which was much thought of, because, at one time, when King Ferdinand was sick, a good woman had prayed to the statue for his recovery, and he, when he did recover, repaid the service by sending the statue a golden crown. The statue became so famous after this that the Spanish women, when in sorrow, used to kneel before it and chant their plaintive wail, which is so simple that I think you can understand it, though it is not in English. It runs—

> Santa Maria,
> Madre de Dios,
> Madre de gratia,
> Madre purissima,
> Madre castissima.

One day, the priest of the church in which the statue stood observed, to his horror, that its crown was gone. Hue and cry was at once started, and pretty soon it was found that the crown had been taken by a young soldier named Manuel. The archbishop hastened to Bolivar, denounced the thief, and demanded his punishment. The liberator was shocked. Manuel was one of his favorite soldiers, a young man of great promise. But sacrilege was the most heinous of all crimes, punishable with death, and, according to the old law, with torture besides.

A court was convened, and Manuel was brought before the general, by whose side sat the archbishop.

"Didst thou steal the crown?" roared Bolivar.

"I did, general; I cannot deny it. I did. The way of it was this: When I got home from our last campaign, I found my poor old mother starving. Just think, a poor old woman, over seventy, and no food to eat! Oh! it killed me to see her. Madre de Dios! Seventy years old, and no food; I had no money to give her. You know, general, we were not paid off." (The general nodded his head, and the archbishop blew his nose.) "I had nothing, not even a crust of bread, to give her. I went out of my mind. My poor old mother, who would have given her life for me, starving! I went out and entered the church. I knelt down before the Blessed Virgin, and prayed to her for help. I was praying even for so little as a piece of bread, when—I am afraid you will not believe me, gentlemen, but it's true—the Blessed Mary of Grace stepped off her pedestal, took off her crown, and laid it in my hand."

"What! the statue?" shouted Bolivar.

"The statue, as true as I am a living man."

There was a dead pause in the trial.

"I think, general," said the archbishop, after a long silence, with a queer twinkle in his eye, "that this is a case of a miracle."

The general looked at him for a moment, and a queer twinkle came into his eye, too.

"Prisoner," said he, in a voice which was not as harsh as he perhaps intended it to be, "the archbishop says this was a miracle, and he is a judge of miracles. Miracles are his business. You can't be punished for a miracle, so you are acquitted. But if I ever hear again of your fooling with statues, I'll have you shot. The court-martial is adjourned."

And I dare say the two good old men, as they walked off arm in arm, thought they would eat their dinner that day with a better appetite, because they had not sentenced the young soldier to death.

THE WOMAN FROM NAPLES

A.D. 1838-1540

BY the will of Ferdinand the Seventh, his successor was to be his daughter, Isabella, who was less than three years old when he died; and, until she grew up, her mother, Christina, whom the people called "the woman from Naples," was to be regent. To this will Ferdinand's brother Carlos refused to submit, on the ground that, according to his understanding of the law, women could not reign in Spain; he gathered round him a party of friends who were willing to fight for him. He was a narrow-minded, pig-headed, fat-witted Bourbon, who could never quite thoroughly get it through his head that the world moves.

I dare say that he would have cut less figure, but for the temper of the people at the time. In the cities, and among educated Spaniards, the long domination of the Church had disgusted them. The priests were hated and loathed as fiercely as they had once been reverenced. To a mob at Madrid, Seville, or Cadiz, a priest in canonicals was like a red rag to a bull. In Madrid a white-haired old priest in his robes passed a party of workmen.

"Old man," cried one of them, "why do you wear a woman's petticoat?"

"Because," said the graybeard, intrepidly, "I am a priest of God."

"Take that for your God," said the workman, knocking the old man down.

The priest rose, wiped the blood from his face, and tendered the other cheek, " Strike there, too," said he to the ruffian; and the crowd, admiring his grit, shouted, "Good for you, father!"

Isabella's reign had hardly begun when cholera, which was then raging all over the world, broke out in Spain. Ignorant people said it was the work of the monks; that they had poisoned the wells. Riots broke out, monasteries were attacked, and the priests murdered by scores, while in the chief cities mobs went round shouting, "Down with the monks!"

"ALL THE DAY LONG I AM HAPPY."

On the other hand, in the country parts, and especially in tile pasture country of the north, Navarre, the Asturias, the Basque provinces, and Galicia, where old fashions prevailed, where only one person in eight could read, and there were no books or newspapers, where the peasants wore the garb which their ancestors had worn in the Middle Ages, and tended their flocks and fished the bays just as they had done before the discovery of America, the priests were as strong as they ever had been. The peasants would stand no trifling with the Church, and when they heard from their curas that Don Carlos was a true Christian, who told his beads early and often, and who, if he became king, would probably restore the Holy Inquisition, while the woman from Naples and her friends were little better than infidels, who had robbed the Church already, and were likely to rob it again, they said they were for Don Carlos, and they fought for him in their old, gallant, stupid way.

They were so loyal to their faith that they kept up the war for seven years. Don Carlos did not do any fighting. He preferred to walk the boulevards in Paris, to dine at his clubs in London, to skim the bay of Naples in his yacht with ladies; but he read the accounts of the Basque peasants dying for him with a good deal of interest.

His best general was an old officer of the army whose name was Zumalacarregui. He may remind you of the old fighting monks of crusading times: a hard, cold, iron man, who hardly ever spoke, never did any man wrong, never spared a sinner, or kissed a girl; but who went right on with his work as if there were no such things in the world as love or mercy or tenderness or human weakness. This old warrior won so many battles that the people of Madrid and Seville and Cadiz could not contain their rage, and whenever a crowd assembled shouts arose, "Down with the monks!"

The people of Spain generally were against Don Carlos. It seemed to them mean to try and cheat a little three-year-old girl out of her throne. They got up a good deal of sentiment about sweet little innocent Isabel. I believe the sentiment did not last after the sweet little innocent grew to be a woman; but while she was a baby it was strong. The regent struck back at the priests by laying hands on the property of the regular religious orders. In this way the government fought the Church with its own money.

A SERENADE.

But the woman from Naples did not make her way into the Spanish heart. Her husband died in September, 1833; in December of the same year she was secretly married to a private soldier named Munoz, by whom she had ten children. The Spaniards said that she was so busy trying to get money for these children that she had no time to think of the kingdom. She made her husband a duke, and spent her days in riding with him, and her evenings in singing and dancing in his company.

Against the Carlists, as the followers of Don Carlos was called, the queen regent sent a valiant and skilful general named Espartero, a native of La Mancha, and after several years' fighting, he put them down. Then said Christina, "There are some towns here which are giving me trouble about their fueros which I have taken away. Go and put down these people with a little cannon shot and a few cavalry charges."

"Madam," said Espartero, "they may, as you say, be put clown with a little cannon shot and a few cavalry charges. But I will not be the man to put them down. I would rather resign my command,"

Christina promised to restore the fueros. But in a few days she changed her mind, and said that she would not restore them, whereupon Valencia and Barcelona broke out in revolt. Espartero said it was none of his business. Thereupon the regent flew into a temper, and went off to Paris. The Cortes was not distressed at losing her, and appointed Espartero regent in her place. This was in 1840.

He proved an excellent regent, but was not calm-tempered enough to manage the government in such troubled times. Christina intrigued against him, and all the hungry politicians who wanted office and plunder, and to whom Espartero would give neither, worked against him. In 1843, weary of strife, he resigned, and the Cortes declared that little Isabella, who was thirteen, had come of age, and she was crowned queen. Then Christina came back to Madrid, and ruled the country under her daughter's name.

ISABELLA

A.D. 1843-1868

ISABELLA, as I have told you, became queen when she was thirteen years old. She had only been half educated, and had been encouraged by her mother to indulge her whims and impulses, however foolish they were. You will not be surprised that she grew up a self-willed young woman, with an ungovernable temper.

When she was fifteen, the queen-mother ordered her to marry her cousin, Don Francisco. Isabella refused. She hated Francisco. He was a puny, awkward, shy youth, with a squeaky voice, and in his ways more like a girl than a boy. Isabella called him Fanny. She said she would have none of him. But that night, Christina, with two men, went to the girl's room, and lectured, upbraided, scolded, threatened, and bullied her all through the long hours of the night; when morning came, with a broken spirit and eyes swollen by crying, the girl surrendered. Christina had her married immediately, for fear she would change her mind. She told her mother that she could never love her husband; and, indeed, she never did. She took pleasure in calling him Fanny before people, and in flirting with other men in his presence. When he demurred, she put him down with a look. She grew to be a great, tall, swarthy woman, with broad shoulders and a rough voice. He always looked as if he had been her little boy, and not her husband.

Thus married and settled, the young queen established a court after her own heart. It was full of profligate men and women, who did nothing but gamble and drink and dance and ride on horseback day after day. The only serious occupation they had was to gamble in stocks, and at this they made vast sums of money, through their possession of secrets of state. All good Spaniards—the virtuous Espartero among the number—avoided the court as a plague-spot. Many of them left the country. Spanish gentlemen travelling abroad blushed when the queen was mentioned. She held high revel, as though there was nothing to live for but pleasure, and that was to last forever.

It did not. A time came when the people resolved on a change, and demanded the return of Espartero to power. He did not last. He could no more govern that intrigue-ridden country, with the queen and her court against him, than he had been able to do it in 1843. He was driven out of office by lies told by the gamblers and intriguers, which the queen affected to believe. A rough soldier named O'Donnell succeeded him. He rode roughshod over every one, and when the queen's husband, " Fanny," opposed a bill to confiscate some Church property, which had thus far escaped, the fierce rough-rider threatened to shake him till his teeth dropped out. But intriguers upset him, too, at the end of three months; and then the most adroit, the most foxey, and the most cold-blooded man in Spain, Ramon Narvaez, became prime-minister. He was overthrown a good many times, but he always got back to power, he knew so well how to manage the Cortes and the queen.

Narvaez was not a great statesman, but he preserved order in Spain, collected money enough to carry on the government, and steered his bark through the rocks and shoals upon which other prime-ministers had gone to wreck. Isabella herself did not much care who managed the government, so long as she had her fun. When that was interfered with she was a tigress. Once, when she had been driven out of Madrid by a riot, which was put down in due course, Concha sent her word by the banker Salamanca that she could come back, if she came without her favorite Marfori. He had scarcely got the words out of his mouth when the furious queen flew at him, as if she meant to throttle him, calling him vile names, and spitting in her rage.

Of course, she did not like liberty. When her cousin, the Duke of Parma, visited her at Madrid, he said to her:

"They tell me you have got some old-fashioned institutions here— Cortes and elections, and things of that kind. Why do you not give them all a kick over, and be mistress in your own house?"

"Ah!" replied the queen, with a sigh, "I wish I could."

There were laws enough in Spain to secure personal liberty. But they were a dead letter. Under Isabella a man could be seized in his own house and shipped to the Philippine Islands, and his property confiscated, without any reason being given him for the act; or, he might be taken out of his house at Madrid, and ordered to live in a remote village at the farthest end of Spain, never to leave that village under peril of his life.

Under Isabella, labor in Spain was despised more than it had ever been. The sons of well-to-do people would not work. They would live on a crust of bread and a paper cigar, but they would not put in six hours a day at a desk or a bench. They preferred to beg. Under Isabella, beggary became a regular business. Beggars had to take out a license as livery-stable men do here. If they had powerful friends, they got a petty office under government. The salary of these offices was very small—only a hundred dollars a year or so; but those who held them generally got rich by taking bribes. With money anything could be got from the government, and every one in the service of government took money.

Fortunes were made by speculators; Queen Christina is said to have made forty millions of our money by gambling in stocks. A governor of Cuba reckoned to make a million in three or four years—also by bribery. Another class of people who got rich were the smugglers. Spain had an absurd tariff, which had been framed in the hope of encouraging home manufactures; the result was that foreign goods were smuggled into the country, and the tariff yielded no revenue.

The women of Spain, under Isabella, were generally idle, ignorant, and devout. They went to mass and confession regularly. But I am afraid this excellent practice did not improve their morals or their behavior. Queen Isabella herself was devoted to her religion. When she started out on her wildest and most helter-skelter spree, she gave a ring or a string of beads to a statue of the Virgin, which she kept in her bedroom. Spanish ladies were less gentle than American or English or French ladies of the same period; they were cruel to animals. I suppose that this fault was due to their fondness for bull-fights, as the poor quality of the books written under Isabella was due to the indifference of the people to letters. The only books sold in Spanish book-stores were works of devotion and translations of the worst kind of French novels. It is only in our day that really good Spanish books have once more been written.

In the year 1868, the Spanish people rose in disgust at the imbecile and impure life of this vile woman. They did not want her life. They only wanted her to get out. The streets were filled with people who called after her the most dreadful names. The prime-minister, Don Jose Concha, threw up his office and went into the country. Isabella was told that she must go. She telegraphed' to the Emperor of France, who was at Biarritz, begging for help. But Napoleon the Third knew too much to interfere.

On September 30th, 1868, on a bright sunny morning, Queen Isabella, with her husband, her four children, her favorite, and her confessor, alighted from a railroad carriage at Biarritz in France. The French emperor, the empress, their son, and attendants were waiting on the platform to receive the strangers. When they met, Isabella burst into tears, and the empress, who had known her a long time, cried out of sympathy; the emperor stood like a man of stone, with a stern, sad face; the little King of Spain hopped round like a tomtit, holding a child by each hand, and fidgeting with his feet. There was a short talk in a waiting-room, and it is now known that Napoleon then told Isabella he could do nothing for her.

The Spanish party boarded the car on their way to Pau. Just before the train started Isabella cried, in Spanish, "I have not kissed the empress good-bye." Eugenie sprang upon the gallery of the car, and offered her cheek. That pure cheek had never before been pressed by such impure lips. Isabella tried to kiss the empress on the other cheek; but Eugenie had leaped down and was gone.

From Pau the ex-queen went to Paris, where she lived in splendor, having laid her hands, before leaving Madrid, on all the valuable property she could carry away.

So she fades out of history.

SPAIN IN OUR DAY

A.D. 1868-1890

WHEN Isabella had been got rid of, without bloodshed, the best and wisest public men of Spain met in Madrid to decide how the kingdom should be governed. For the moment, authority was placed in the hands of Marshal Serrano, General Prim, Senor Sagasta, and Senor Zorilla, who were all honest men, well thought of by the public. When the Cortes met, Serrano was made regent, and then the question arose who should be king, for it was agreed that the Spanish people were not sufficiently educated in politics to carry on a republic.

Several gentlemen were proposed. There was Louis Philippe's son, the Duke of Montpensier, who was always ready to take anything that offered. There was Leopold of Hohenzollern, a rather hungry German, who quite fancied the idea of being king. The people preferred Espartero, but that wise old statesman had had enough of public life, and positively refused to accept a throne in the place of the olives and oranges he loved to raise. Others were mentioned, but at last the choice fell upon Amadeo, the second son of King Victor Emanuel of Italy. He also refused the crown, not once, but twice and thrice; but the Spaniards persisting, he finally accepted.

He was sworn in on January 2, 1871. He was a tall, open-faced young man, as honest as the day, meaning to do right, and intending to allow no one to swerve him from what he believed to be right. His idea was that Spaniards should govern Spain through their representatives in the Cortes, and that he had no right to set his will over theirs.

But he had not the least notion of allowing any party to use him. He did not believe in the show or flummery of royalty. He walked the streets alone, dressed like any other gentleman, and he was as ready to chat with a poor man who was in rags as with a grandee of Spain.

This did not suit the blue-blooded Spaniards, who were sticklers for dignity and display. Nor did the simple, lady-like behavior of the queen please the noblewomen of Spain; they thought a queen should be something grand and overpowering. Both the nobles and their wives began secretly to sneer at the king; they called him a Savoyard, because his grandfather was King of Savoy—Savoyard, in French slang, having the same meaning as huckster or beggar. Taught by this example, the rabble of Madrid shouted after him "Savoyard" in the streets; and one day they shot at him as he passed with the queen in his carriage.

THE GREAT SQUARE AT MADRID.

He could not manage the Cortes. Those who had voted to make him king, thought he should favor them; he said the King of Spain should have no friends and no enemies, but should use his authority equally for the benefit of all. So, gradually, all parties worked to make him trouble; and be, without the least regret, resigned the throne on February 11th, 1873, having occupied it a little over two years.

Then a republic was proclaimed, and the executive power was placed successively in the hands of Pi y Margall, who held it five weeks; Nicolas Salveron, who lasted about as long; Emilio Castelar, who ruled a few weeks longer; and Serrano, who had been regent before. Finally, on December 31st, 1874, the republic was abolished, and Don Alfonso, son of Isabella, a young man of seventeen, was elected king.

He had been well educated by a bright and good woman, Madame Calderon de la Barca, and had never seen much of his mother. He was a brave, frank lad, who, when they offered him the throne, answered that he had no objection to try what he could do. If the Spaniards got tired of him, he hoped they would tell him so, and he would step out as Amadeo had done.

HOW THEY THRESH GRAIN IN SPAIN.

He reigned until he died on November 25th, 1885. His reign was quiet, and every one loved him. In all his eleven years of power he made no serious mistakes, and the intriguing politicians of the Cortes gained nothing by quarrelling with him.

When he first became king, he married his cousin, Marie Mercedes, daughter of the Duke of Montpensier. It was a genuine love match, and Alfonso's heart was broken when she died, six months after the marriage. The Spaniards insisted on his marrying again. This time his wife was Mary Christina of Austria, who outlived him. She is now regent, during the minority of her son Alfonso, who will presently be King of Spain.

Within the past twenty-five years great changes have taken place in Spain. The vast domains of the Church have passed into private hands, and in many cases are being intelligently tilled. Railroads have been built in every direction, and with this help the people of each province have been made acquainted with their neighbors 361 in the others. There has been a surprising revival of trade and industry. The Spanish people, who had been stationary for a century, have begun to increase in numbers. The courts now generally administer even-handed justice. There is an excellent police, and crime is pretty generally punished. Good roads have been made in the country parts, and the streams have been bridged. Common schools have been established everywhere, and the law obliges Spaniards to send their children to them. In the towns there are excellent universities. Newspapers are published in all the cities, and books are printed which it will do you no harm to read. Steady efforts are being made to put an end to the race of beggars. The brigands have been wiped out.

Take the prospect altogether, and you can hope that a new day is dawning for Spain, in which that country shall be as famous for the virtues of its people and the prosperity of their homes, as it is for the beauty of its scenery, the exquisite charm of its climate, and the loveliness of its women.

Lightning Source UK Ltd.
Milton Keynes UK
UKHW040718290622
405123UK00001B/89